WITHDRAWN
HARVARD LIBRARY
WITHDRAWN

Nebuchadnezzar's Dream

Nebuchadnezzar's Dream

or

The End of a Medieval Catholic Church

ROGER LENAERS

GORGIAS PRESS
2007

First Gorgias Press Edition, 2007

Copyright © 2007 by Gorgias Press LLC

All rights reserved under International and Pan-American Copyright Conventions. No part of this publication may be reproduced, stored in a retrieval system or transmitted in any form or by any means, electronic, mechanical, photocopying, recording, scanning or otherwise without the prior written permission of Gorgias Press LLC.

Published in the United States of America by Gorgias Press LLC, New Jersey

ISBN 978-1-59333583-0

Translation by L. M. Teugels of *De droom van Nebukadnezar of het einde van een middeleeuwse kerk* (Leuven, 2001) and *Uittocht uit oudchristelijke mythen* (Leuven, 2003).

GORGIAS PRESS
46 Orris Ave., Piscataway, NJ 08854 USA
www.gorgiaspress.com

Library of Congress Cataloging-in-Publication Data

Lenaers, Roger, 1925-
 [Droom van Nebukadnezar of het einde van een middeleeuwse kerk. English]
 Nebuchadnezzar's dream, or, The end of a medieval Catholic Church / Roger Lenaers. -- 1st Gorgias Press ed.
   p. cm.
 ISBN 1-59333-583-0 (alk. paper)
 1. Catholic Church--Doctrines. 2. Church renewal--Catholic Church. I. Title. II. Title: Nebuchadnezzar's dream. III. Title: End of a medieval Catholic Church.
 BX1751.3.L4613 2007
 230'.2--dc22

2006037926

The paper used in this publication meets the minimum requirements of the American National Standards.

Printed in the United States of America

Daniel answered the king ..., 'To you, O king, as you lay in bed, came thoughts of what would be hereafter, and the revealer of mysteries disclosed to you what is to be. ... 'You were looking, O king, and lo! there was a great statue. This statue was huge, its brilliance extraordinary; it was standing before you, and its appearance was frightening. The head of that statue was of fine gold, its chest and arms of silver, its middle and thighs of bronze, [3]its legs of iron, its feet partly of iron and partly of clay. As you looked on, a stone was cut out, not by human hands, and it struck the statue on its feet of iron and clay and broke them in pieces. Then the iron, the clay, the bronze, the silver, and the gold, were all broken in pieces and became like the chaff of the summer threshing-floors; and the wind carried them away, so that not a trace of them could be found. But the stone that struck the statue became a great mountain and filled the whole earth.'

Daniel 2:27.29.31-35

Contents

Preface 1

Chapter 1. Speaking Without Being Understood 5

Chapter 2. Farewell to the World Above 11

Chapter 3. Leaving Ancient Christian Mythology Behind 23

Chapter 4. No Book of Oracles but a Book of Witness 39

Chapter 5. The Indissoluble Tie with the Beginning 51

Chapter 6. Watchdog in the Sanctuary of the Tradition 61

Chapter 7. Speaking about the Unspeakable 77

Chapter 8. Primeval Stone of Our Doctrine of Faith? 91

Chapter 9. Equal in All Things 103

Chapter 10. A Reversed Pyramid 111

Chapter 11. Beware of the Artists! 127

Chapter 12. Better Coarse but Wholesome Bread 145

Chapter 13. The Holy Seven 163

Chapter 14. Five Once-in-a-Lifetime Catholic Rituals 173

Chapter 15. Taking And Eating, Taking and Drinking 191

Chapter 16. Guilt and Punishment 209

Chapter 17. Mentally Ill or Close to God? 221

Chapter 18. Where Do We Go in Times of Trouble? 229

Chapter 19. Clearing Away the Transformer 241

Epilogue 251

PREFACE

A professional theologian might find the ideas that are developed here not nuanced and even questionable, a dangerous kind of vulgarization, unable to do justice to the complexity of the theological issues. This is because the theologian looks in a detailed, even microscopic way at the problems within his specific discipline. When one popularizes, however, one looks with the naked eye, and just sees what everyone can see. Where the use of a microscope allows one to distinguish black and white spots, the naked eye sees only shades of grey. A synthesis that is to be useful for the lay person should therefore simplify without falsifying. This is not an easy task. Maybe it will be reassuring to know that the author is somebody who because of personal interest and pastoral needs has tried to keep track of the developments within Christian doctrine and within modern thought and sensitivity for almost fifty years (including his theological studies). And also that he has written a lot about these issues in the past fifteen years, in his native Dutch. And that he now feels the need to collect the harvest of this long period of reading, thinking, discussing and writing, and present it to the public, convinced that it will help clear the way for a faith that feels at home in the twenty-first century.

This book is an effort to translate the one and perennial faith in Jesus Christ and his God in the language of today. Western civilization in the future will no longer think as it used to do in the past, just as an adult no longer speaks and thinks like the child s/he once was. Faithfulness to God's offer of salvation, as it reaches us through the Church, demands that we should take leave of the images and representations with which we felt at home in the past, as well as of the language in which the Church has cast these images. Indeed, by the internal dynamics of evolution, which is God's own creative act, the rock of modernity has cut itself loose from the great mountain range of history, and it is striking the clay feet of medieval faith with great force. The impressive monument which is the Church of twenty centuries, with its golden head in Rome, awaits the same fate as the grand statue that Nebuchadnezzar saw in his dream. This book intends to demonstrate why this clash is inevitable.

At the core issue is the problem of language—language not only understood as a system of words, but involving the whole appearance of the Church. The traditional language of the Church has become a foreign language for the Westerner of the third millennium. It is a language of insiders that is only understood by the fast-shrinking remnant of faithful who are still familiar with the imagery of the past. Quite a lot is spoken and written about this today. However, usually only a description and an analysis of the problem are offered, as well as the pessimistic prospects based on them. Or one hears calls for a new evangelization—as if such would stand a chance if one stuck to the language of the past. But what is mostly missing yet really indispensable is rephrasing the richness of our faith in images and concepts that are familiar to contemporary people. Without such rephrasing all evangelization will be empty. The participants at the Second Vatican Council apparently realized how dangerous the widening gap between **proclamation** and the modern world was going to become. And they finally understood that it made no sense to proclaim in the liturgy the 'Word of God' in a language of which 99 percent of the faithful did not understand one iota. Church Latin was probably the most eloquent symbol of this alienation between the modern human and the proclaiming Church. In its attempt to bring the Church up to date, and as an overture to the grand symphony of ecclesiastical renewal, the Council replaced Latin with the vernacular in the liturgy. But what is the use of replacing a symbol, if one leaves reality unchanged, that is, if one sticks to the religious worldview and symbolic expressions of the past? For the texts translated from Latin which are served up to the faithful, remain also in English, German or whichever idiom a foreign language, only accessible to the initiated. And liturgy, as important as it might be, is only one part of ecclesiastical life. The Church needs a radical reform, which should touch upon all its aspects. Its entire message and appearance needs to tune in to modern humanity.

This is exactly the intention of this book. In it the author wants to venture into what is not done enough: to peel our doctrine of faith out of its shell of medieval imagery and ideas, and to reshape it into the language of modernity. This new formulation of our faith will inevitably be far removed from the traditional one; so much so that it might give even the impression of being heterodox, that is: of being no longer in conformity with the true doctrine. But this is not at all the case. The readers will have to make this out for themselves.

It might seem strange that this book has no footnotes. But an idea or a position does not become more probable if someone else has already said this before. It is up to the readers to judge whether they deem acceptable and intellectually honest what is found in this book. As to the absence of a bibliography: why and for what purpose should an author list what in the course of so many years he has read and appropriated, as a whole or in part? As a matter of fact, more often than not this appropriation has happened so unconsciously that he even no longer knows who exactly has sown in him this or that particular insight that he made his own. At the end of this preface, the author therefore wants to acknowledge all those, living or dead, those still known to him and those already wrapped in the clouds of his oblivion, of whose thoughts and feelings it has been given to him to become the inheritor and new mouth-piece.

Louvain, Belgium, January 1, 2006.

CHAPTER 1

SPEAKING WITHOUT BEING UNDERSTOOD

THE END OF A SECRET LANGUAGE

The Merriam-Webster dictionary lists as the first meaning of the word 'language', what most people associate with this term: 'the words, their pronunciation, and the methods of combining them used and understood by a community'. However, sign-language is a language also; and the arts of painting, music, and dance 'speak' their own languages. The same dictionary therefore, in a second definition, stretches the term and defines 'words' as 'a systematic means of communicating ideas or feelings by the use of conventionalized signs, sounds, gestures, or marks having understood meanings'. The latter definition includes the broader spectrum of non-verbal communication: tone, rhythm, volume, expression and movement—the whole range of body-language. Also body-language reveals, betrays, 'translates' thoughts, images, feelings. Language in its broadest sense includes every means of making internal thoughts and feeling available to others, so that they can share the experience. This evidently requires that the other grasps the communicating character of the language-act and understands at least part of its message. The precise way, however, in which this wonderful process of communication unfolds, does not matter for the present discussion.

The question we would rather like to ask is: why do we want to share our internal life with others? And the answer is clear: to establish the deeply needed connection between ourselves and **oth-**

others—we are not ourselves without others; to be confirmed or corrected by their reaction (again through language), so that we can move on; often also to induce others to do something. Moreover, language has an internal function towards the 'speaker'. What was vague and unformed inside him or her gets attention and receives a form, so that s/he gets a grip on it.

Not only individuals, but also groups and cultures express their thoughts, images, values, certainties, and fears. They do this collectively, in explicit doctrines, rules and laws, as well as in traditions, practices, habits, rituals and taboos. They do this also by means of the shape, size and architecture of their buildings; through the artifacts in and on the buildings; and by means of the dress and the manners of those who lead the activities and the rituals in these secular and religious buildings. All this is part of the language of a cultural group.

The Christian cultural group in its Western form has over the ages developed various means of expressing its collective thoughts and feelings: its own language in the narrow and broad sense of the word. It has formulated laws and creeds, shaped rituals and enforced them, built churches and monasteries, and decorated them. It has given expression to its conscious and unconscious ideas, expectations, fears, joys, certainties and doubts, in words and in images, in colors and in sounds. But then something very strange happened. A system of communication that everybody understood for over a thousand years, has, without migration of nations or barbarian invasion, suddenly become a foreign tongue, a dead language that is only understood by those who are really devoted to it.

CHURCH LANGUAGE HAS BECOME THE LANGUAGE OF A FOREIGN CULTURE

Those belonging to the conservative wing of Western Christianity might be flabbergasted and dismayed by this sudden break. For them this is a shock, because they cannot or do not want to understand the important fact that every language, also Christian language, is conditioned by its temporal origins. The language of the Christian message originated in a particular culture and in a very specific geographical setting, by which it is marked throughout. In the first century of the Common Era it served as the expression of the experiences and the ideas of an initially small group of people, who found inspiration and leadership in their quest for the transcendent God in the figure of Jesus of Nazareth. The language of that first group spread out because more and more people found an answer for their own quest in the message that it expressed. They joined the group and accepted its language voluntarily, later also because its leadership enforced it on them. And each time they further unfolded that language.

In the course of this unfolding, the language of the Church has undergone minor changes, but in essence it has remained the same as in the beginning. Culture evolved very slowly in the first millennium. The imagery of the Christian Middle Ages did not differ substantially from that of the Late Roman Empire. This is understandable because the message of the gospel was wrapped in the language of the dominant culture—including all the deformations, shortcomings and contaminations of that culture—and therefore it was accepted without much ado. Every new generation recognized itself in the formulations of the message and stuck to it.

But in the fifteenth century, Western society underwent a movement of change that would result in an all-overturning cultural revolution. Modern Humanism was born. That Humanism engendered the modern sciences of the sixteenth and seventeenth century, and these in just a few centuries changed the face of the earth. As a rule an evolution in the control of the material world entails a parallel evolution in the realm of ideas. In Marxist terms this is called the alteration of the spiritual superstructure of a society as a result of changes in the material base. But when the superstructure changes, language also necessarily changes along with it, as language is the expression of the thoughts and the feelings of a culture, hence of its superstructure. Over time, words may start to carry meanings and shades of feeling that are different from those they had in the beginning. Practices become obsolete. Rules become meaningless. Images become incomprehensible. The word 'king' serves as a fine example of a word whose meaning has shifted: today a king merely stands for the highest authority in the state, who has to follow the rules of the state himself. In the past, however, when the Church employed the title 'king' to express something meaningful about God and Jesus Christ, it denoted the highest authority endowed with absolute power, who issued the laws, but stood himself above the law. In the West, democracy has replaced autocracy. The word 'king' has remained, but its contents have shifted. The same has occurred with many other words. What the average churchgoer thinks and feels, when he hears Paul speak about the 'law' and the 'flesh' in the Letter to the Romans is therefore very different from what Paul intended when he wrote that letter. Inevitably, the result is confusion. The intended evangelization only generates misunderstanding and distortion. This holds for the bulk of ecclesiastical and liturgical language and also for the language of Scripture, which underlies both. That the message of the Church no longer gets across, is in the first place due to the fact that its imagery and underlying world-view and conception of God, in short its whole language game has remained that of medieval times, whereas Western society is moving away from the Middle Ages with increasing speed. One who thinks and feels in a medieval fashion, speaks in a medieval fashion. For the modern thinking and feeling human this language has become a foreign language, as foreign as the already abandoned ecclesiastical Latin.

THE RESULT: INTERNAL TENSIONS WITHIN THE CHURCH

Not everyone in Western society has already entered this process of drastic changes. A great many prefer to stick to the old ways. Their vision of the world has not yet evolved. They cling with great faith, even blind stubbornness, to the imagery, forms, and expressions of the past. This results in the tensions between the conservative and the progressive wings of the Church. In the past, such tensions did not exist, as thoughts and actions that deviated from the norm were not tolerated, and if necessary wiped out with the help of the dungeon and the stake. Examples are the Cathars, the Waldensians, Jan Hus, the Anabaptists, Giordano Bruno, the Marranos, the Alumbrados and heretics of every kind. Luckily for the nineteenth century liberals and the twentieth century modernists, times have changed; otherwise they would have been added to the list of victims and burnt at the stake. But the result of this tolerance is that the one and only Roman Catholic Church, like a new Rebecca, bears fighting twins in her womb.

Unfortunately, most of the leading figures in the Church belong to the group of those who stick to the imagery and forms of the past. Indeed, they owe their position, influence and income to the inherited structures of the Church and hence to the same old vision of the world. They are not willing to develop openness toward deviant ideas, as this would clash with their position in the

Church. If they would do so, they would quickly be removed from their hierarchical position, as happened to bishop Raymond Hunthausen in Seattle or in France to bishop Gaillot. But the faithful at the grassroots who have developed a modern way of thinking and feeling do not recognize themselves in this past, and they, often impatiently, demand that the church engage in a search for new forms of understanding and language that correspond to their new ways of thinking. They engage in experiments, and try to provide a solid foundation for their often crude and experimental new images and formulations, which are often considered 'heretical' by the hierarchy. Their conservative twin brothers, however, can only see them as disturbing trouble-makers who deviate from the traditional, and in their eyes unchangeable, doctrine. Convinced that the traditional formulations are the only way to capture the one and only truth, they decry all efforts to reformulate this faith as error, unfaithfulness and unbelief. This attitude excludes any dialogue from the outset, as dialogue includes reciprocity. As to the modernity-minded faithful, they would be mistaken, if they placed all their hopes in a rather pragmatic revision of the language of the Church—and language, as everybody knows, also includes thought forms and practices. Even if they were to succeed in clearly articulating and pushing through some pertinent reforms, such as decentralization of the church administration, admission of women into the ranks of the clergy, democratic participation in the nomination of pastors and bishops, abrogation of the encyclical *Humanae Vitae*, and abolition of mandatory celibacy, they would still be far removed from the final goal to be achieved. For in doing so they would still remain at the surface without delving into the deeper layers that resist any attempt at reform. Language and articulation always come in the second place, first comes that from which these derive their raison d'être and which they try to convey: the potent thrust of the vision of the world which language puts into words. If the traditional language of the Church has ceased to speak to contemporary people, then this is not because it is incorrect or unclear, but because, on the contrary, it very clearly and correctly conveys a world of ideas that has been outstripped by the flux of time. Therefore the next step in our examination will be a chapter about the whole gamut of ideas that is condensed in the catchword 'modernity'. This is a very crucial chapter, because only a general breakthrough of these ideas in the Church can prepare the way for a vital renewal of the Christian self-understanding today. And without this renewal, the Church has no future in the modern Western world.

Chapter 2

Farewell to the World Above

From Heteronomy to Theonomy

Until the sixteenth century, Christianity, like any other culture of the past, conceived of our world as totally dependent on another world that was imagined and modeled after our own world, the only one we know. Until today, many Christians still adhere to the same worldview. This other world was conceived as ruled by a mighty king, as was common in the past, who was, in Jewish-Christian thought, surrounded by an entourage of angels and saints. This ruler issues laws, controls whether these are kept, punishes or forgives those who break them at his discretion, and rewards those who keep them. His domain is spontaneously localized above our own world, and is thus called 'super-natural', or 'Heaven'. He knows everything, even the most hidden things. In comparison with his knowledge, our knowledge is close to ignorance. Fortunately, however, this ruler occasionally reveals to us what we need to know for our own good but that remains inaccessible to the efforts of our mere intellect. The at least latent goodwill of this other world founds our hope that by supplications and the offering of gifts we will receive what we cannot obtain on our own. Hence the supplicating prayers, sacrifices, and the many other ways to placate the ruler above, which are especially useful when one fears having angered him. Fear for his anger is one of the many signs that he is portrayed after the model of dread-inspiring earthly rulers. On the other hand, in the imagery of the faithful (Christians, Muslims, and many Jews), this other world guarantees eternal post-mortal bliss in the heavenly domain to those who have obtained merit through good deeds. For despite everything that has just been said, this other world is indeed a good, even a perfect world. One only needs to know the rules of the game.

TYPICAL CHRISTIAN HETERONOMY

Unlike the two other Abrahamite religions, Judaism and Islam, Christianity teaches that about two thousand years ago, Jesus of Nazareth descended from Heaven to our planet, not only endowed with divine power and knowledge, but as a true God in human form, and returned to the same Heaven after his death. Before his ascension into Heaven he arranged for a representative, Peter, on whom he bestowed some of his power, which the latter in turn transmitted to his successors. These grant the necessary authority to their various subordinates on the hierarchical ladder, in descending order, which allows even the lower ranks to issue commands. Each of the apostolic successors of Peter is assumed to be connected to the omniscient other world through his link to the divine-human Jesus of Nazareth. This ensures that the hierarchy knows better than the People of God what is true and what is false, and what the other world requests. In other words: they possess a divine and thus infallible magisterium. This is an extremely simplified and therefore somewhat distorted summary of traditional Christian thought. Such a worldview is generally called 'heteronomous', because our world is, in this view, completely dependent on the other (Greek: *heteros*) world, in which all the laws (Greek: *nomos*) for our world are laid down.

However, the existence of this second world is an axiom, that is, an undemonstrated as well as irrefutable proposition. An axiom might appear self-evident, but it remains a freely accepted and hence not compelling starting point. If one accepts an axiom, one does so because it appears meaningful and trustworthy. The same holds for the acceptance of the existence of a second world. Humankind has apparently a spontaneous inclination to adhere to this axiom. Otherwise the matter-of-course way in which heteronomous thought has prevailed throughout human history, would be inexplicable. A Christian who still wants to adhere to this axiom is in respectable company: the entire Old and New Testaments, the entire Patristic literature, Scholasticism, all the Councils including the Second Vatican, the entire Christian liturgy, all the dogmas and their elaboration in Christian theology are based on this axiom.

Moreover, as to the basic and underlying pattern, Jesus himself, and the 'apostles and prophets' on whose words the Christian proclamation is based, all thought in a purely heteronomous way.

AUTONOMY

In the sixteenth century Western world, however, the acceptance of this axiom began to show a small crack. The emergency of the exact sciences in that epoch slowly led to the insight that nature follows its own inherent laws that can be calculated, and the effects of which can be predicted and often averted. Once lightning was discovered to be a mere electrical discharge, and the lightning-conductor and Faraday's cage were found to be effective means against its devastating impact, penitence psalms, holy water and palm branches had soon served their turn as antidotes against lightning strikes. The first generation of these new scientists undoubtedly remained traditional believers and hence heteronomously thinking Christians. However, by their discoveries of the inner mechanisms of the cosmos, they unwittingly excluded all interference from another world into ours. The possibility of such interference would indeed invalidate all scientific undertaking, as this would mean that a supernatural force would be able to shake the newly discovered scientific certainties, which would in turn disable the entire technological culture that is based on them. It follows that the axiom of the heteronomy of the cosmos collapsed in modernity. The cosmos does not follow supernatural directions: it follows its own way, its own (Greek: *autos*) laws (Greek: *nomos*). A new axiom, opposed to heteronomy, the axiom of autonomy, entered the stage and gradually drove out the old.

Moreover, since the human is part of the cosmos, indeed even the culmination of cosmic development, he should also be autonomous and be able to find his own (moral) laws within himself. The path to this second conclusion was already prepared by the eulogy of human greatness and dignity in fifteenth and sixteenth century Humanism. The new axiom of autonomy penetrated gradually and often unconsciously into Western culture, first into its intelligentsia, and in the eighteenth and nineteenth century also into the broader basis of the masses. The first symptoms of the acceptance of the new axiom were the successful battle against the persecution of witches in the seventeenth century, the abolition of torture as a legal instrument in the eighteenth century and, at the end of that century, the first declarations of Human Rights. These were followed in the nineteenth century by the abolition of slavery, and the unstoppable breakthrough of the democratic idea, which was then called 'liberalism' and immediately condemned by the autocratic thinking Church authorities. The result of this grand movement, which was initiated in the Western world by Humanism and the sciences, is called 'Modernism', which includes 'Postmodernism', the latter being not the abolition, but the mere self-criticism of Modernism. We are not only the contemporaries of, and the witnesses to, this Modernism, we are its carriers and its vessels.

Not only lightning, but an ever growing number of other physical and psychical phenomena that were earlier perceived as the result of supernatural interventions, such as epidemics, earthquakes, sudden recoveries, clairvoyance, dreams, apparitions, voices from another world, stigmata and possessions (by the devil and the like), were now recognized as the effect of inner-worldly forces. Encounters with the other world therefore occurred less and less often, until they all but ceased. As a result, the automatic assumption that the supernatural world occasionally punishes or rewards, and is always ready to interfere, also diminished. This does not mean that the existence of this other world was bluntly denied; no, the other world still existed but it hardly ever showed any signs of life or activity. But it is only a small step from the acceptance of the inactivity of a supernatural world to the assumption of its inexistence, and the West took this step in the nineteenth century, simultaneously announcing the 'Death of God' and displaying the birth of modern atheism.

THE CHURCH AN ACCOMPLICE TO THE ORIGIN OF ATHEISM

The axiom of autonomy does not automatically lead to atheism. Rather, the emergence of atheism, especially in its virulent form, antitheism, is triggered by historical and therefore random factors, the most important of these being the negative attitude of a rigid institutional Church. In other words, had the Church been more open to the new contemporary values, the Enlightenment could have taken a very different course. But, convinced that heteronomy was at the core of the Christian message, rather than just being one possible paradigm, Church authorities denied the autonomy of the cosmos, so self-evident to the modern mind, with recourse to knowledge from the other, unverifiable, world. Moreover, they mobilized all their remaining inner-worldly means of power to fight the notion of autonomy, because of the latter's claim that scientific findings cannot be denied on religious (or philosophical) grounds; and that in case of contradiction between dogma and science, the correct answer is to be found in science rather than in the dogma. The result was a panic that together with the dogmas the entire Church and its divine foundation would collapse. The supporters of the Theory of Evolution were the victims of this panic in the nineteenth century, as were the so-called Modernists in the twentieth.

With the same fervor authorities of the Church fought the growing awareness that the human, as the summit of evolution, is autonomous. Such autonomy would include that humans do not depend on any external authority whatsoever that can interfere with their freedom, and that they have unassailable and absolute rights, such as freedom of conscience, freedom of thought and religion, the right to absolute respect, the right of having a say in issues that regard them, in other words: democratic rights. This was unacceptable for the autocratic Church. As late as 1832, Pope Gregory XVI in his famous Encyclical *Mirari vos* condemned solemnly 'that false and absurd maxim, better termed the insanity (*deliramentum*), that liberty of conscience must be obtained and guaranteed for everyone'. And even now, in the beginning of the twenty-first century, after two centuries of modernism, inner-ecclesiastical democracy and equal rights for women are still taboo for Rome.

The preservation of the authoritarian ideas of the past was also fostered, at least at an unconscious level, by the all too human fear to give up the patiently established positions of authority and their accompanying material advantages. For, whether one likes it or not, the Vatican loves to wield power and to have it make inroads everywhere. Of course, there is nothing wrong with power in and by itself. However, craving for power and abuse of authority are great wrongs, and these are always around the corner. 'Power corrupts, absolute power corrupts absolutely', is the by now well-known adage of Lord Acton, the undaunted critic of Vatican I and an honest contender reacting against the Pope's infallibility that was proclaimed there. Even for a Church that proclaims the Gospel it seems to be extremely difficult to distance itself from power and wealth, despite the fact that the Gospel calls for exactly this at every page.

MODERNITY AND THE 'DEATH OF GOD'

The Church's resistance against what was becoming self-evident for every thinking human being, was extremely vexing in the eyes of the humanists. As a result, the odium which the Church had incurred by this attitude spread to the point of assaulting the very axiom on which it based itself: the existence of an all-controlling second world to which people have to submit themselves, and of which the Church claimed to be the official representative. And because 'God' had always been localized there, He passed away together with this second world in modern culture. This demise had been prepared for a long time: everything that was previously considered as divine interference had slowly been exposed as an inner-worldly phenomenon. This would not have been devastating if people would have had an open eye for the sacred depth in and under these earthly phenomena, because then they would have found God all the time, albeit in a different way than before. But modernism reduced the amazing wonders of the cosmos to a hyper-complex interplay of mechanical forces which it tried to master with mathematical equations. In order to liberate itself from the God-on-High, whom the pre-modern Church used as a ploy in its struggle to ward off the basic concerns of Humanism, Modernity also closed itself off from being touched by God-in-the-Depth. Fascination with the abilities of human thought and technique finished the job: it made people blind for the deeper dimension of the material world. It is apparently difficult for the inner eye to simultaneously see with the same sharpness what lays at one's feet and what shows up at the horizon.

The fact that heteronomy was conceived as an integral part of the Christian message was already devastating in the nineteenth and twentieth centuries. In the future, it threatens to become an even greater disaster. This is so because the Western world distances itself ever faster from the pre-modern world-view, which was built on the axiom of heteronomy. To secure the future of the Church, rethinking the Christian message in terms of autonomy is a pressing need. This is a basic form of enculturation: the Christian faith has to be translated into the culture of the twenty-first century; it has to disseminate itself in a world of globalization, the UNO and the Internet. This world, however, lives by the conviction that the human and the cosmos are autonomous. In any case, Rome has it wrong when it feels it has to repeat the old formulations over and over again, and ever more articulate, and to threaten with punishment those who do not appear to listen. The modern believer is not a grade-school student anymore, just as the modern human no longer understands, and even misunderstands, the language that Rome speaks. Shouting and banging on the table will not make that language any more comprehensible.

FROM AUTONOMY TO THEONOMY

Is it possible, however, to reformulate in the modern language of autonomy the perennial experiences of faith which are expressed in Scripture and Tradition in heteronomous categories, without turning traitor to the core, that is, the reality 'God'? The 'Death of God' appears to be a necessary consequence of autonomous thinking. Is there still a place for God left in such thinking? There most certainly is a place left, and not just the tiny place that remains reserved for the 'God stop-gap' when all human attempts at explanation have failed. No, his new place is the most prominent place, so prominent that, in comparison, his old role as the God-in-Heaven was only that of an outsider who only occasionally appeared on the cosmic stage and on the stage of everyday life, and as such never can have been the true God. Autonomy is not the grave digger of the true God, but only of the unsatisfactory imagery of a God-in-Heaven, who is a human, all too human, construct and in any case in modern times an inadequate presentation of the God who reveals himself in Jesus.

For the modern human who does not know any 'outside' world, any intervention in the cosmic processes by a divine power outside and above our world is inconceivable. That is why many biologists of evolution no longer see a place for a creating God. Misled by the heteronomous idea of God which they come across everywhere in Christian thought, they are convinced to serve the autonomy of the sciences and their discoveries by discarding this ever-meddling God and ascribing the wonder of the cosmos and its origins to purposeless, blind coincidence. In Chapter 7, where the relation between creation and evolution is treated, this mistake will be corrected. But also for the modern faithful such external divine intermingling is inconceivable. This is not because there is no creating God at all, as atheist scientists think, but because they see God as the innermost depth of every cosmic process. God is never acting from outside, because he is always inside.

This reconciliation of autonomy and belief in God is called 'theonomy'. One who thinks theonomously confesses God (in Greek: *theos*) as the deepest ground of everything and therefore also as the internal law (Greek: *nomos*) of the cosmos and the human. In this theonomous thinking, there is only one world: ours. But this world is sacred as it is the ongoing self-revelation of the sacred mystery that we call 'God'. This automatically raises the question as to the occurrence of evil in the cosmos: this problem remains a long and sharp thorn in the flesh also of theonomy. But it is no bigger problem here than in heteronomous thought, in which the devil was invited to force a solution. Unfortunately the poor devil cannot do anything more than to shift the problem a little: where does the evil that is projected unto him come from?

ALL SPEAKING ABOUT 'ABOVE' COMES FROM 'BELOW'

The absolute unanimity of heteronomous thinking during the entirety of ecclesiastical history makes it very difficult for the Church to give it up and replace it with theonomy. For many this must be more unsettling than an earthquake. One can understand there will be enormous resistance against efforts to translate the Christian message in terms of theonomy. For those who think heteronomously, to uphold the old axiom is a matter of 'to be or not to be'. It is clear to them that the assertion of the new axiom will cause the grand statue of the Church of twenty centuries to fall to pieces.

Nonetheless, the heading above this section intimates that this collapse is inevitable. The infallibility of a dogma presupposes that it is uttered by an infallible authority. But all human knowledge is limited and therefore fallible. In the past, infallibility was therefore extracted from a second world that had a monopoly on omniscience and that was so kind as to occasionally lighten up the darkness of our human ignorance. In heteronomous thought, all valid speaking about 'above' comes directly from this eternal and absolute 'above' and it owes its absolute reliability and immutability to it. But that leaves unanswered the critical question as to how we know that a formulation really comes from the axiomatic Heaven and not from some genial or confused human mind. To be sure, such questions were taboo in the ecclesiastical family of the past: they smacked of doubt and doubt led to unbelief; and unbelief was sinful. These questions were, of course, allowed when discussing the alleged authority of Mohammed or the founder of the Mormons, but it was 'overlooked' that an honest outsider or presumed objective spectator has the right to ask the same questions about the authority of the Church.

However, if there is no super- or extra-cosmic authority who knows everything and whom it pleases to share his knowledge with a select few, then everything we think and say about God and his realm turns out to be inner-worldly, human, the expression of our human thinking, feeling and searching. And these expressions are ever changing. If so, every proposition is a child of Time and bears the features of this restless and contradictory father. In other words, it is only true to a certain degree: however faithfully it keeps in touch with, and unfolds, the chosen point of departure, it can never express more experience of reality (which is another name for truth) than what has been gathered by humans up to that point. Therefore every proposition is liable to correction and revision.

Also the formulations of the Church are temporary and culture-bound and therefore relative to a certain degree. If one absolutizes them, by connecting them to the God-in-Heaven and having them share in his absoluteness, then one overloads this human endeavor. True, it was possible to think this way in the heteronomous past, and in conservative circles in the Church this is still possible, just as inflexible Muslims can still do this with regards to the Koran, which they refuse to be subjected to criticism. But for a theonomously thinking Christian this has become impossible.

It is obvious what this means for declarations of dogmas and conciliar pronunciations. If a Pope or a Council declares something to be a dogma, it not only means that every member of the Church has to subscribe to it, under penalty of sanctions—in the past this included physical punishments, now only spiritual sanctions to be executed by God-in-Heaven. It means first and foremost that this declaration is assumed to be infallibly correct, guaranteed by God-in-Heaven, and therefore no longer subjected to revision or reformulation. This guarantee is based on the (historically contestable) founding of the Church by Jesus of Nazareth, who, as the earthly manifestation of God-in-Heaven allegedly conferred upon the Church, and more specifically upon its leadership, the privilege of infallibility. This entire structure inevitably collapses when there is no longer an 'above' and a 'below'.

THE CORRECTNESS OF FORMULATIONS IS RELATIVE

Dogmatic propositions are liable to revision also for another reason, namely because, as the heading of this section reads, the correctness of all formulations is relative. The following should make this clear.

Is the formula '1+1=2' correct? 'Of course', we all exclaim. 'It all depends', says the computer scientist. If we ask him why this is so, he will say that it depends on the numeral system you use. In our decimal system, 1+1 is of course 2. But in a binary system, that is, a system that uses only two figures, as is the case with computers that only know the numbers 0 and 1, 1+1=10. Because the figure 2 does not exist in computer language, the formula 1+1=2 does not make any sense in this language, and is therefore not correct. Only the formula 1+1=10 is correct in computer language. Conversely, even though 1+1=10 does make sense in the decimal system, it is utterly incorrect there. As a matter of fact, we probably owe our decimal system to the fact that we have ten fingers. If we would have had only three fingers on each hand, we would have developed a seximal system, and 4+4 would not have been 8 (this figure would not have existed) but 12.

The two formulas, 1+1=2 and 1+1=10 are both correct, but each within its own system. Correctness and incorrectness are therefore relative, which means: dependent on the chosen point of departure. But after one has chosen such, one has to continue consistently, otherwise one will make mistakes.

The same holds for formulations of faith: their correctness depends on the selected axiom of departure. Their correctness, not their truth. Truth has to do with being real, with existential value, with depth and the enrichment of life. Correctness is an exclusive matter of formulation, which has to stay in the track of the chosen point of departure and which has to follow the rules of logic in its progress, first and foremost the rules of identity and contradiction.

This point will be continued, but first I will give a second example to illustrate the above statement that correctness and incorrectness are relative, that is, dependent on the chosen starting point. As is well known, Euclid based his geometry on the axiom that only one line can be drawn parallel to a given line through a point not on the given line. In the nineteenth century, however, the Russian mathematician Lobatschevsky developed a completely coherent geometry, based on a different axiom, namely that two parallel lines can be drawn through that point. All the propositions in this geometry are incorrect from the point of view of Euclidan geometry, whereas all the propositions of Euclidan geometry are incorrect in Lobatschevky's system. Nevertheless all the propositions of Lobatschevky are as incontestable as those of Euclid. Everything depends on the chosen axiom of departure. And this choice is free.

THE CORRECTNESS OF FORMULATIONS OF FAITH IS ALSO RELATIVE

The two examples above should prevent the reader from considering the ideas presented in this book as a chain of heretical thoughts. Nothing is less true, despite the fact that those who follow the traditional axiom of the heteronomy of the human and the cosmos might get this impression. The proposed ideas are merely a different, but equally valid translation of the one message of faith, based on another axiom.

The traditional formulations are the expression of a pre-scientific, still heteronomously thinking culture, and hence they are only valid in that culture and do not enjoy an absolute or eternal validity, despite conservative views on the matter. Modern believers do not reject the traditional formulations as erroneous. They know—or should know—that these formulations correctly translate the same experience of faith and encounter with God through Jesus Christ as do theirs, they are merely based on a different axiom. The formulations of reality that for the conservative believer are indestructible and absolutely binding, may in the eyes of the modern-thinking believer be valuable, and at times even genial efforts to grasp the unthinkable and ungraspable, but from his point of view they are historically outstripped. They are only absolutely binding for those who, like our ancestors, think heteronomously. But modern believers, who have assimilated the values of the Enlightenment and have said goodbye to the so-called 'first naivety', take their point of departure in the opposite axiom of autonomy. For them, the *Catechism of the Catholic Church* that was issued by Rome in 1993, is therefore only a brilliant synthesis of the ideas of the late counter-reformatory Church. It does not do justice to their contemporary approach of the God that attracts them and it will barely help them to find this God.

Their criticism not only affects the *Catechism*, but also our Profession of Faith. The disappearance of the second world above us makes it difficult for believers to be honest when uttering the words 'he came down from Heaven', 'ascended into Heaven', 'is seated at the right hand of the Father', and 'He will come again in glory to judge the living and the dead'. Everybody can see that. But there is more going on. If all intervention in the cosmic order has become unthinkable—since there is no supernatural instance which would be able to deregulate the natural flow of events—then also the conception of Jesus without a human father has become unthinkable, and even so the resurrection, understood as the reanimation of an utterly dead organism; and sacred formulas such as 'He was conceived by the power of the Holy Spirit and born of the Virgin Mary' and 'on the third day he rose again', as well as 'the resurrection of the body', become obsolete, because all these declarations presuppose the deregulating intervention of God in the cosmic order. If this is the case for the profession of faith, then also for its source, the Bible, from which the former has been distilled. The latter aspect will be further elaborated in Chapter 4.

CHAPTER 3

LEAVING ANCIENT CHRISTIAN MYTHOLOGY BEHIND

THE CRISIS OF THE CHURCH IS THE RESULT OF AUTONOMOUS THINKING

The Western Church lives through a crisis. Everybody can see that, and there are ample sociological studies and statistics to confirm this. For the authorities in Rome this situation is highly disturbing because, in their view, humanity needs the Church badly: *extra ecclesiam nulla salus*—outside the Church no salvation. This is warranted by messages from on high that leave no doubt on the matter. They find this crisis incomprehensible, because the Christian proclamation is the best there is, far surpassing everything its competitors have to offer. Past experiences confirm this: the Christian message has always been received with open arms in the West, and has been infused into every aspect of Western society. Admittedly, sometimes necessary force had to be employed, as with the Saxons who were driven into the ecclesiastical sheepfold under great resistance by Charles the Great. And those with diverging opinions often remained faithful to the one and true doctrine, at least on the face of it, because they knew that diverging opinions were harshly subdued. But this can neither be the whole explanation for the success of the Christian message in the early Middle Ages, nor for its thorough influence on every aspect of life. Apparently, people wanted to be Christians. And all of a sudden they do not want this anymore. Why is that? The message has remained the same. Why does it not sell anymore? Look at the Catholic schools that have to close because of enrollment going down; at the churches that remain more and more empty on Sundays, not to mention on weekdays.

If there is nothing wrong with the message, then those to whom it is addressed must be to blame, that is at least the opinion of the Catholic leadership. The people have become unwilling and unreceptive to the Good News. For the Vatican the culprits are once again secularization, modern humanism, and prosperity. The modern Christian allegedly seeks his salvation only on earth, and the human has come in the place of God. In addition, unruly progressives would contribute to this situation through their worldly obsessions with a democratic and participatory Church, the abolition of obligatory celibacy, the permission of women to the ministry, and their revaluation of sexuality. They act as a fifth column behind the already suffering ecclesiastical front.

A meager consolation would be that it is not the first time in history that the Church's words falls on deaf ears, and that the 'mystery of lawlessness' (2 Thess. 2:7) is not a recent phenomenon. At the time, the parable of the sower tried to make sense of the disappointment that the good seed only finds a fertile soil with a few. Already Paul sighed, quoting Isaiah, 'Lord who has believed our message?' (Rom. 10:16). And then of course there is the devil, who is always trying to prevent the seed from germinating and prospering. In any event, conservatives never put the blame for rejection on the side of the message. On that side, the precious water of eternal life always flows. But listeners do not seem to be thirsty. And they cannot be thirsty because they are always satisfied with the bountiful pleasures of this world.

LARGE STEPS ON A WRONG WAY

What is the solution to this problem? Convinced that one has to learn from the enemy and that the Children of Light ought to be no less clever than the Children of Darkness, the Church administration is using the attainments of modernity, such as radio, television and the Internet, as weapons in the struggle against this detestable modernity. No means are spared in this undertaking, as is clear from the popularity of the late John Paul II with the media; the papal trips to all the lands of the Lord; a touristy Holy Year which includes a full indulgence; a record amount of beatifications and canonizations; the stimulation of the cult of Mary and of pilgrimages to locations that relate to her; the support of organizations and journals that try to turn back the clock or at least to stop its turning. Other remedies, such as the publication of a 700 page official *Catechism of the Catholic Church*, and the ever more explicit repetition of the traditional formulations of the faith betray the opinion of the authorities in Rome that members of the Church are of good will, but are ignorant and a little deaf. And for those among the baptized that are not ignorant or deaf but clearly of bad will, there is always the means of discrete force. Heavy-handed force as was available in the good old times is unfortunately taboo: Amnesty International would immediately sound the alarm. But it is possible to tighten the authoritarian reign, to enforce oaths of fidelity to Church leaders, to deal harshly with dissident or critical movements, to appoint only Church dignitaries that promise to follow the Roman path, to put innovators on a side track, to intimidate rebels, to drag suspect authors before the Roman church tribunals, to silence them by firing them as professors of theology.

In all this the ship of Peter, originally a modest fishing boat on the Sea of Galilee, but meanwhile transformed into a Super-Titanic, steers straight into waters that are full of icebergs. But the steersmen on board as well as the steersmen on land, retired at the age of 75, keep confident that this is the only correct course. They have been sailing it for centuries already and all this time no iceberg has ever been sighted on this route. Moreover, this route has been prescribed by God himself. It would be treason to the essence and the task of the Church to deviate from it.

"THE ORDERS HAVE NOT BEEN CHANGED"

From this perspective, the message has been laid down once and for all; we have inherited it and it has to be transmitted unharmed, that is, unchanged, to the next generations. This reminds us of a passage in the delightful dream- and fairytale book of Antoine de Saint-Exupéry, *The Little Prince*. During his wanderings, the little prince arrives on a tiny planet where he meets the official lamplighter and starts a conversation with him. Suddenly the man gets up, lights the only lamp of the planet, and comes back. They continue their conversation and as suddenly as the first time, the man gets up, puts out the lamp and comes back again. The little prince is surprised, but becomes even more surprised when this lighting and extinguishing of the lamp is repeated shortly afterwards, and then over and over again. When he asks the man why he does this, the lamplighter explains that he has received an order to light the lamp every evening and put it out every morning. But the little planet had started to turn faster and faster over time, so that the evenings had followed ever closer upon the mornings. However, 'the orders have not been changed'.

There can hardly be a better way to illustrate the senselessness of a faithful but blind devotion to the past. 'What was good in the past', say its supporters, 'remains good forever, even today'. This is a fatal mistake. As a rule, a good (and a bad) habit or idea originates in response to a situation, but loses its validity and reason for existence when that situation disappears. Human history is one large process of change. Sometimes change goes so slowly that it goes unnoticed, so that each generation appears to be a clone of the previous generation and the great-grandfather can foresee which problems the great-grandson will encounter (the same as he encountered in his time) and how he can overcome them (in the same way as he did). In such periods of time, when the river of evolution flows unnoticeably slowly, elders are regarded with great esteem: they are the wise, they foresee the future, they know what will happen because they know what happened in the past; they are the ones that are respected, from whom one expects the necessary answers, and their answers are accepted with great faith and confidence. In such a cultural phase everything remains as of old: nothing will change with respect to the habit, the practice, the 'order'. And rightfully so. Changes are not necessarily ameliorations.

But today evolution has been caught up in a current and not even fathers, still much less grandfathers, know which questions and which problems youngsters will encounter. Recourse to the past, to the orders that were given to handle the then-actual circumstances, is to no avail in a new situation. One who only knows a horse-drawn cart cannot design the rules for traffic on a highway.

THE BASIS IS DIVIDED

Whereas the leaders of the Church are almost unanimously convinced that the course that was chosen in the past has to be continued—in other words that the traditional 'language' has to be maintained—the basis is more divided. The large majority is not the least concerned about the drainage of the Church and is not interested in the means to counter this course of events. In their eyes, the Church is no more than a service organization which they only very occasionally need: for the baptisms of their children, for their First Communions and their confirmations, often for their weddings, almost always for their burials. A second group (who *are* concerned) consists of conservatively thinking pious Christians, unfortunately not only elderly, who expect all salvation from the Church authorities and who nurture the latter's illusion that they have it right in everything they say or do.

Fortunately, there is also a third group, mostly consisting of engaged Christians, who worry as much about the situation as the authorities in Rome, but who feel and think in a modern way and therefore do not see a solution in the remedies the authorities prescribe. 'These remedies are no good', they say, 'because the diagnosis is wrong'. Neither modern ideas or prosperity, nor the devil or the incredibility of some Church leaders are the problems. And they have good arguments for this. In the past there were plenty of kings and dukes and princes of the Church and even ordinary Christians who lived in prosperity, even bathed in wealth, and who were not the least challenged in their Catholicism. Why would this suddenly be the case today? And were the popes and the bishops in the very pious Middle Ages so credible? Moreover, the explosion of unbelief in the nineteenth century occurred mostly among the needy proletariat, and not among the wealthy bourgeoisie. In addition, researchers and psychologists have become more and more convinced that contemporary humans are quite religious and looking for ways to satisfy their vague religious needs. But they don't like the quality of the product of the Church and rather visit all kinds of gurus, prophets and sects and cannot seem to get enough of their dubious merchandise. The success of these non-ecclesiastical and often anti-Christian religious movements, be they sects, alternative religions, or one of the many forms of New Age thinking, sheds doubt on the value of the above explanations, and calls for a better solution. And also for better remedies than those which are promoted by the Church authorities.

The latter have it right, on the other hand, when they refuse to seek the reason for the decline of the Catholic faith in the quality of the product. At least on this point the group of critical believers agrees with them. Because, if the product were no good, they (including the present author) would long ago have said farewell to the Church and accepted another offer. This means that the problem must be found in the wrapping of the product, and in the presentation by its sellers, that is, not in the product itself but in its marketing; in other words: in the language in which the message is proclaimed. The present package bears an expiry date of 1789. That is the birth year of the French Revolution, the first explosive revelation of the modern spirit. Therefore it is absolutely necessary to offer our quality product to the people of the twenty-first century in a modern package, that is, in the language of the twenty-first century. The present book is an attempt to do this.

In Search of a Modern Formulation for the Old Message

A preliminary note is due. Is it absolute necessary that everybody buys our product, that is, that everyone becomes a Christian, preferably a Roman Catholic, and remains it, and thus at least sociologically belongs to the Church? This was the uncontestable certainty up and until the nineteenth century, laid down in the well-known adage that was first formulated by bishop Cyprian of Carthage in about 250: 'Outside the Church there is no salvation'. Most missionary activity has been driven by this certainty. To be sure, God's plan with this world, the foundation of his dominion, includes in good Jewish-Christian thinking that the world becomes gradually infused with divine grace, which will turn it into a society that pleases the Lord. The biblical parabolic images of yeast and salt do not suggest, however, that the whole world should be turned *into* yeast or salt, but rather that it will be become a better world due to the yeast and the salt. The decline of official Church membership is in that respect not terribly alarming. The situation only becomes alarming when the baptized are no longer active Catholics but rather consoling statistical figures. And this seems to be more and more the case. It is also alarming when people with an 'honest and good heart' (Luke 8:15), who would be potential members of the Church, do not find what they are looking for in the proclamation of the Gospel and do not see their religious needs fulfilled there. Even if it is repeated a hundred times that the proclamation is the bread of eternal life, this bread has become as hard as stone from old age. Seekers get the impression that they are offered rocks instead of bread. The message does not touch them and will never touch them, because it is spoken in a language that has no existential sound for them. It has never outgrown the 'first naivety', the phase before modern critical thought and before the declaration of human rights.

To reformulate the entire heteronomously formulated doctrine of the Church with its armory of articles of faith, rituals, traditions, practices, spiritualities and rules in theonomous language would require the work of a lifetime. In the present book this can only be attempted for some of the most central elements of the Christian heritage. For each of these elements, its heteronomous character has first to be clarified, as this character makes the doctrine or the ritual or the rule no longer acceptable for the faithful who has left heteronomy behind. Thereafter, the traditional religious formulation has to be carefully analyzed so as to lay bare the religious experience behind it. It is the latter that interests us, because, whereas the formulation is the product of abstract thinking, cast into the thought molds of a certain era, the experience is the ever new, living encounter with divine reality. This experience constitutes the essence of religious faith and requires an actualizing reformulation in theonomous language. An example should make this clear: If Jesus of Nazareth lived in our time, and we children of modernity would meet him, we would use an entirely different language to express the same experience of sacred depth that his disciples lived through in their encounter with him. We would neither come up with images such as 'King' or 'High Priest', 'Lamb of God' or 'Word' or 'Sitting on The Right Hand of God', nor with dogmatic definitions of his relation to God as the Second Person of the Holy Trinity. This does not invalidate these earlier formulations; rather it means that these are no longer compelling for the modern human because they no longer convey a revealing insight.

In translating traditional images into modern ones there is one important rule: where an image is based on a super- or extra-cosmic world that intervenes in ours, this image has to make way for a different one in which God surfaces as the deepest ground of the cosmos, to which the human also belongs. But the cosmos and the human are concrete realities. What happens to them can always, at least to a certain degree, be experienced. In the two-world scheme, processes can take place so completely in the divine, that is, the other, world that they no longer manifest themselves in our human world as an asset of depth, liberation or renewal. Take, for example, the removal of original sin from the newborn through baptism. Or what the tradition holds about Jesus' crucifixion: that by dying on the cross he saved the world, conquered death and Satan, paid Adam's debt and re-opened the gates of Heaven that had been closed since Adam's sin. None of this is verifiable within our world. In the autonomous scheme that knows only one world, such processes are not real; they are at most beautiful, but in any event idle, products of fantasy. This is not only the opinion of the modern unbeliever but also of the believer. Both ask rightfully to what in this concrete reality these formulations refer. The unbeliever will shrug his shoulders in rejection and ask this question with a compassionate smile. The believer who is the heir to a long shared tradition of faith will ask this in the hope of finding out which existential, good news can be discovered in these heteronomous formulations. S/He knows that they are part of a mythical language, designed in the past and as such outstripped by the present, but that they bear a kernel of actual good news and that they are as such the expression of an everlasting value-loaded experience. S/He wants to participate in this and rephrase it in a way to make it accessible to others also.

The insight that there are two possible axioms that lead to different formulations of the same experience should make us tolerant. Progressives should not consider conservatives stubborn and naïve: the tradition of past theological thinking witnesses to a fantastic sharpness and subtlety and has found answers to all the difficulties that flew from its images; unfortunately the answer was often that nothing is impossible for God. The heteronomists, on the other hand, should stop accusing their more progressive fellow believers of rejecting the revealed truth and stop condemning them as heretics, iconoclasts and unbelievers. At stake are simply two different but equally faithful approaches to the same mystery which is always larger than our minds and our hearts. Because such is God: always larger. However, as autonomous thinking grows stronger and more and more accepted, less and less will remain standing of the traditional, that is, heteronomous, Christian formulations and the practices that are based on them. Just as the rock in Nebuchadnezzar's dream did not leave anything standing of the statue that reached unto Heaven.

THE PAINFUL NECESSITY OF A FAREWELL

It is of course possible to stay faithful to the axiom of heteronomy, mindful of the adage that the old wine is better. But that is betting on the wrong horse. Everything indicates that the new axiom will gradually dominate the entirety of humanity. Western scientific thinking—which is the cradle of the new axiom—and the assets of modern technology are conspicuously dominating ideas and certainties all over the globe. The traditional doctrine of faith that was based on the axiom of the two worlds is like a town that was built on what appeared to be solid ground but that now appears to be no more than a mighty ice field. But alas, a mental climate change is in effect, causing the ice field to melt at an accelerating tempo. We can keep on dreaming of a new Ice Age, but we would do better to leave heteronomy behind before the whole enterprise starts to sink, and go aboard the life-boat with only our most precious possessions, leaving behind with great sadness the rest of our centuries-old treasures, knowing they will go down forever. They are, after all, transitory, like every work of human hands. We will have to live as displaced persons for a long time, housing in temporary quarters that will be missing a lot in comparison with the spiritual comfort we enjoyed in the past. Only much later will a new town emerge in which we will regain some of our past security and welfare. Meanwhile we will have to do without our past certainties and accept that we have to leave many questions unanswered.

There is, for example, the important unsolved question as to what will replace our former descriptive certainties about the 'extremes'. What, in this new perspective, happens to us when we die? In a view that has no place for another 'world' in which one ends up after this life ends, there is evidently no place for a final judgment, a Heaven, a Hell and a Purgatory. And what remains of reward and punishment? All these traditional images and certainties cannot but collapse, like the statue in Nebuchadnezzar's dream, if it is assumed that there nothing else than this cosmos, albeit a cosmos that is full of the God of Jesus of Nazareth. They collapse because they were considered to be realistic descriptions, whereas they were in fact ancient Christian myths. But the good news that is coagulated in these untenable images calls out for new images in which it can again become liquid and nutritious.

FAREWELL TO THE ANCIENT CHRISTIAN MYTHS

The majority of the doctrines of the Church are in fact ancient Christian myths. This does not hold only for the examples that were just given. It also applies to the Fall in the Garden of Eden, the virginal conception of Jesus, or his ascension to Heaven. It even holds for some doctrines that appear to be the supporting columns of the ecclesiastical building, such as the incarnation and the resurrection. The word 'myth' is often used to define something as unbelievable, as a fairy tale. But in reality, myths are the profound stories of a people or a culture about the forces that dominate human life and the relations between these forces and us. These stories are utterly reliable for a given people or for their culture. Christianity developed in the ancient Greek and Roman culture that knew many such myths. But these were pagan myths and hence they were for the Christians utterly unacceptable because they could not be reconciled with their own specific Christian myths. Christianity therefore soon developed its own myths. This was inevitable. About the Mystery and its relation to us we can only speak in images, that is, in myths. The inherent danger is that these myths will be held for reality. But myths are not messages; they are the presentation of an experienced deeper reality. The festive existence of the Immortals on the Olympus is such a presentation. For most ancient Greeks this was in every sense true and real. The bliss of the angels and saints in Heaven is just such a myth. For medieval people this was equally true and real. But after the Enlightenment, this can only be an image, a myth, no less than the Gods on the Olympus. This means: we no longer take it literally but at the most as a way of presenting a *logos*, that is, an idea or a truth. As long as people accepted these tales as true representations of reality, they did not ask the question as to which *logos* lies hidden beneath the *mythos*. In the past, only rare enlightened spirits such as Socrates asked such questions. Now everyone that bears the mark of the Enlightenment asks them. We have to, even when it concerns the stories and images of the ancient Christian mythology. We can no longer believe them, presented the way they are.

For the modern believer this means a very painful exodus. Speaking about the exodus reminds us of the departure of Abraham from Ur of the Chaldees, leaving his clan and his Babylonian culture behind to search for a land as yet unknown to him. And of the adventure that made Israel, according to its own mythical past, the People of God. This memory means also that this book is not about destroying holy icons but, just as with Abraham and Israel, about a liberating departure. This exodus should lead the reader towards a renewed encounter with the divine, just as happened to Abraham at the Terebinth of Mamre and with Israel at Horeb.

The asset of the Enlightenment was not that it taught Western people to think with precision and clarity. The medieval philosophers and theologians thought in a very precise and clear manner, but they always took for granted that the biblical stories and the doctrines that were built on them were trustworthy accounts. The role of the Enlightenment consisted of opening the eyes of Western people to the fact that these stories were no accounts at all, not more than those of the Gilgamesh epic or the Iliad. The world in which these stories take place cannot be reconciled with the world as we know it, characterized by unshakeable physical, chemical and electro-magnetic laws. Eventually, therefore, the adherents of the Enlightenment saw themselves obliged to erase this totally different world, to which also the Christian myths belong. But they forgot to question which *logos*, which deeper truth and enriching message had been symbolized and expressed by the ancient Christian myths. They forgot, because they were so annoyed by the stubbornness with which the Church—out of fear of what was coming at it— kept on presenting its images as realities. And because, on top of it all, it had the nerve to reject modernity in its totality on the basis of these images. Aggression narrows the view, makes one blind. In its aggression against the Church, the Enlightenment became blind for the depth of the Christian myths. And in its blindness it threw out the baby with the bath water.

Modern-day believers are looking for this baby. They are no less averse to the Church's denial of the inner-worldly reality and its laws of thought than modern unbelievers. Also for them, there is no longer a God who would intervene from his world into our own, revealing truths, threatening with punishments, granting supplications, rewarding the righteous, descending in human form into our world, walking around in it, shaking its physical laws. Also for them, this is obsolete mythic thinking, ancient Christian mythology, sometimes poetic and moving; sometimes irritating, sometimes strange, even verging on the bizarre. They find it obsolete not because it is mythic, but because those ancient Christian myths clash too fiercely with their experience of reality. However, unlike the Enlightenment, they want to discover the richness that lays hidden beneath this mythic language to reformulate it in the language of the twenty-first century. This new language will be mythic in its own way. As has already been said, speaking about the mysterious Ultimate Reality can only be done in images and thus in myths. But today these have to be the images and the myths of the twenty-first century that can be eye-openers for the people of the twenty-first century. Occasionally the believer can still use something of the old mythic language as deliberate imagery, but not as the record of actual happenings, as they are still regarded by the average believer, and even by the bulk of church authorities. In most cases, however, they will have to leave this language and look for a better one.

THE CLASH BETWEEN AUTONOMOUS THINKING AND CHURCH DOCTRINE

Important in all this is that it is impossible for modern people to keep thinking in the heteronomous system without ending up in a terrible self-contradiction. This is precisely what makes the exodus so necessary. Such a contradiction is like a biting acid that slowly but steadily dissolves the acceptance of the message itself. This is probably the reason for the recurrent, previously unthinkable, results of recent surveys: that the average believer disagrees with Rome on many issues, not only on the papal guidelines regarding sexuality but also on what church authorities present as the essential points of belief, to be found in the already mentioned Vatican *Catechism of the Catholic Church*. This widespread dissent is not necessarily the result of unbelief or bad faith. It is equally often the result of an incapacity to subscribe to statements that run counter to what modern humans—often still unconsciously—consider as self-evident as cars, televisions and refrigerators. A classic example of such incapacity is their acceptance of the theory of evolution.

In contradistinction to, for example, the Mormons, Jehovah's Witnesses and other kinds of creationists, most modern Catholics subscribe without problems to this theory. If they did not already absorb it with their mother's milk, they probably absorbed it later. But as will become clear now, the acceptance of this theory brings them unwittingly into conflict with the religious doctrines that they, at least for the time being, still profess. This is because the theory of evolution flagrantly contradicts the biblical presentation of the creation by explaining the origin of the species, up to and including that of the human, as an infinitely slow, natural process of development, the laws of which it has all but disclosed, and not as a work of creation by God-in-Heaven. In the wake of billions of years, the unicellular and the multicellular species, the mollusks, the vertebrates and the mammals develop subsequently as the result of random mutations and natural selection. Eventually, the animals with hands and brains split themselves of as a distinct group in the family of the mammals, and this group divided itself into even smaller groups, among which were the primates from which the human species developed.

It can only come as a surprise then that in the entire above-mentioned *Catechism* (date of publication 1993, not 1493!) the word 'evolution' does not appear once, not even where it should be expected, that is, in the discussion of the Creation. The word that *is* mentioned there is 'original sin'. This original sin occurred 'at the beginning of history of man' and was 'freely committed by our first parents' (par. 390). About these 'first parents' it is further related that they were 'constituted in a state of holiness' (par. 398) but lost this harmony and purity by refusing to obey an explicit prohibition from God. As a result, the soul lost its control over the body and the harmony between man and woman made way for a relationship of lust and domination. And as the great surprise that tops it all: only then death would have made its first entrance into human history (par. 400).

How can such formulations be reconciled with the theory of evolution? To start with, it does not seem likely that humanity would have originated in the way presented by the theory of monogenism that is warranted by the Church, that is, with one man and one woman who, by sheer coincidence, reached the threshold of humanity at the same time. It is much more likely that this happened to several pairs at distinct locations and times, as is claimed by scientific polygenism.

But much trickier questions are lurking elsewhere. Where in the gradual evolution from pithecanthropus (literally: ape-human) to homo sapiens, as the human is called scientifically, is there a place for a human pair that would be blessed with the perfection and the knowledge and the inner harmony ascribed to them by the Tradition? And how is the immortality of this pair to be fitted into the history of the evolution of the living beings? Before them and after them everything that breathes dies, from flea to brontosaur and from pithecanthropus to homo sapiens. Further, how could this human pair that just emerged from the twilight zone of animal conscience suddenly have possessed such a lucid knowledge of

God, including knowledge of his explicit commandments (whence could they have learned these?), that they could have rejected these with a firm and deliberate 'no'? To explain this 'no', the presence of a devil was necessary, himself being an originally good spirit who, by himself, even though his 'self' was good, turned completely and irrevocably evil, and this without the help of another evil seducer.

If it were only about a so-called 'primeval event, a deed that took place at the beginning of the history of man', as the *Catechism* has it (par. 390), roughly one million years before our time, it would be easy to classify this with other past events and go on with today's business. But this is not the case: this primeval event has disastrous consequences for today's business. The tragedy of human mortality comes exclusively from there and everything that is wrong with the human and with society: repression and humiliation, cruelty and suffering, all the disasters and the pains of human history, up to and including the birth pangs of women and the difficult labor to gain our daily bread. This procession of disasters does not make it easy to assent to the jubilation about the *felix culpa*, 'the truly necessary sin of Adam', during the Easter night service. It is about time that this late-Roman hymn makes way for a more contemporary song about the way Jesus' freely accepted death can bear a saving meaning for us.

CONSEQUENCES FOR THE DOCTRINE OF ORIGINAL SIN

The concept of Original Sin is the foundation of the classical theory of the hereditary nature of this sin. The desperate attempts of the Catechism to arrive at a satisfying formulation of that doctrine demonstrate how obscure it has become for the modern human who is seeking insight. In paragraph 404, the question is at least not shunned: 'How did the sin of Adam become the sin of all his descendants?' The answer is found in the unity of the human race. 'Still, the transmission of original sin is a mystery that we cannot fully understand'. To further this understanding, the *Catechism* pulls out a theological trick which ends with the statement: 'that is why original sin is called "sin" only in an analogical sense: it is a sin "contracted" and not "committed"—a state and not an act.' And in par. 405 it reads, again, that 'original sin does not have the character of a personal fault in any of Adam's descendants'. If there is no personal fault, then there is personal innocence. And how can we reconcile this with the catastrophic course of events, which has all the characteristics of a punishment? Such a complicated solution is very difficult to understand: a sin that is in fact not a real sin (the essence of a sin—personal choice—is lacking) but only an 'analogical' sin (so what remains of the reality?) that yet has to be punished. In the 1442 declaration of faith of the Council of Florence, this punishment still consisted of perennial doom and Hell, compared to which a medieval torture dungeon appears like a vacation resort. This proviso was wisely omitted from the present *Catechism*.

Several other doctrines that are attached to the doctrine of Original Sin will be dragged along in its fall. For example the explanation of baptism as cleansing away original sin; the explanation of Jesus' death on the cross as an atoning sacrifice, with its consequences for the understanding of the Eucharist; the dogma of the Immaculate Conception of Mary, which will lose its ground without the foundation of original sin, as well as the dogma of her ascension to Heaven with soul and body, which is based on her conception without original sin; and as a result of the fall of the two previous dogmas, also the dogma of the infallibility of the pope will collapse. This is more than enough disastrous news. Again the image pops up of the tall statue in Nebuchadnezzar's dream that reaches unto Heaven and utterly breaks apart.

THE NECESSITY OF A TRANSLATION

The contradiction in the simultaneous acceptance of the theory of evolution and the doctrine of original sin is only one of the many clashes between unconscious autonomous thinking and traditional heteronomous religious concepts. Autonomy is nowadays accepted by almost everybody, as shows from the behavior of even the most conservative Christians. Why else would they visit a doctor when they are ill, instead of invoking the formerly competent saints or taking pilgrimages to their holy sites? Or why would they defend democracy and human rights, even if these were condemned by the Church until deep in the nineteenth century? And why do they protest against religious compulsion even though such compulsion was traditionally considered to be very Christian and the Church has applied it liberally, even with the help of torture and the stake. The answer is always the same: because by their behavior they show that they recognize the autonomy of the human and the cosmos, even though their mind often still denies it. But this often unconscious acceptance of autonomy brings the supporters of heteronomy into a hidden conflict with many traditional Christian ideas. One who takes the attainments of modern thinking seriously cannot but grow further and further away from ideas that are still presented to him in medieval garb. The whole of Christian doctrine therefore needs urgently to be translated into the language of the twenty-first century. This translation will start in the following chapter. The most important themes from dogmatics and spirituality will subsequently be treated; the Table of Contents shows what they are. For each of these themes, the heteronomous character of their traditional formulation will first be laid bare. Thereafter an attempt will be made to find a modern translation for the religious experience that lies behind it. The result of this tentative translation will not always be satisfactory. The contrary would be a miracle. We are embarking on an exploration of barely discovered land on which for that reason there are no paths yet. Paths will materialize there, however, when many people begin to come and go.

Chapter 4

No Book of Oracles but a Book of Witness

Scripture as the Source of Our Faith

This book will undoubtedly evoke worried and even condemning reactions. Such a book is dangerous, it will be said, it is more liberal than religious, yes, even heretical. In most cases this criticism will flow from an honest concern for the integrity of the traditional religious heritage, big chunks of which seem to be washed away by the flood of the author's personal opinions. Religious matters are indeed matters of inheritance. Whoever wants to present something as Christian heritage, should be able to demonstrate that he is not trying to sell his favorite ideas under the label of Christianity. Otherwise this person will become a new Joseph Smith coming up with a new book of Mormon. Every Christian has to be well aware of the fact that he belongs to a religious community that has its living roots in the first century of the Common Era. What cannot in one way or another be traced back to the centuries-old tradition of this community, cannot lay claim to Christian identity. Therefore it is necessary at this point to treat the ancient and perennial sources from which a contemporary religious view should draw in order to claim Christian identity and to avoid the stigma of heterodoxy. Catholic theology identifies these two sources: Scripture and Tradition, both written with a capital.

A SOURCE OF FAITH BUT NOT AN ORACLE

The first of these two sources, Holy Scripture, seems easy to find. Take the Ignatius Bible and there it is, a to z. However, the reality is more complex than this. You may be holding the book but you will only access its contents when you read it and understand it. This is where the problems start. First, there is its volume: depending on the edition, the text takes up over 1000 pages in small print, spread over two columns. Which Catholic has ever read the whole book, let alone internalized it? The second and even larger obstacle is the distance between our way of speaking and thinking, and that of these two to three thousand year-old texts. A translation cannot take away this barrier. This distance weighs heavily on the comprehensibility of the text and is often the cause of misunderstanding and incorrect interpretation, with the effect that one might elevate one's own mistakes to a source of faith.

What does it mean concretely that this book, with its often confusing and sometimes contradictory texts, is a source of faith? Is it maybe a divine book of oracles, each and every one of its words waiting to be weighed on a gold scale, because it lifts up a corner of the veil that hangs over the mystery of God and the world? Is everything affirmed in this book correct, everything claimed in it the truth? Should we agree with everything that is written in it, merely because it is in this book, even if it contradicts the insights and certainties of a society that in the meantime has developed further?

One gets this impression, not only when listening to Jehovah's Witnesses, but also when hearing the recurring reaction of Catholics that are confronted with new presentations of the ancient tradition: 'But in the Bible it reads…', 'But doesn't Jesus teach…?', 'But Paul writes…'; after which the door of conversation is closed and the discussion is over. It shouldn't be this way, because even if it is written the way it is and even if the author meant it as it stands there (which is not always the case), it still remains his personal opinion, his belief, which does not exclude, of course, that this already was, or has become the belief of a church community. The author is, however, not a divine oracle. What he writes is and remains a human word. Just as all the others he has everything he claims to know about the 'above' from 'below'. If Paul thinks that a woman should remain silent during a service, or that she has to wear a head covering when she prays, then this does not imply that

God orders her to do this, only that Paul would like to have it this way. For he belonged to a culture in which women were still second class people. When John says that the Word was God from the beginning, this is his personal way of grasping the relation between Jesus and God; but his views are not such that they oblige me to see it the same way. The tradition knows of other ways to approach this relation. True, the views of this author have received an enormous following and this for good reasons. Therefore I should try to understand these reasons, so that I can come to grips with them in an intelligent way. Even the words in the Gospel that are ascribed to Jesus himself, are still human words, which means that, like most human words, they are open to various interpretations, so that it is not always possible to decide once and for all whether they have to be taken literally or not; whether they are a minimum requirement or an ideal; whether Jesus spoke like everyone in his time—which implies that his words are temporal—or whether he spoke from a deep experience of God—which implies that they are eternally valid; whether they are the answer to a concrete question, or rather have a general bearing, applicable everywhere and at any time. And finally, did Jesus himself really speak these words and did he say them in exactly this way? We can only hear what the evangelist, who was a human just like us, has Jesus say from his personal belief in him.

Is Scripture Not the 'Word of the Living God'?

We can put it this way: when Paul wrote a letter to a church in Asia Minor, was every sentence, every word of his, divinely inspired? Paul himself in any event never thought this was the case. If he would have suspected that countless future people would take each word that flowed from his pen as decisive for their thinking and acting, convinced that it came directly from God, he would probably have stopped writing letters out of sheer anguish. Or he would have inserted at regular intervals: 'This is my opinion, but please feel free to think otherwise'. Similarly, the gospels are not the fruit of divine dictation. This might be suggested in the circular mosaics above the crossing of the Saint Peter's basilica in Rome, in which the four evangelists look up, their six-foot-long goose feathers ready to write. These mosaics reflect the ideas of the people in the time they were composed, which explain their imagery. But did it really happen that way?

Even disregarding the heteronomous world in which this idea of inspiration originated, it still contains a whole gamut of contradictions to the critical mind. How can the Word of God contradict itself, one wonders, by having Joseph with Mary and their baby return to Nazareth after the presentation of Jesus in the temple (in Luke), and at the same time have them flee to Egypt to protect the child from the murderous plans of Herod (in Matthew)? Or by ascribing two different family trees to Jesus? And how can the Word of God be at odds with historical or scientific facts, for example by classifying hares with the animals that chew the cud, as in Leviticus 11:4–6; or by having the sun stand still above Gibeon, as is stated in Joshua 10:13? In addition, that eternal and unchangeable Word of God contains statements that cannot be taken as perennial or unchangeable with the best will in the world. Think about the catalogs of sins and corresponding punishments in Leviticus 20 , or the commandments to stone adulteresses and homosexuals. Even the Church's magisterium does not seem to honor the unchangeable and eternal validity of these commandments, because it discards countless commandments from the Old Testament without any scruples, even very holy commandments, such as circumcision, the Shabbat rest, or the prohibition against consuming blood (a capital offense, see Leviticus 17:14). How can the magisterium afford to do this, if these commandments are God's own words, declared to be eternally valid down to the smallest detail by Jesus in his Sermon on the Mount (Matt. 5:18). The magisterium does not even take each and every word of Jesus himself seriously, as with his prohibition against swearing oaths. It is not necessary to delve even deeper into the jungle of difficulties that relate to the traditional view that Scripture is a collection of God's own words.

As a matter of fact, this view implies that we make human words divine, because we lift them out of their historical limits and essential inadequacy, and assign them unassailability and absoluteness, characteristics we reserve for the sacred Mystery that we call God. To do so would be a disguised form of idolatry. The decisive argument against the traditional presentation of divine inspiration is, however, its heteronomous character. This in the first place makes it untenable in modern times.

That the words of these authors are the expression of their personal (albeit also communal) beliefs, explains the divergences and even contradictions between them. If so, we shouldn't be afraid to think or to speak in a way that deviates from a specific current of the scriptural tradition, even if this has become the main current, as long as our words originate in our belief in Jesus Christ and are nourished by a side-stream of the same tradition. The tradition is indeed a river delta with many arms. This frees us from the obsession to smooth out all bumps, to harmonize what does not fit in and even to flatten out stark contradictions with all sorts of tricks, so that we can forget about them without feeling uneasy. The diverse statements of Scripture represent various aspects and phases of the Tradition, which in their turn reflect various ways to express faith in God and Jesus.

THE FIRST WITNESS TO THE TRADITION

If Scripture is not literally God's word, and if it is not infallible, then what is it? It is the oldest collection of texts that the ancient Church has handed over to us as the residue of its beliefs and in which the Church community keeps on recognizing its own religious insights. The words of the New Testament authors (and what the Church borrowed from the Old Testament) teach us what certain local churches or specific branches of the universal Church in the first and second centuries thought and believed. Practically none of these authors belonged to the group that knew and met Jesus in person. Almost all of them had to rely on testimonies and professions of faith of people that actually knew and followed him. Their own encounter with him, from which they drew their certainty, was an encounter of faith. From this perspective we are not worse off than these authors, since our situation is not that much different from theirs. Indeed, just as we have to rely on them to learn something about the historical Jesus, they had to rely on the first witnesses. And just as with them, without a personal encounter with Jesus through faith in him, the data transmitted to us will not go beyond the level of interesting facts, comparable to what we know about the Roman emperors. It will remain fodder for the brain, not food for the heart. Our God-filled existence, reached through a faithful encounter with Jesus, is not the effect of knowledge, but just as it happened with them, the fruit of a faithful surrender, which enriches our hearts and gives us the inner certainty that we are on the right track.

If the human character of Scripture is so clearly established, is it still possible to call it the 'Word of the Living God', as many a lector concludes the reading of Scripture in the Service of the Word? Most certainly so, for the simple reason that it takes two partners to establish an encounter. The record of such an encounter is marked by the input of both. The Bible is the sediment of the encounter with God of many generations of faithful Jews and Christians. Much divine 'speaking' is therefore present as the background of their human words. Precisely for this reason do we speak about Holy Scripture, which means as much as divine Scripture. This does not imply that each of its sentences and words are divine, incontestable, forever valid and above all criticism. Incontestable is only God's speaking itself, which can only be embodied in the contestable words of human beings. The imperfection of this embodiment entails that different and even better embodiments were and are still possible, even such that could be hardly reconciled with the one embodiment that we know.

Revelation

This being said, what remains of the revelatory character of Scripture? Here a word about revelation is in order. Also this notion is suffused with heteronomy in ecclesiastical discourse. It suggests that something that we cannot discover by ourselves, but that is indispensable for us, is graciously communicated to us from another world that knows everything. Is it, however, possible to speak meaningfully about divine revelation after this other world has vanished?

Sure. How often do we say, 'this was a true revelation to me ', when we suddenly experience an unexpected richness of insight. Something revealed itself to us. 'Revelation' denotes the active side of illumination. But illumination is something that one receives: one 'becomes' enlightened. This 'becoming' points to the passive side of the event. Also in theonomous thinking it is entirely possible to say that God reveals himself by communicating himself, by letting himself be known in the depths of our human psyches—a revelation that rises into our conscience. This conscience is, however, marked and defined by the culture and the abilities of the subject who receives the revelation. Therefore divine 'speaking' (which in itself is a human metaphor) becomes human hearing, interpreting and speaking, with all their characteristics of ignorance, fallibility, clumsiness, mistakes; and with a portion of bad will and selfishness, because these dwell in each of us and influence our thinking and speaking, and not for the better.

The term 'revelation', therefore, receives two characteristics in the theonomous view it did not have in the heteronomous view. The first is that the light in the human being shines bottom-up, rising up from deep inside us into our consciousness, and not, as it was conceived earlier, shining down upon us from on high. This means, for example, that the Roman Curia, despite all its claims to a teaching authority from on high, does not necessarily know God's plan of salvation any better than a faithful base community in Bogotá that tries to listen to God's moving presence from within; and that it should not force this community to think and to speak in the Curia's way.

The second is that this light does not reach us like a pure laser beam, in one color, clear, perfect and unchangeable, but broken up into as many facets of color as there are people. Not one of these facets in and by itself, no single human word about God, can therefore be *the* Word of God, eternal, infallible, and perfect. Consequently, such words, even the words of Scripture, can never lay a claim to absolute truth. They remain human words, often filled with richness and opening paths towards God, sometimes poor and even misleading. If we assent to them, we don't do so because they are infallible in and of themselves, but because they touch us existentially and enrich our lives, like the fantastic word of the author of the First Letter of John: 'God is (the) love' (4:8). This word can become the sustaining foundation of somebody's life, but not because one abstractly knows that it is true (from where would we draw this certainty?), but because one experiences it as fulfilling and meaningful, as a revelation, not as Revelation. The revelatory nature of a word is identical with its potential of reality, and this can be recognized by the existential fruits it produces.

WHAT FOLLOWS FROM THIS?

To give words of Scripture the status of infallible—be it sometimes unclear—oracles, that lend themselves to disparate, even contradictory interpretations, is to disregard the human way in which God comes to us. To use them as the unshakeable foundation on which an equally unshakeable building of binding doctrinal certainties can be erected, is a dangerous game. Scripture is not a magic box with divine answers to human questions. Other confessions or sects may use it as such; a modern Christian shouldn't do this. Neither should we present the words of Scripture as infallible truth to others, to be accepted without discussion. What we can do, however, is to suggest them as an aid inasmuch as we ourselves feel helped by them.

We Christians proclaim that for us the divine light shines in its full brightness in the person of Jesus of Nazareth. Indeed, we have experienced some of this brightness ourselves. First through the written testimonies about him, albeit that these testimonies are subjectively conveyed, limited and one-sided, and shaded by the Jewish or pagan past of their authors; and later through an internal, equally limited and one-sided personal experience which increasingly fills, enriches and illuminates our existence, as we adhere more and more faithfully to Jesus of Nazareth and believe in him in an ever more existential way. But also the Old Testament is for us a sparkling fire of divine light because it contains the sediment of all the incomplete, one-sided and limited experiences of Israel with God—experiences we see, moreover, culminate in the God-experience of Jesus of Nazareth. Therefore Scripture, the Old Testament as well as the New, is for us a (still) richer finding place of the self-revelation of God condensed in human words than the Iliad, the Upanishads or the Koran.

Obviously, a theonomous view of Scripture reduces to naught the practice of presenting one's own views (which of themselves may be very valuable) as irrefutable, even infallible truths, with the help of some quotation from Scripture, and to dismiss the views of others as untenable or heretical, as if Scripture were indeed a book of oracles from which one can pull some quotations to knock out an opponent. Often, such quotes are not only severed from their scriptural context, but their original meaning and resonance are often quite different from what the new user is making of it in support of his or her own views. Of course, there is also a correct use of scriptural argumentation: when one wants to show with scriptural references (with due respect for text and context), not that the idea one stands for is irrefutable, but that it chimes with the overall vision—or with a particular vision—that was (is) alive in Tradition. For Scripture is the main witness to Tradition, more than the entire Patristic literature and the Roman documents taken together. Fortunately, the superstitious practice in which one opens the Bible at random and reads the passage on which it falls open as a kind of holy telegram, sent from the heavenly realm as an answer to the seeker's questions, has at least disappeared.

READING THE BIBLE. WHICH WAY TO GO?

All these speculations should not blind us to what is probably the biggest problem with Scripture. For almost a thousand years, direct contact with this primary source of faith has been reserved to the small segment of society having had the privilege of learning Latin: the clergy and monks. All others, the majority of the people of God, had to content themselves with sermons, if at all dealing with Scripture, and with the so-called 'Bible of the poor': the scant fragments of the Bible hewn in stone on the facades of the cathedrals, sculpted on pulpits and capitals, shown in frescos on the walls and the vaults of the churches, in oil paintings on altar retables and canvasses, carved in wood on decorative panels and depicted in stained glass windows. As a rule, this iconography was restricted to the scenes of Creation and Fall, the Infancy narratives, the Passion story and the Last Judgment; or scenes from the life of Our Lady as related in the apocryphal Proto-gospel of James. Therefore it can hardly be said that the masses were familiar with Scripture.

When shortly after the invention of the printing press the Reformation started to spread explosively, the Bible, translated during the same time, soon came into the hands of all who could read, not only of those who knew Latin. Alarmed Church authorities reacted by greatly discouraging autonomous reading of the Bible in the vernacular, as part of their counter-reformatory strategies and as a remedy against possible digressions from the only correct official Roman doctrine. The remedy ended up being worse than the disease it claimed to cure. Out of necessity, catholic piety sought its food elsewhere, in the cult of Our Lady and the Saints, in the rosary prayer, in pilgrimages and processions, in messenger-appearances, in private revelations, in worship of the Holy Sacrament, in care for poor souls in Purgatory, in the earning of indulgences, and more often than not in superstitious practices. Protestant piety nourished itself with Scripture and is therefore still today more familiar with its content and its language.

The breakthrough of modernity with its autonomous thinking worsened the cause of the Catholic camp even more drastically, for the heteronomous sphere in which Scripture breathes, now appeared as a real blockage to the transmission of its message. Access to this message is presently only possible at the cost of a continuous transposition, for Scripture speaks the language of an entirely different culture and way of thinking than the modern one. That language can only become ours up to a certain point, and only with the help of a cultural-historical and scientific knowledge enjoyed by just a small group of privileged people. Unlike in the past, however, personal reading of the Bible is no longer discouraged by Church authorities but rather recommended, and no means are spared to help the average faithful step across the high threshold of estrangement and to convince them to read the Bible: more accurate and also freer translations of the Bible, Biblical exhibits, Biblical study circles, Biblical calendars, Biblical days, Biblical weekends, Biblical years and so on. These initiatives cannot be praised enough. Yet they only reach a small percentage of the basis. For all the others, the large majority of Church people, the estrangement continues undiminished. This estrangement raises the question whether propaganda (or publicity) for making people read the Bible really pays off. Even if people can be moved to take up Bible reading, most of them will give it up before long. Modern readers who are ill-prepared for this job, will not be able to understand rightly the message it contains. They are not familiar with the world of thought of the Bible, and on top of it the intra-ecclesial developments have already rendered obsolete much of the faith imagery used there. The texts are replete with personal and geographical names that are meaningless to them; they have no knowledge of the historical backgrounds and of the practices and ideas of those days. Under these circumstances, reading the Bible will not really nourish them in the way it is supposed to do. Have a try yourself with the Letter to the Romans; read it with the eyes of a twenty-first century person without being upset or annoyed, if this is at all possible. Therefore instead of recommending the whole Bible with its 2000 columns one would do better to make anthologies of those texts that are still more or less easily accessible. But even then many explanations would be needed, as well as a general introduction to guide modern readers through the difficulties that confront them in reading a literature that is 2000 years old or even older.

A last critical remark concerns the never questioned practice of reading passages from Scripture Sunday after Sunday in Christian congregations, texts that are for the large majority of the faithful (if they are already listening) barely more understandable than the Hebrew or Greek original. But here we enter the domain of the liturgy, which is another part of Tradition. This is the subject of the following chapter.

Chapter 5

The Indissoluble Tie with the Beginning

Tradition Our Only Source of Beliefs

From Chapter 4 it can be derived that Scripture is the first and foremost source of Tradition—of 'Tradition' with capital 'T', which is not the same as 'tradition' with a small 't'; just as 'Scripture' with capital 'S' is not the same as 'scripture' with a small 's' 'Tradition' with a small 't' is the whole set of transmitted customs and thought forms. 'Tradition' with capital 'T' refers to the multifariously transmitted 'deposit' of experiences the faithful had in encountering Jesus-Messiah. These are experiences of salvation, well-being, fulfillment, renewal, meaningfulness and existential enrichment, because for those who believe in him, Jesus is the apogee of God's self-revelation. In the past, and often still today, this Tradition was considered a second source of beliefs. In fact it is the only one, because Scripture also is such a transmitted 'deposit', albeit the first one and in that sense the most original. Besides Scripture, Tradition contains all the other expressions of the common belief in Jesus as our Messiah, such as the liturgy and extra-liturgical prayer, professions of faith, pronouncements of Councils and Synods, popes, Doctors of the Church and bishops, spiritualities and mysticism, catechisms, pious practices, and even canon law—and not only those of the past but also those of today. This 'second form' of tradition is also holy to us, because it, too, opens a door to the Christ who lives in the church community and, through him, to God.

However, what is true for Scripture (see above) is also true for Tradition. Tradition, too, is tremendously dependent on the factors 'person, time and place'. Tradition is the residue and outcome of an ecclesiastical vision within a very specific cultural framework. And cultural frameworks are always in motion; sometimes infinitely slow, which makes them appear immovable, sometimes awfully fast, as in our days. In all its richness, this 'deposit' is therefore basically temporary. The more radical the changes in culture, the more radical too will be the ensuing changes in religious imagery and formulations. Much of the religious heritage is therefore already long past its expiry date. From this it follows that we have to approach Tradition, especially today, with the attitude recommended by Paul in the oldest text of the Tradition, his First Letter to the Thessalonians (5:21): "Test everything and keep what is good", because today is such a time of fast cultural changes. This entails that today's images and formulations will drastically diverge from those of earlier days. Despite all those changes, however, the tie with Tradition should remain intact; otherwise we would cease to be part of the community of faith that was born from the public appearance of Jesus of Nazareth. A Christian cannot just profess anything whatsoever. Reincarnation, for example, has never been part of Tradition: it is neither found in Scripture nor in any other source. The same holds for the idea of God as an impersonal power or as just another name for nature. Such ideas have drifted along with the stream of modernity; reincarnation, for example, came in as a reaction to the image of resurrection of the body, that has become untenable for modern thinking people. This book is a quest for formulations of belief that stay in line with Tradition and continue it, but at the same time are compatible with twenty-first century culture. As such they must basically diverge from the formulations that originated in the Middle Ages and in the Tridentine era. Of the many aspects of Tradition, three are particularly important: the Creed, the liturgy, and magisterial pronouncements. The former two will be treated in the present chapter, the latter in Chapter 6.

THE CREED

A major witness to Tradition is the Creed, the profession of faith, which is also called 'symbolum'. The Greek word *symbolon* refers to a means of recognition. The Creed was a means of recognition which gave one legitimate membership in the Christian community, a sort of badge that provided access to Christian gatherings. It taught what one had to profess as a Christian. When we refer to the symbolum today, we think specifically of the 'twelve articles of faith' that are recited after the sermon in Sunday mass—'are professed' is too flattering a word. Historically, however, there were plenty of Creeds or symbola. There is a Western and thus Latin formulation of the Creed, and an Eastern and thus Greek formulation, and both exist in several variants. The Western Creed has been transmitted in a Roman, a North-African, a Gallic, an Irish, and a Spanish variant, among others, and also in the Eastern Creed one had various local—longer or shorter—versions. The rule of thumb for dating these creeds is: the older the shorter. This shows that, with the progress of time and influenced by the spirit of the time, the fairway for the faithful has been increasingly narrowed down. The specifications almost invariably dealt with the person of Jesus and his relation to God.

All these creeds are very concise summaries of the religious view that is expressed in Scripture. Therefore, all the items that create problems to modern people in Scripture simply resurface in the Creeds: the imagery and language of Tradition, including the Creeds, are incurably heteronomous. If we want to use the 'twelve articles of faith' today to express what we really profess, we will certainly come off badly. We will need time and again to switch on a spiritual adaptor to translate the bulk of these articles in theonomous language. If not, we can only recite the creed, but not truly profess it. This has already been demonstrated with some examples at the end of Chapter 2. The various chapters in this book attempt to show how the religious content that is formulated in the Creed, will suddenly take on a different, more brilliant meaning, in a modern presentation. A formulation that is adapted to the modern understanding and which allows us to truly profess our Creed will follow in the epilogue.

The Christians of Thessalonica to whom Paul addressed his first letter, would probably have been flabbergasted when hearing the Creed as sung or recited in the Latin High Mass of old. They would have wondered if this Creed still dealt with the same faith as they themselves professed. 'Of course it deals with the same faith!' would have been the answer in the year 381, when the Creed of the Council of Constantinople was settled. And also today, the official answer is still the same: the faith never changes, nothing is added to it, nothing is taken away from it; it only develops and makes explicit what was implicit in it. The original message contains (and conceals) infinitely much more than one could suspect in 60 AD, to the point of covering all the items of the Catechism of the Catholic Church with its roughly 700 pages. Everything contained in this Catechism has allegedly surfaced very gradually, as the fruit of the patient workings of the Spirit of truth which will guide the Church 'into the full truth', as the author of the fourth Gospel has Jesus say after the Last Supper (John 16:13). This centuries-long development of faith content is called 'evolution of dogma'. The provisional end point of this 'evolution of dogma' are the dogmas of the nineteenth and twentieth centuries: the infallibility (albeit solely under strict conditions) of the Pope (1870); the Immaculate Conception of Mary (1854); and her ascension with body and soul into Heaven (1950). Fortunately, also the innovative views of the Second Vatican Council which have sprouted as surprising young twigs from the old and half-moldered trunk of the counter-reformatory Church, are part of this development. Those are, strictly speaking, not called 'dogmas', yet they are therefore no less valuable, not less Tradition.

Whenever Protestant fellow Christians asks their Catholic brothers and sisters which scriptural base they have for ascertaining the three aforementioned dogmas, they have in all honesty to admit that these cannot be found in Scripture, not even with a magnifying glass. 'But', they are quick to add, 'that is also not needed'. God's Spirit guides Tradition and does so infallibly. This is reflected in the so called *sensus fidelium*, the faith sense of the Church community. If the faithful all together, or at least their representatives (even though not elected by them), hold that something is true, then it is true. It is as simple as that. But if the main witness to original Tradition, Scripture, does not give us a clue, how can we know that we have stayed on the flying route of the original tradition? By means of which automatic pilot?

The official stock answer is obvious: 'By means of the Holy Spirit!' But we should not hastily speak that way. The question is not whether God's Spirit is active in the Church. This is part of the bedrock of Tradition. If God's Spirit was intensely active in Jesus Christ, then it is also active in the community of those who have, as it were, merged with him into one body, that is: in the Church, not as a human institution with all its inherent flaws but as God's new creation that shines forth through that institution. The more one thinks in an evolutionary perspective, the more evident it becomes that the community of the faithful will only gradually discover the full richness of the original message. Finding truth takes place in progressive steps. For God's Spirit is the creative, incessantly renewing Spirit.

The crucial question is which criterion we have at our disposal to distinguish enriching evolution, called forth by the creating Spirit, from distortion, unleashed by unholy gravity. It is all too obvious that several phenomena in the history of the Church do not in the least bear witness to the Spirit of Jesus. After all it could not have been otherwise. The evangelical message has been disseminated in the cultures it christianized, but in turn it often became polluted by them, blended with its unevangelical counterpart, resulting in a mixture that was dragged along as ecclesiastical truth sometimes for centuries. The history of the Church appears to be a traveling pageant of deformations and aberrations and even shameful crimes, committed by the faithful and their pastors, approved if not recommended by princes of the Church and their theologians, and most of the time sanctioned and sanctified with the help of scriptural quotations.

One of the saddest examples of this course of events is the centuries-old Christian anti-Judaism. This started already in the New Testament and ever since the Crusades has festered more and more fiercely and taken on ever more brutal forms. Convinced that they were doing God a service, Christians of all walks of life have decried their Jewish fellows, who belonged to the same people as Jesus and Mary, as God's murderers, and under that pretext they have persecuted them without mercy. That Christians have done this for centuries without the slightest scruple, yes even regarded it as a God-pleasing work, can hardly be taken as a sufficient criterion for attributing their dealings to the workings of God's Spirit.

Dogmatic evolution time and again refers to the above-quoted verse of the Fourth Gospel (16:13): that the Spirit will guide the Church 'into the full truth'. This huge building seems thus to rest on a very narrow supporting base. Moreover, this verse should not be taken for an infallible pronouncement that can be applied randomly to all sorts of inner-ecclesiastical phenomena. The stability of the construction becomes even more doubtful if one considers that the quoted verse can also be translated differently, that is: 'The Spirit will lead you to live in the full truth'. 'Truth' in John usually means truthfulness, authenticity. If so, this verse has less to do with doctrine than with forms of life. The equally often invoked verse John 14:26, also taken from Jesus' speech after the Last Supper—that the Spirit will teach the disciples everything and remind them of what Jesus has said—is not really of any avail. For it presupposes that the later developments can be traced back to the words of Jesus and hence to the gospel.

What then, is the essence of Tradition in which we want to stay at any price? First and foremost the experiences with Jesus, lived by those who encountered him and believed in him. We know of these, because they have been recorded in the New (or Second) Testament, which builds on the religious experiences of Israel that have been recorded in the Old (or First) Testament. What is manifestly at odds with Jesus' spirit, as it speaks from these Testaments, can of course not lay claim to any validity. It can be a tradition but it is not part of Tradition with capital 'T'. Persecution of Jews, aggression, religious coercion, striving for riches, pomp and honorary offices, or authority exerted as power instead of service, cannot be the fruits of the good tree of God's Spirit, notwithstanding how long and deep these have been thriving in the Church and unfortunately still often continue to thrive.

On the contrary, what certainly belongs to the kernel of Tradition are those developments that build further on its solid bedrock. One can think of the awareness of the dignity of the human person and the recognition of inviolable rights that come with it, such as the rights of the integrity of the body and of freedom, and consequently the abolition of, and fight against, slavery and torture; a democratic disposition, not only outside but also within the Church; equal rights for women, even though the Church still has a long way to go in this regard; rejection of discrimination and racism, and social justice. One can also think of ecumenism and the recognition of the salvific power of non-Christian religions, of the preferential option for the poor and the socially disadvantaged in our society; of our sense of responsibility for the Third World; of peace efforts; of the conservation of nature as God's creation; of the struggle against merciless globalization and the glorification of high finance. But it has taken time before the sanctity of all this has penetrated the collective ecclesial consciousness. It is precisely in this maturation process that God's Spirit is at work.

Yet, almost everything in genuine Tradition is formulated in a heteronomous way, in images and practices theonomously thinking people simply no longer know what to do with. One of the clearest examples of this is found in the liturgy. Because of its central position in religious experience, a separate section will now be devoted to this topic.

LITURGY: FROM A SECRET LANGUAGE TOWARDS A COMMUNITY LANGUAGE

The renewal-minded participants of the Second Vatican Council probably assumed that introducing the vernacular into the liturgy and patching up the texts and the liturgical rules would do the job. That was a big mistake. Ever since Pius V's Missal, composed by order of the Council of Trent, the liturgy had been a sleeping beauty in the woods. The conservative Vatican authorities would have liked to let her sleep for another couple of centuries. So, when she had been awoken against their curial will, they tried everything to lull her back to sleep. The changes could alas not be reversed; but now it should be over with trying to reform everything! Rest had to return—the rest of the grave. But soon it became clear that the clock could not be turned back. After an initial period of enthusiasm (new brooms sweep clean), the faithful at the grassroots realized that liturgical language was still an alienating ritual, a solemn abracadabra, replete with references to things that the average faithful, who earlier had been fed with unintelligible and indigestible Latin, were not able to locate, and with images that reeked strongly of a musty past. Swept along by the democratic wind that had started to blow in the Church as well, carrying along a sense of responsibility for the greater good of the people of God, the faithful at the grassroots started to renovate, fix up, adapt, re-write and re-create. The idea was to bring the liturgy back to its original purpose of communal prayer of the Church, so that it would no longer be the hedged-in private garden of the Church authorities, who are constantly spying around to check whether everyone stays on the paths that had been laid out in the past.

Liturgy is usually understood as the liturgy of the mass. However, it encompasses much more. Not only the other six sacraments but also, among others, the many devotions and blessings, the canonical prayers of monks and monastic nuns, burial rituals, processions, litanies and church songs. However, because most Catholics are only acquainted with the liturgy of the mass, the remarks that follow confine themselves to this particular form of liturgy.

We have been raised in the false conviction that the liturgy of the mass, with its formulations and its stereotypical sequence of gestures and prayers, is something sacrosanct and eternal. In reality, however, it is a building that has been constructed, refurbished, demolished and reconstructed during many centuries, depending on the taste and the ideas of the time; a colorful patchwork made of many pieces of fabric, witnessing to changing historical sensitivities. The transmitted liturgical prayers of the mass have at some point in history been created by the faithful, from their contemporary situation and as the expression of the faith understanding of that period. They have not descended from Heaven. Therefore, if it was good then to create one's own language of prayer, it cannot be wrong today, despite all the Roman prohibitions. The objection that the unity of the Church would be endangered and suffer great damage if every nation, or worse, every parish would cultivate its own style does not hold. It does not harm the unity of the Church that a follower of the Western rite gets lost in the Eastern liturgy. Or that Western churchgoers are flabbergasted by the way the Eucharist is celebrated (and really celebrated, with singing and dancing) in Central Africa. Moreover we are not nomads who pitch their tent in ever new pastures; we are members of a local church, which is itself a self-reliant cell of the larger Catholica. In Paul's words: where is the body if all the cells are the same? Further, unity is not the same as uniformity: unity denotes an internal cohesion; uniformity only means external equalization. The danger of a loss of quality because of the excessive freedom of fieldworkers is certainly real. The stylistic level of the traditional liturgy was indeed high quality. But there are remedies against loss of style, such as mutual control and the proverbial wear and tear of time, which in the long run removes the rubbish and only keeps the rubies; moreover there is the golden rule that one better sticks to the old unless he has something better to offer. The aim is not to be new, but to be good, that is, good for today's people. The language of prayer should without any doubt remain rooted in the original Tradition, but it should not sound like the prayer of a late-Roman orator, a medieval monk, or a Tridentine theologian. Therefore the liturgy in the Congo has to be different from ours and our liturgy has to be different from Vatican liturgy; the liturgy in a village of mountain farmers should not be the same as that in a metropolis; and a liturgy for children should be different from that in a nursing home.

The lapidary proverb *lex orandi, lex credendi*: the practice of prayer is the rule of belief, is particularly applicable to the liturgy. The saying contains a play on the two meanings of the Latin word '*lex*'. The former '*lex*' denotes an accepted habit; the latter refers to a norm that has to be kept. This means that the religious imagery that has settled in the liturgical language, has become a binding part of Tradition. This creates the danger of remaining stuck in an outdated pattern of belief, one that reflects the bygone culture that has informed the formulation of eternal faith in the temporary language of prayer. The ongoing search for a language in which a concrete community of faith recognizes itself is therefore a service rendered to Tradition, which, as a living fruit of God's Spirit, has to change continually. Because for years they have faithfully recited what was printed in the liturgical books (in the past this was indeed called 'reading' the mass), most pastors' ability to continually renew their language of prayer has been blunted and it is only gradually recovering. Improvising prayers is a skill that every pastor should command, but apparently none of them has learned how to do this properly. The result is usually very disappointing.

If the pastor can allow himself some freedom with regard to the formulation of the prayers and the choice of the songs, that choice is denied to him by the higher authorities with regard to the Sunday reading from Scripture. Moreover, the Roman Curia insists that the used translation of Scripture stays as closely as possible to the biblical original. It does not allow the use of a modified, freer or elaborated rendering, meant to prevent misunderstanding, to clarify a text that might provoke anger, and to interpret obscure words or images. This stubbornness punishes itself, because in this way the message of faith that is read aloud, will to a large extent not be understood and will not nourish religious life. Nevertheless, such a growth in faith is the purpose of the lection in the liturgy, most probably also in the mind of the curial lawmakers. The reform of the liturgy by the Second Vatican Council has at least ended the nonsensical practice of reading these texts aloud in a language nobody understands any longer, and to call this proclamation of the gospel. Yet, with the current practice of reading Scripture aloud we are not much better off. The Roman authorities make these choices as if still living in the past, but prescribe them to people of the present. They never seem to wonder what good fruits this rain of God's word can bring forth that is Sunday after Sunday poured out over the not- or half- or ill-understanding churchgoers. Sometimes there is only one remedy, one which is rather palliative in nature and not really healing: to replace a prescribed reading that is manifestly beyond the understanding of the gathered congregation by one that is more accessible. And if the threshold is even then still too high, to lower it by clearing away some of the obstacles during the reading. This means: touching up, despite the prohibition to do so, and with the risk of making mistakes; substituting unknown terms such as metretes and didrachms and denars and the like with their modern equivalents; replacing misleading terms by less misleading synonyms; inserting commentary (just as it is already done in Mark 7:3); skipping verses that disturb the train of thought or that are a crux even for the exegetes; leaving out unnecessary foreign names, *et cetera*. For that which the listeners do not grasp, cannot be the Word of God addressed them; it cannot awaken in them a faithful response. And since without a homily the lection remains a closed and sealed book for the average faithful and since it is not possible to deliver two or three homilies in one service, it seems reasonable in some cases to confine oneself to just one reading instead of the two or three that are prescribed by the hierarchy. Apparently these have the illusion that it is better to listen to three readings without grasping one word of them, than to just one of which the meaning can be explained.

Above, mention has been made of the Roman authorities making liturgical choices in our place and imposing them on us. Hence, these too have to do with Tradition, at least in the sense that they are like watch dogs in that holy house. This will be the subject of the following chapter.

Chapter 6

Watchdog in the Sanctuary of the Tradition

Teaching Authority or Magisterium

When a major or minister issues a decree, he thereby limits the freedom of the citizens. Those citizens are nevertheless willing to accept the decree, and this not only because they would otherwise be punished. Indeed, the citizens have empowered these officials to curtail their freedom in a number of cases, provided it serves the common good. They have done so by electing them and giving them a mandate. An average Joe cannot issue decrees, even if he has nothing but the common good in view, because he has not been mandated to do so, not by me and not by anyone else.

Also the hierarchy of the Church, consisting of the Pope, the Curia and the bishops, issues decrees, commands and prohibitions, and in doing so it curtails the sacred good of the freedom of the faithful. Because all people are equal for the law and have an inalienable right to personal freedom, this can only happen with the faithful's consent. And this consent should be given by them freely, not out of fear for punishment, but because they feel that concern about the common good can be entrusted to these authorities. In most cases these undoubtedly have the common good of the faithful in view—leaving aside the question whether the common good will indeed be served by their decisions. But on what do they base their right to curtail our freedom? Certainly not, as with the major or the minister, on a mandate that they received from me and others. No, they claim to have received a mandate from God-on-High, who stands above everything human, thus also above human rights including the right of self-determination, and who can even abolish those rights. Such an approach only makes sense in a heteronomous frame of thinking. Outside this frame, all the hierarchy's claims to obedience are just hanging in the air. The ease with which the faithful nowadays put aside decrees from Rome—such as the prohibition against contraception or the prohibition on liturgical experiments—might well be the result of a yet unconscious feeling on their part that the hierarchy's right to speak has hardly a leg to stand on.

HIERARCHY IN THE HETERONOMOUS PAST

In the past, no single Catholic would have reacted this way. *Roma locuta, causa finita*: 'Rome has spoken, the matter is closed' was then the adage. To greet a bishop, one kneeled and kissed his ring. To greet a pope, one even kissed his feet. Was this a sign of belief? It was at least as much a survival from a time when popes, bishops, abbots and prelates of every kind were also political and economical rulers, ecclesiastical princes with an aura of superiority warranted by God and with the necessary middlemen to inculcate this sense of their superiority into their subjects. Even today the word 'bishop' evokes an atmosphere of power and superiority rather than an evangelical atmosphere of service and entrusted responsibility. The pomp and circumstance that even today still surrounds the ordination of a bishop, not to mention the enthronement of the bishop of Rome, conjures up uneasy memories of feudal times. Moreover, these ceremonies largely circumvent the evangelical idea of simplicity. And last but not least, ordination is an awfully heteronomous concept; but about this more in Chapter 14.

This itself surviving past makes of the actual bishop, at least psychologically, someone entirely different from what the *espiskopos* (literally: supervisor) was or was supposed to be in the early Church. He was not master and lord, not 'your Lordship' or 'your Eminence'; he did not have a palace nor did he carry a staff, but he rather carried the burden of the community with whose care he was entrusted. As a matter of fact, this community was originally not larger than the size of a small parish today. The fiction of his being a shepherd, a meaningful concept in a culture of nomads and cattle-farmers, can be seen in the shepherd's staff with which the bishop still solemnly strides today. Originally, this was a stick with a bent end used for grasping by its leg a sheep that wanted to escape and to hold it back—an instrument of power, that is. This shepherd's fiction, however, has served its time, despite the fact that the late Pope Wojtyla tried to keep it alive in his document *Pastores gregis*—Herds of the Flock—about the bishop's office. One who has to look after half a million or even more sheep is no longer a shepherd, even if he is still called so. He is, rather, an agrarian mega-industrialist or a minister of cattle-breeding. Besides, the faithful are no longer bleating sheep. And if, out of reverence for the Bible, we would like to give the title 'shepherd' a chance, it would suit a local priest much better than a bishop. For that local priest knows his sheep, as could be expected from a shepherd. He knows them, at least, a little bit—and at any rate much better than the bishop. Finally, as to the ever-repeated thesis that the bishops are the successors of the apostles, no single historical argument in support of it is to be found, quite to the contrary. The distance between the group that used to travel around with Jesus and today's residing bishops is in any case enormous.

Also the concept of a 'pope' is the result of a long development that can hardly be called a blessing. It certainly no longer has the connotation of the Italian *papa*, from which it is derived. In the course of many centuries, it has appropriated (to its own detriment) the image of an autocratic ruler over a billion Catholics. This has become a sad stumbling block on the path towards ecumenism because of the claims involved in it to absolute power and infallibility. The fact that Rome was the capital of the immense Roman Empire played a considerable role at the dawn of this development. Indeed, part of the prestige of the capital, which was then the political center of the civilized world, reflected onto the local Roman church community and its bishop. Moreover, it did not take long before these local bishops referred to their lineage with Simon Peter (again without historical proof) of whom they claimed to be the legitimate heirs on the Roman bishop's seat, as well as to the priority position the Gospel accorded to Peter. In the following centuries they aggrandized this priority a thousand-fold, whereby they did not demur from having themselves called *Summus Pontifex*—that is, High Priest, which was in Ancient Rome the title given to the head of the pagan (!) college of priests—and in the Middle Ages also *vicarius Christi*—deputy of Christ—and even *vicarious Dei*—deputy of God on earth. Anyway, if today hundreds of thousands gather to cheer the successor to Simon Peter, they don't do this because they find Simon Peter so extremely important. It has much more to do with the power of the media, mass psychology, and personality cult. It has in any case nothing to do with the Gospel.

The Roman Curia serves as the executive organ of this patiently constructed papal authority. One would have no problem at all with this organ, if it would see itself as a serving and helping hand. But this is not the case. The curia commands and prohibits, admonishes and punishes, uproots and plants, and produces—after Jesus has freed us from the old laws—an endless avalanche of new laws. It does so without any mandate from below, but only on the basis of its heavenly mandate which through the mediation of the pope has allegedly been assigned to them by the supernatural world above. From the point of view of modernity this construction is of course a pious *fata morgana*.

The stark smell of power and glorification that exudes from the titles 'bishop', 'cardinal', and 'pope' goes back to a period of time when the magisterium made claims to heavenly origins and threatened its subordinates—into which the sisters and brothers of the New Testament had been meanwhile metamorphosed—with excommunication, Hell and damnation if they would not comply. This smell is so penetrating that it cannot possibly be removed. It would be better, therefore, to replace designations such as 'bishop' by new, historically less compromised names, such as is done in the evangelical Church in the German-speaking countries that now speak of 'superintendents'. This term recaptures the New Testament *epi-skopos*, which is now translated literally without the false (un-evangelical) undertones that resonate with the word 'bishop' as the poisonous fruit of the centuries-long un-evangelical exercise of power. Genuine healing, however, can only be achieved by establishing democratic rules for electing leaders, in line with a totally new, theonomous concept of hierarchy. What does such a concept look like?

HIERARCHY IN THEONOMOUS PERSPECTIVE

The word 'hierarchy' consists of two Greek terms: *hieros*—sacred, and *arche*—guiding principle or authority. Therefore it means, in fact: sacred government. 'Government' is an inner-worldly term, free from heteronomous connotations and is therefore not at stake in our discussion. This is, however, not the case with the qualifier 'sacred'. This qualifier belongs to the sphere of encounter with the divine and will therefore be filled in differently in a heteronomous and a theonomous perspective. In heteronomous language, 'sacred' points to the ineffable mystery of God-in-Heaven. Wherever it is also used for qualifying people and earthly matters, such as places, practices, times and institutions (the hierarchy being one of them), it refers to a special quality that has descended on them from God-in-Heaven. In this perspective the hierarchy is an institution that has been ordained and empowered from on high, including its external form of an autocratic power structure. The latter is, however, time- and culture-bound and therefore, at least outside of the heteronomous perspective, very questionable. Equally heteronomous is the idea that this power would reside in its fullness with the Pope, who would receive his right to command, prohibit, teach and punish through an unbroken chain of succession going back to Peter, directly from Christ himself. Precisely because this hierarchy is grounded in the heavenly domain, the Pope allegedly partakes in the fullness of power, knowledge and holiness of this domain, and he bestows these powers in descending order onto the lower ranks in the hierarchy, which he himself appoints. The entire hierarchy thus conceived hangs from the heavenly dome, like a chandelier hangs from the ceiling. When that ceiling collapses because the heavenly world appears to be a beautiful but temporary and dated construct, when, in other words, theonomy replaces heteronomy, then that chandelier, which is the traditional concept of hierarchy, falls down and is shattered into a thousand pieces.

Does this mean that theonomy tolls the death knell for the hierarchy and that this institution has to be abolished? By no means. Every human organization, including the Church, needs a government and structures of authority in order to continue to prosper. Therefore every organization spontaneously develops such structures. But it does not follow that the ecclesiastical structures of authority have to be conceived of as descending from God-in-Heaven, with the highest concentration of power at the top and total powerlessness at the bottom. A theonomous conception of the Church is designed along different lines. It rather imagines a bottom-up structure of power, developing from below, from God-in-the-Depth whose creative force infuses the entire People of God, moving it to generate the necessary forms of authority and leadership, much like every living organism develops its necessary organs and functions from the inner dynamics of life. This way of thinking is based on the ancient Christian awareness that God's Spirit inhabits the body of the Church, and builds it up in the service of the new world that God wants to establish. This ecclesiastical body is something universal and local at the same time. Therefore the local Church communities—and they more than any others—are one hundred percent Church, the living body of Christ, inspired and moved by the Spirit.

With this as our starting point, a free thought experiment would yield the following outline of a theonomical hierarchy. The need to expand and grow will impel a local Church community to look out for a suitable pastor, who is able to inspire them and enhance their vital energy and coherence. They do not necessarily have to search for such a leader by themselves; it is possible that one just befalls them. However, under no circumstances should a leader be imposed or forced onto them: it is up to them to choose for themselves who will guide them, preferably unanimously, and otherwise with a majority vote. In a democratic culture the need will moreover be felt to have a board that assists and controls the pastor. In this way a local organizational structure will develop, one that can be called holy, because it has grown under the impulse of God's creative Spirit. Yet, every local church essentially relates to other local churches, who together form the Church as such, the body of Christ who continues to live throughout human history. Therefore a local church should be willing to collaborate with other churches, to learn from them, and to share with them all that it has and realizes. God's Spirit is a unifying spirit. Eventually, there is only one 'body of Christ', however much each local church embodies this in its own way.

Such unity takes its first shape on the level of what is now the deanery: the pastors and boards of several adjacent local churches choose a common leader and his (or her) board. This newly created larger entity is less coherent than the local churches, and will serve a more occasional and administrative purpose. This is, however, not the end of the story. The Church is more than this. The deans and their boards, as representatives of their group of local churches, choose in their turn a common leader and his (or her) board. We have now reached the level of what is currently the diocese. In this way the choice of representatives and the delegation of tasks will go on until a last representative and his (or her) board are chosen. With every step the lower level delegates some of its responsibilities to the higher level, so that the latter has its own domain in which to function. The lower level, however, may request accountability from the higher level as to what it has done with the delegated responsibility.

As to the appointment of pastors, it should not be the sole decision of the local community that is directly involved: the groups and communities with which it co-operates, and the higher level that has a controlling function, should also be heard before a decision over the appointment of a new local leader is taken. This role should at least take the form of using a veto right when there are good reasons to assume that a proposed candidate will make fruitful co-operation impossible.

THE CONSEQUENCES OF THIS DEMOCRATIC MODEL OF HIERARCHY

In this theonomous concept of the hierarchy, not only internal coherence but also the right of decision is at its fullest on the level of the local church communities and gradually declines when moving up to the top of the hierarchical structure. Given this bottom upwards scheme, the higher organizational structures will have less bearing on the religious life of the faithful than the lower ones, in other words, on that what makes the Church the Church. To state it more blunty: with respect to the vitality of Christian communities and the healing role of the Church in the world, the Pope is—not in a juridical sense or with respect to his dealings with the outside world, but existentially, which is in the end the correct gauge—less important than the bishop, and the bishop is less important than the local pastor. Moreover, the Pope and the bishops should not be exalted exceedingly. This is clear from the following: when a local community is left without a pastor for a year, its religious life will suffer much more than when a bishopric or the Holy See remains vacant for a year. Ongoing interventions, admonitions, prohibitions and punishments on the part of Rome distort the right proportions seriously.

In addition, this attitude (and that of certain bishops) disrespects an important principle everyone holds dear with respect to secular society: the Principle of Subsidiarity. Following this principle, each level is fully authorized to do what it is able to do by itself; only those things that exceed the capacity of the lower level will be entrusted to a higher level, for example in matters that require co-ordination or agreement with the other churches. In the current heteronomous system of hierarchy, things are reversed. Here, the papacy concentrates all the power in itself and, through the Curia, always has the last word, even in the smallest and farthest little chapel in the world Church. When the lower levels stand up for their rights, such as the right to choose their own bishop, they are immediately reminded of their position of dependency. This makes clear that a change in the basic axiom not only leads to the translation of the formulations of the faith, but has also far-reaching practical consequences for inner-ecclesiastical life.

A theonomous approach to hierarchy such as is proposed here wards off more than one danger at once: first the danger that the Church continues to be identified with its higher authorities; second the danger that our Roman Catholic Church continues to appear as an autocratic, historically outdated institute in our democratic world, an anachronistic relic that therefore increasingly loses credit; further the danger of creating conflicts by imposing on churches bishops that are rejected by the faithful; and finally the danger that institutions such as the Curia continue to ignore the adulthood of the people of God and to restrain their Christian freedom. As to the first of these four dangers, one may ask oneself to what extent someone who didn't receive his authority from a community is entitled to speak in the name of that community. Nevertheless, the media and therefore also public opinion keeps on identifying the position of a Catholic community, such as a diocese or a church province or even that of the Church as a whole, with the personal opinions of a leader that has sometimes been forcefully imposed upon these communities by a higher authority. Moreover, all too often the official representative to the bishops conference for a special domain such as the media, education, or social action, turns out to be a bishop that is considerably less competent in this discipline than many laypersons, who unfortunately have just this disadvantage: to be laypersons. Nevertheless, such a bishop thinks he can make authoritative statements on that matter, relying on the assumption that through a supernatural ordination he has received from the omniscient and almighty Heaven a special competence that ordinary faithful lack. The foregoing is a fine example of heteronomous thinking; which will only hold till a final clash with autonomous thinking will shatter it completely.

What then is, in theonomous perspective, the competence and the function of the authorities on each of the higher levels of the hierarchy? Their task is to co-ordinate and to control what happens on the lower level, to inspire that level, and, if necessary, to reproach. Theirs is, in other words, the function of supervisor, in line with the original meaning of the Greek term *episkopos*, from which the term 'bishop' derives. It is not incumbent on this supervisor— and this is also true for the bishop of Rome—to issue commands and prohibitions. Nor is it is his main task to lecture the members of the Church, as if they were a bunch of children. Think of what the author of the First Letter of John writes to his faithful in 2:27: 'As for you, the anointing that you received from him (the Spirit of Jesus) abides in you, and so you do not need anyone to teach you.' If this is so, however, what then remains of the teaching authority of the leadership of the Church, the so-called magisterium?

THE MAGISTERIUM

The leadership of the Church repeatedly underlines that its teaching authority, the so-called magisterium, belongs exclusively to the Pope and the bishops. This is clearly the result of a heteronomous perspective on the Church. In this view, this teaching monopoly, just as their authority, is bestowed upon them from on high and descended on them at the time of their ordination. The latter is itself is a product of heteronomous thought, as will become clear in Chapter 14. Those who have not been consecrated cannot lay claim on these privileges.

It is to be noted that the hierarchy only started to claim the monopoly of the teaching authority at the time of the counter-reformation, and that Rome kept on affirming this monopoly with ever greater insistence in the following centuries. Indeed, it was the best way to close ranks in what remained of the Catholic Church after the reformation, and to prevent further schisms. This late origin is no coincidence. In the centuries before the Council of Trent, the bishops had been busy with things quite other than instructing their flock. They were often the younger sons of noble families to whom the bishop's seat was given as a consolation prize because the succession including noble title and worldly power had unfortunately gone to their elder brother. They usually had much less knowledge of theology than of hunting and handling weapons, and spent more time collecting and spending (or wasting) the revenues of their expansive properties than meditating and proclaiming the faith. They owed their bishop's ring and scepter to a prince's favor, which they had to pay with all sorts of services such as providing soldiers and even joining him in battle, something to which they were not at all averse. Where would they have gotten their teaching competence? From on high? Owing to their often simoniacal ordinations?

But even after the Council of Trent, bishops do not owe their teaching competence to a special illumination from above, which at their episcopal ordination would allegedly have transformed their ignorance to wisdom, but to their own intelligence, their theological training, and their religious insight. Today as in the past, a bishop who was only a theological dwarf before his ordination will not turn overnight into a theological giant through this ordination. Just as before his ordination, he will think either correctly or incorrectly afterwards also. Only in a heteronomous worldview, in which another world can be invoked to make the impossible possible, does a bishop owe his teaching competence to his ordination.

INFALLIBILITY

The guaranteed correctness of what the hierarchy proclaims, in other words the infallibility of the magisterium, is only thinkable in a heteronomous perspective. All God-talk, theonomy comments, is human talk. Traditional Muslims may still believe that the Koran contains God's innermost own words, which Mohammed heard from the mouth of the Archangel Gabriel. But as soon as this messenger world becomes a *fata morgana*, this no longer works. True, God's Spirit who speaks through the members of the faith community that is the Roman Catholic Church certainly also speaks through those who rule the roost there. Yet, the human 'medium' colors the Spirit's speaking with all the colors of the rainbow, it distorts it, renders it unclear and deficient and fallible, just as happens with any human speech.

But fortunately, the Spirit never ceases to utter his self-revelatory speech, and because of this the result will slowly cleanse itself: in the course of the history of salvation little by little we grow closer to the truth. But this process is never finished and the result is always susceptible of improvement. And nobody in the Church possesses the truth exclusively in such a way that others would depend on him to tap it: we all are and remain disciples of the Spirit and not of some human authority. Whoever realizes this will never impose his own views on others as the right answer to all questions, as has been, and still is, the order of the day in the teaching Church, especially in its headquarters on the Vatican hill. These are, of course, fully entitled to have a preference for a specific formulation of the faith or for a specific practice, and to communicate, and even to recommend this preference to their fellow Catholics, as well as the grounds that can be adduced in favor of it, as a possible enrichment of the latter's lives. But they do not have the right to impose that preference. How do they know that their preference coincides with the eternal truth and that, conversely, all other ideas, such as those that are represented in this book, are dreadful mistakes? They can adduce arguments, but no proofs. And arguments call for counter-arguments. Someone having a preference can only trust (which is a form of belief) that his preference corresponds better to the motions of God's Spirit. The Spirit, however, is not bound to this preference and blows in others as it pleases.

In all this we should not lose sight of the following. The idea that the hierarchy possesses an (infallible) teaching authority from Heaven is a statement made by the selfsame hierarchy, which for the trustworthiness of this statement has recourse to the infallibility of its own teaching office. This suspiciously looks like a *petitio principii*, a logical category mistake which consists in taking that which has to be proved as the basic argument for the proof. But apparently, if something is repeated often and long enough it acquires the patina of self-evidence, with the result that in the long run everyone accepts it uncritically. This is exactly what has happened with the hierarchy's claim to infallible teaching authority. And it is exactly on this unfounded claim that the Church bases the ecclesiastical practice of condemning deviant opinions and of punishing their authors—until some three centuries ago by means of the dungeon, the wheel and the stake, and today, because of a lack of such effective instruments, by means of excommunication, dismissal, and the prohibition to teach and write. And as is often the case, this centuries-old practice has turned from a claimed right into an acquired right. That a layperson, no matter how strong a believer or how much in possession of theological training, is still not allowed to deliver a sermon during mass is again one of the lamentable products of the monopoly of truth that the hierarchy arrogates to itself.

A Word about Dogmas

To conclude these reflections about the magisterium, a few words about the term 'dogma' are due. Dogmas are useful things. They are milestones on the long highway of the tradition and show us in retrospect the stages of the journey that have been covered. But milestones also indicate that the journey is not yet finished. They are not signposts that read 'Forbidden to go any further'. One may not request from people that they pitch their tent on that spot, nor, what is even worse, that they return to that point. For the journey has to go on. The quest for the truth must never end.

These milestones have not descended ready-made from Heaven. They have been placed there by human hands; they are a human work. In the history of the Church they were mostly the result of an intensive searching, thinking and discussing process conducted by bishops who, without consulting their flock decided in a final settlement what (in their eyes) was the truth—a truth that had to be accepted by all the faithful. Only in the last few centuries were these milestones sometimes the work of the one person who had gradually amassed all the decision making power in the Church unto himself.

What follows, in heteronomous perspective, from the declaration of a dogma? First of all, that such a declaration is infallibly true and that its correctness is guaranteed by God in Heaven. Consequently a dogma is not only unsusceptible of change and improvement, but to reject it boils down to repudiating God. To guarantee this, appeal is made to the founding act of the Church by Jesus of Nazareth who, as the visible embodiment of God-in-Heaven would have bestowed on his Church and especially on its leadership the privilege of infallibility. And second, from now onward the faithful have to confess this dogma on the penalty of sanctions—in earlier days physical sanctions, nowadays only spiritual sanctions to be put into effect by God-in-Heaven. This entire construct, however, collapses like a house of cards at the slightest blow of a theonomous wind, because in the theonomous view there is no place left for such a guaranteeing 'above'.

The bad reputation that the word 'dogma' has acquired in modernity is related to the suggestion of spiritual pressure and rigidity that adheres to this word due to its heteronomous usage. The following two remarks may help at least partially to free this word of its negative connotation.

The first is that the Greek word *dogma* literally means: what seems right to someone, that is, somebody's opinion and the decision taken on that account. The Greek root *dok-* (or *dog-*) always contains a notion of subjectivity, of a personal view. When this root is used, no objective certainty is being claimed. Conversely, when in Greek one refers to objective and reliable knowledge, one employs the root *id-*, which means also 'to see', or the word *epistèmè*. An ecclesiastical dogma is therefore the shared opinion of a smaller or larger group of representatives of the Church population. Thus, for example, at the Council of Nicea the definition that Jesus was 'of the same substance as the Father' represented the opinion of the large majority of the participants. But these did not form the majority of the then living bishops: only five of the numerous Western bishops had traveled all the way to the remote town of Nicea on the southern shore of the Black Sea. And of those present a considerable number only subscribed to this dogmatic formula and the ensuing condemnation of Arius out of pure caution. They did not want to get in trouble with the Emperor Constantine, who (not yet baptized!) presided over the council and who supported the Arian condemnation so as to secure the unity of his Empire. Similarly, the almost one billion contemporary Roman Catholics owe the dogma of papal infallibility to the decision of only 700 church leaders, most of whom were not even elected and mandated by the people of God, but were appointed by the sole actor who wished to be declared infallible. Shocking at the promulgation of the dogma was also the numerical disproportion between the delegations. The Italian bishops constituted a phalanx of 250 men, that is 35% of the participants that were entitled to vote, many of them being theologically incompetent but so much the more loyal to the Pope. On the other hand, central Europe with twice as many Catholics as Italy had to content itself with only 75 bishops. These were mostly good theologians, but at the ballot they were powerless against the Italian bloc. Should the truth depend on such factors? This is enough reason not take the proclamation of dogmas too seriously. They are no oracles.

There is a second remark. To ensure the absolute trustworthiness and immutability of dogmatic pronouncements, heteronomous thinking invokes the special assistance of the Holy Spirit who allegedly prevents Church leaders from making mistakes. Apart from the obviously heteronomous stamp of this reasoning, it is assumed that the Holy Spirit is particularly active in those voters who form the majority in a council. However, was it indeed the Holy Spirit who made the majority of the participants at the Council of Florence declare in the *Decretum pro Jacobitis* of 1442 that 'all those who are outside the Catholic Church, not only pagans but also Jews or heretics and schismatics, cannot share in eternal life and will go into the everlasting fire ... even if he has shed blood in the name of Christ'. This declaration looks more like the product of the spirit of an intolerant epoch that could only conceive of God as intolerant, than like the product of God's Spirit. Five hundred years later, when under the influence of modernity one had started to think differently about tolerance and intolerance, the majority of the bishops at the Second Vatican Council declared equally solemnly and equally inspired by the Holy Spirit exactly the opposite, namely that all religions in their own way offer paths towards salvation, and not towards everlasting fire, and even that certain non-Catholic Christian communities (the 'heretics' and 'schismatics' of Florence) deserve to be called 'Churches'. This indicates that what is ascribed to the Holy Spirit is at least as much the expression of the spirit of a given epoch. This is another reason not to be too much upset about dogmas. They are human work and will lose their validity in the course of time, just as currency bills.

To avoid any deadly misunderstanding: the foregoing does not mean to say that dogmas are errors and that the teachings of the Church and the dogmatics that are based on them are no more than tons of scholarly nonsense. To the contrary, they all remain valid as long as one stays within the framework of the axiom of heteronomy and as long as one continues to think along the line of the same unconscious presuppositions as before. But all this ceases to exist when one switches over to a different axiom. This is exactly what started to happen at the Second Vatican Council, although the participating bishops were not yet explicitly aware of the changed axiom. Nonetheless, it was already unconsciously working in them. The message of faith that in the course of many centuries has coagulated into the familiar formulations and practices of a heteronomous nature, needs therefore to be reformulated because of the shift of axioms that has now taken place. This reformulation should not be condemned as unbelief and heresy by the supporters of heteronomy simply because it differs that much from the traditional formulation; just as the followers of the Euclidian geometry should not stigmatize the propositions of Lobatschevsky as unscientific nonsense simply because they are so much different from Euclid's propositions.

CHAPTER 7

SPEAKING ABOUT THE UNSPEAKABLE

THE GOD-IMAGE OF THE THEONOMY

The God-image underlying this book has already been outlined briefly in Chapters 2 and 3. One who is not prepared for such an image of God will at first be astonished, as this image barely resembles the clear-cut imagery with which we have been raised, namely that of Scripture and Tradition. If one said 'God' in the past, he evoked a clear image with which every Christian (and every Jew and Muslim no less) was familiar from childhood on, that is, the image of an almighty and super-holy being, enthroned with royal pomp in a separate world called 'Heaven', ruling over humanity and the cosmos with absolute power, yet at the same time an approachable person, invisibly present everywhere and at all times, watching over everything, rewarding the good and punishing the bad as a righteous judge, if not in the present (because rarely this rewarding and punishing was experienced during one's lifetime), then certainly in the hereafter, and then without any excuse and for eternity. Depending on the perspective, he appeared as strict and righteous or as compassionate and forgiving.

The modern human feels ill at ease with this clear-cut imagery. God has changed in his perception. He is no longer a 'he', nor a 'she', despite feminism, no longer a 'somebody' but rather a nameless 'something', infinite and ungraspable, sometimes experienced as a vague and all-permeable force (like 'May the Force be with you' in the Star Wars fantasy), or a power comparable to the ancient Fate. This uneasiness with the clear portrait of the past is not unfounded. This portrait looks too much like an infinitely magnified photocopy of the inner-worldly powers and reminds too much of 'Big Brother is watching you'. But the uneasiness with this traditional God-image is as much due to the fact that God is projected outside the cosmos and as such outside the reality that we can experience, in a second, separate, world. How will theonomy fill in the image of God in a way that remains within the Tradition and that does not swap the God of Jesus for its own fantasy images? Because this is the God with whom a Christian is concerned. If he says 'God', he refers to the Mystery that lights up through Jesus, through his words and actions. In this, Jesus' words have to be treated more cautiously than his actions, because they are more likely to have been colored by the heteronomous images inherent to the world in which he lived and thought. What follows now is an effort to show that the theonomous God-image effectively remains anchored in the Tradition that started with Jesus, however heteronomously colored this Tradition may be.

Two Ways to Think about the Creator-God

The term 'creation' serves as an instructive example to demonstrate the difference between the heteronomous and the theonomous God-image. The fact that God is the creator of the cosmos is one of the most firmly anchored articles of faith of the Tradition, simultaneously defining the position and the essence of the cosmos and its relation to the divine Mystery. This is a relationship of absolute dependence. In religious language it is said that the cosmos has been created by God. Like everything else we say about God, the notion of 'creation' comes from our world. In this world, an artist who creates, produces things that previously did not exist, making visible and audible what he previously only carried as an idea or image in his mind. 'Creation' is therefore just another word for the self-expression of the mind in material forms. It is a kind of birth process. This creative activity of human beings in the cosmos has become the model for God's dealing with the cosmos as a whole. In the heteronomous language to which religious experience apparently spontaneously resorts, images of artists such as the potter (Jeremiah 18), the clay-worker (Genesis 2), the wood-worker, the painter or the composer, pop up quasi-automatically. These images all express the idea that the work of art is at birth totally dependent on the artist, but once born it becomes not only independent but even totally separated from its creator. After the birth process, the umbilical cord is cut off. If the artist takes off or even dies, the work of art continues to live its own life. If the artist lives and stays around, he can later, if it pleases him to do so, apply some cosmetic surgery to his work of art: he can correct it and refine it. This whole gamut of images has been transposed to the relationship between God and the human. God creates the human and from now on this creature is free to go its own way in its own world, which is different from God's world. Nevertheless he will always remain under God's watching eye, and the latter cannot but notice that the human being, like a new Pinocchio, alas often uses his freedom in a different way than his creator expected him to do. In such cases the creator will have to intervene with punishments to correct this aberrant behavior. But the creator-God intervenes in the cosmos as well, which is, no less than the human, the work of his hands but lacks the freedom to act at its own will; and there He corrects his work with divine plastic surgery: working miracles and answering our prayers.

Can theonomous thinking retain this idea of creation to express the relation between the cosmos and God? Does this imagery not automatically include a separation between God and the cosmos, sending God into exile in a second world, which is against theonomy's own axiom? No, it doesn't. For there are forms of creation in which the artist and the work of art are two different entities indeed, but nevertheless remain so inseparable from each other that the end of his creating activity automatically means the end of the work of art as well. Think about dancing, improvisation on the organ, or singing. These forms of art do not simply coincide with the dancer, the organist, or the singer. But neither do they lead a separate existence. As soon as the artist stops creating, the work of art ends as well. The creation is in fact the creator himself, but not in the sense of full identity; it is, rather, a glimpse of his inner self, a snapshot of his inexhaustible being, one of his many possible self-revelations. Or think about our speaking. Our speaking never exists apart from us, and can, as opposed to a sculpture or a painting, never lead an independent existence. Nevertheless, our speaking does not simply coincide with us. It is only an utterance of our inner being, a limited glimpse of our true essence. This essence fully surpasses every word in which it expresses itself, because every word is only one of its innumerable self-expressions, always leaving an infinitely large part of this essence unsaid, thus never coinciding with it or exhausting it completely. In the same way, the cosmos is God's creation, not his creature that lives apart from Him, as traditional thought has it unconsciously, but his self-expression in material forms. Understanding God's creating activity in this way not only guards us from the now untenable anthropomorphous God-image of heteronomy; it also guards us from pantheism, which is entirely foreign to the Tradition. Indeed, the creating God does not coincide with the cosmos; He always surpasses it, just as the artist surpasses the work of art in which he (only) partially reveals his hidden essence. This means that in theonomy the notion of creation can still function in a meaningful way. Its function is that of an eye-opener: it opens the eye for the mystery in which we live. However, the danger remains that the confession of 'God, Creator of Heaven and Earth' will always provoke images like those on the vaulted ceiling of the Sistine Chapel, and will always mean the beginning of a relapse into heteronomy.

Because we have invented a name for this holy Reality, namely God, as if it related to someone more or less equal to the many other 'someones', we usually talk about him without awe. This is a form of serious blindness. Because in fact we talk about an ungraspable and breathtaking Mystery, from which all the cosmic energies and processes are only the amazing handwriting, the astonishing self-revelation. We encounter this Mystery everywhere, in ourselves and outside ourselves; we can see and hear it in everything. We only need to get tuned in to it. As soon as we start to see it and to hear it, it no longer sounds unrealistic that we have to 'love it with all our heart', as it reads in the Old and the New Testament. The beauty and the fabulous richness of forms and the infinite ingenuity and the marvelous characteristics of nature will become as many glimpses of His still infinitely richer being. As soon as one realizes this, all arguments in favor of the existence of God will become needless: we then encounter this divine Mystery, which reveals itself in everything, everywhere.

ABOUT CREATION AND EVOLUTION

As has already been noted in Chapter 3, the theory of evolution is self-evident for most modern Western people. Strangely enough this is not the case for the lesser half of the citizens of the United States. They are creationists. They are convinced they have to save God's activity as a creator by denying evolution. In their eyes, creation and evolution contradict each other like water and fire. However, in the eyes of theonomously thinking Christians, they don't contradict each other at all. No, they coincide. They are the same reality, approached from different angles. When talking about creation, they focus on the (gradual) self-revelation of God in the cosmos and in the human. This self-revelation is not static, as in 'He spoke and the world came into being', but continues in an evolutionary and unthinkably slow way, as a billion-years long ascent towards ever richer levels. As long as there were only physical forces, rays and waves—waves of light, electro-magnetism and gravity—the Mystery revealed less of its inner essence, expressed itself in a less rich way, than when life originated. And in the phase of the first forms of life, it expressed itself in a less rich way than when life had already developed itself in a billion forms; and before human life originated, in a less rich way than in the phase of hominization. And in Jesus of Nazareth even endlessly richer than in the *homo sapiens*, who ultimately is only a transitional form, the missing link between pithecanthropus and the fully human being.

When a theonomous Christian speaks about evolution, he leaves aside this aspect of God's self-expression and focuses instead on the process of growth that, as the result of this gradual self-expression in the course of cosmic time, has been initiated and is still being enacted. This evolution follows the laws that have been largely unveiled by contemporary evolutionary biology, building further on the foundation laid by Darwin's theory of natural selection and De Vries' theory of mutation. In this process, everything runs its natural course. No outside intervention is involved, that is, there is no creator in the heteronomous sense of the word. He is not necessary any more than a foreign hand was necessary for Mozart to express himself in his concerti. These concerti followed all the musical laws and were at the same time the audible expression of Mozart's inner being. Nobody will hesitate to speak about the creative inspiration of Mozart. Why then should we hesitate to speak about the creative inspiration that becomes visible and audible in the wonders of nature?

This perspective opens the way for a continuous encounter with God: the Mystery 'God' reveals itself in everything. At the same time it calls for a great respect for everything that lives and for nature as a whole. When a believing person is concerned about the pollution of our surroundings, the emission of carbon dioxide, the destruction of the rain forest and the growth of the hole in the ozone layer, then he worries about these phenomena not only as a threat to our health, but even more as a sacrilegious abuse of God's enchanting self-revelation.

A You that Transcends Me

If, in theonomous thought, God is the Last Depth and Inner Being of the Cosmos, is it then still possible to speak about 'someone'? Is God still a person, as Scripture and Tradition teach us so very clearly? Or is God merely the name of a mighty spiritual 'something', the soul of the cosmic body, as Stoicism already had it? As has already been said, many a modern person is inclined to adhere to such a vague image of God, an image that radiates neither warmth nor tenderness towards us, and that cannot be addressed as 'Father' or 'Savior' or 'Grace' or 'Beloved'. Doesn't the axiom underlying theonomy necessarily lead to such a misty and chilly outcome? Some think this is the case. For them, God needs to be 'someone' to whom I can address my complaints and my fears, my protests and my supplications. In their eyes, the theonomous God is not a personal God but a philosophical abstraction, and therefore they do not expect him to last long.

This opinion is again based on the idea that only a God that is defined in heteronomous terms can be the God of Jesus and the Christians, and that true prayer and mystical identity are only possible with a heteronomously conceived God. This is, however, a mistake. What does prayer mean? Prayer is the experience of a more or less conscious encounter with the divine You. How this encounter is couched in words, and with the help of which images it is expressed, is utterly secondary. It can be expressed in the most heteronomous or the most theonomous terms. In prayer, the opposition between heteronomy and theonomy is no longer significant. For the images are not the heart of the matter: they are but a pair of crutches. The heart of the matter is the encounter that we envision. We need the crutches to get to the place we want to go, but as soon as we have arrived there, we can throw them aside. Prayer does not entail the danger that is so inherent to theological speculation, that is, to try to get a grip on God. One who prays does not want to understand God, he wants to encounter Him. In a sense, the language of prayer is comparable to the language of lovers, because that is also a meta-language, a language in which words are merely the embodiment of relations and feelings and no longer fulfill the same role as in ordinary house-and-kitchen language. They are the envelope, not the letter in it.

As soon as we no longer speak from within the encounter with God, but from outside this encounter and about it, as soon as, in other words, the 'You' of the encounter changes into an objective 'He'—no longer a second person but a third person—terminology becomes very important. Then we must try to make conceptual what is not conceptual. There is no other way to communicate the encounter; not even to oneself. Here the choice of language plays a crucial role. Many traditional formulations about this divine You are incomprehensible for the modern thinking faithful, especially those that project this Mystery in a separate world. Theonomy's formulations are therefore not an attempt to escape from the imagery, by, for example, replacing the symbolic 'on high' with the equally symbolic 'in the depth'. We shouldn't and cannot escape from imagery in speaking about God. It is an unfortunate misconception that theonomous language wants to do away with images. No, we have to, and inevitably will, deal with images. However, in this imagery, God is not to be found 'outside' the cosmic reality, lest we clash with the basic axiom of theonomy in which there is only this world of which God is the Depth, and that is the only place where we can find Him. But this impossibility to think God any longer in another world that runs parallel with ours does not prevent us from approaching God as a You. In other words, it does not affect the language of prayer. It only affects the terminological communication of the relation with God to others, that is, theology and dogmatics.

GOD'S ESSENCE IS LOVE

When asked about the essence of the Mystery, theonomy answers with an expressive term that is derived from our human experience. Everything that can be said about the invisible has to be expressed in terms that come from the visible world, and is, consequently, imagery. The image with which theonomy refers to this inexpressible Being is 'Love'. This image includes many things at the same time, too many to explore here. When using this image, however, it is in any case understood that the essence of the transcending Mystery includes knowledge and concern. It immediately appears as a Face, a You who knows us and who reaches out towards us. When the term 'Love' is used, it instantly becomes clear in which direction the cosmos is evolving: it is the steadily increasing self-expression of a Mystery that is Love. This is already clear in the material world that preceded the origin of life. In that world this love reveals itself in the tendency towards unification and the emergence of more complex compounds, as well as in the incredible energies that are hidden in this process. It reveals itself in a more pronounced way in the amazing complexity of vegetable life, in which each cell compounds itself with other cells. On the animal level of cosmic evolution these first impulses of love become even more obvious: there they reveal themselves in coupling and in care for the young, eventually resulting in what will properly bear the name of unconditional love in the human being.

Indeed, Love is the direction which the human being, the climax of cosmic evolution, is called upon to follow. If Love is recognized as the driving force behind evolution, then the evolving human has to learn to step outside himself and to reach out towards the other humans (Teilhard de Chardin calls this 'to de-center oneself'), in order to unite with them. In a world that is as yet unjust and cruel, this also involves dedication to righteousness and justice, to social, political, economical and cultural liberation, and also to personal, inner liberation. One cannot but notice how imperfect the cosmos is up to know, how it is still suffering birth pangs. And one of the most pregnant signs of this is the ever-prevalent social injustice. This injustice, moreover, is one of the reasons why we should abstain from deifying nature, which is only a different name for the cosmos.

Is it, however, possible to call Love a person? Is Love not the very prototype of a force? We should first ask ourselves what lies beneath the word 'person'. This is another term that is found 'below' and that is used to speak about 'above', and that drags all sorts of things with it from below that have no place above. Whether one wants it or not, the term 'person' always carries along the notion of an 'individual'. For us, persons are always individuals. 'Individual' and 'Person' are like conjoined twins: they never separate, except maybe in a philosophical discourse in which their pure, abstract, sterile meanings are explored. But we never use words in their pure, abstract, sterile sense. As soon as we use them they are already contaminated by the good and bad experiences of human beings. Therefore one can safely say that God is not a person because he is not an individual. 'Individual' includes limitation and definition and separation. Therefore painters would do better to abstain from depicting him. They can only minimize the Mystery, reduce it to non-God. Judaism and Islam are right when they abhor any form of representation of God.

However, to be a person can also mean to be a center of knowing and loving, to be a You who can address us as 'you'. And this corresponds fully to the idea of an all-generating Love. Because this Love evidently loves, it 'knows' in the Biblical sense of the word, which includes love; it says 'you' to us; it is a You for us. God is a purely loving, not definable, only acknowledgeable You. Such a You is obviously not cold, rational and distant. Maybe Tradition and modernity can be reconciled if we call the holy God 'personal', referring to the love that says 'You' to us and that wants to express itself and embody itself more and more in us. 'Personal'—to avoid the inextinguishable notion 'individual' that always secretly accompanies the term 'person'.

THE HIDDEN DANGER OF THE INEVITABLE IMAGES

By speaking about the Mystery in this way, theonomy avoids a danger that always lurks in traditional speaking, namely that the imagery is understood as an objective language. Because the imagery is so clearly outlined, one is easily seduced to take the image for the reality. For example, it is said that God is our father, and rightly so because this appellation is central to Jesus' experience. But what can we deduce from this? That God will guard us against accidents or possible aggression of our fellow people, or that he will comfort us in distress and sorrow, all things a father will do for his children? Moreover, for an adult, the relation to his father is different than for a small child. And for someone living in the Middle East in Jesus' time that relation was different than today. There and then, the father was much more a power figure whom even adult sons and daughters still had to obey. What then does the image 'father' teach us about the Mystery that is God? Surely Jesus, an adult man, did not see himself as a toddler in his relationship with Him? His choice of the term *abba* may give that impression. It is often said that this word is Aramaic children's language. This is indeed the case but not exclusively. It is as much trustful adult language. Jesus' way of speaking may give the impression that what holds for a father in real life also holds for the father in the language of imagery, like when Jesus recommends supplicating prayer and gives as an argument that a father will not give his child a scorpion when the latter asks for an egg. The effusions of St. Theresa of Lisieux reinforce the unacceptable view that God can be dressed up as a twentieth century daddy. But it is not as simple as that. When applied to God, the image 'father' does not cover by far all it covers when it is applied to a real father, even an ideally conceived father. It is a sacred principle of theology, for which, admittedly, theologians had to be guided by mystics, that everything we say about God we have to deny at the same time and that what we assert and then again deny, we have to magnify infinitely. The baby hands of our conceptions are way too small to grasp the infinite entity we call God. They do grasp something correct, albeit incomplete. But at the same time they unnoticeably add to it all sorts of familiar notions that do not apply to God, so that we have to deny again what we just asserted. He is (like) a father, but then again not exactly (like) a father. By far not everything that applies to a father applies to God, not even a father's love. God's love is different, because God is entirely different and therefore unconceivable. To call God 'father' in fact says nothing about what He is or does or shouldn't do. On the contrary, it does say everything about the attitude we can and should take towards this Mystery: an attitude of complete trust and resignation, even if we experience something horrible that a father would never allow happening to his child.

THE TRUE GOD IS UNSPEAKABLE

The traditionally pious usually overlook the fact that 'father' is only one of images the Tradition uses to speak about God. If all those images are equally true, then they produce total psychological confusion. Because God is also called 'creator', 'judge', 'avenger', 'bridegroom', 'king', 'master' ... Already this multiplicity and the mutual contradictions such as between 'avenger' and 'father' or between 'judge' and 'groom', demonstrate that every image is denied by another, so that one should not regard any one image as the definitive approach to the Mystery. And the more explicit and colorful the images, the further they threaten to pull us away from the true God, who is inexpressible. Certainly, also 'Love' and 'Depth' are images, and as such mythological language, but this kind of language activates the imagination less. Therefore it is easier to remain aware of the fact that this language is only a finger that points to something entirely different. Theonomical speaking about God is not, as some may see it, a form of mystification, not woolly speech that is devoid of all clarity. Such a reproach supposes that it is possible to speak clearly and neatly about God and his relation to the cosmos, as a sales representative presenting his product. It is with God as with wine. Do we have any idea what wine tastes like and what it is worth when we know what the percentage of alcohol is and the percentage of sugar, from what kind of grapes it is made, where these grew, when and where the wine has been bottled, and more of the like? The wine taster uses an entirely different kind of language. His language can also be called woolly and unsatisfying for the objective mind of the chemist or the geographer. The more precision one applies when speaking about the Unspeakable, the more this reality will be distorted. In heteronomous language, this danger remains immense. One adheres to images as if they were a truthful mirror of the reality. One is much better off releasing these and surrendering oneself to God.

The danger of missing out on a true encounter with God is also imminent in rituals. On the one hand we need them. They correspond to our body-mind nature. But they can become a surrogate and nourish the illusion that one comes close to God by closely following the details of the ritual. Similar to this is the recitation of prayers as if they were more important than the fundamental attitudes of thankfulness, admiration and respect. This is extremely important for a wholesome religious education. The latter does not start with learning to recite traditional little prayers and making the sign of the cross, but in learning to have respect and be thankful. One who has not learned to admire and to thank has not learned to pray.

Theonomy deliberately puts the pith of the matter in worship and surrender. This follows from its representation of God as the Love who wants to express itself in us in an ever richer and fuller way, and therefore compels us to surrender ourselves blindly to its movement. Then it is no longer important whether one calls God 'He' or 'She' or 'It'. Theonomy has passed this three-forked road. As surrender is the heart of the matter, that image will always be the best that leads us directly to an attitude of total surrender and love, the same attitude that is intended by the Arabic word *islam*, that is, submission. It is no doubt easier and more satisfying for our feelings to represent God as our father, at least if one has not lived through very damaging experiences with one's own less than ideal father. Conversely, it is less misleading to approach God as an unlimited Love who is at the same time the creating Foundation of reality. If we think of God in this way we will not be tempted to do away with him when He disappoints us deeply by not saving or comforting us in times of trouble, something a near and guarding father would certainly and even immediately do.

THE SAME GOD AS THE GOD OF ISRAEL AND JESUS

In speaking so differently from the heteronomical tradition, theonomy seems to draw onto itself the reproach that it has betrayed the God of Scripture for the God of the Philosophers. Nothing is less true. The philosophers can at the most arrive at the assertion or the assumption of a mysterious ultimate ground of explanation for all things, or a world soul, or a principle of evolution, or an unmoved mover, or the One from which all flows forth. But no Ultimate Ground of Explanation or World Soul or Fate or Unmoved Mover gives philosophy the right to affirm or even to assume that this could be a 'You' that says 'you' to us and that attaches importance to the human, individually or as a community. It is exactly this last thing that the theonomous Christian confesses in an equally convinced and explicit way as the heteronomous Christian. He does so, because the latter like the former has been apprenticed to Jesus who, as the coping stone of the Jewish religious tradition experienced this Ultimate as a Voice that says 'you' to us, as a Love that addresses us personally with an appeal to surrender. The difference between the God of the Tradition and the God of the Philosophers is not so much found herein that the Tradition approaches God as Father or Master or King or Judge or Bridegroom and the philosopher does not, but rather in that the philosopher doesn't pray to the Mystery but only reflects on it and tries to get some sort of a hold on it.

That the verb 'pray' also serves as the synonym for 'ask', indicates that prayer takes as a rule the form of supplicating prayer. Nevertheless the most fundamental form of praying is not supplication but adoration. Adoration is the superlative of admiring worship but not only that: it is total surrender; it is the readiness to accept everything that the Mystery will allow to occur to us, all the good and all the bad. The next form of prayer is thankfulness, the fruit of the realization that we receive everything from the Mystery, including ourselves. Asking comes only afterwards. It takes its rise from the experience of our being unfulfilled, which is the sign that we have not totally surrendered ourselves to the Mystery, that we are still estranged from it even though it is our deepest self, so that we remain unfulfilled and unsatisfied. The authentic supplicating prayer translates this need for fulfillment, as will be shown below. In its everyday form, however, it looks more like the whining of a child to daddy or mommy to get what it wants but which it cannot attain by itself. The critical questions that are evoked by this form of supplicating prayer in an autonomous and theonomous perspective will be dealt with explicitly in Chapter 18.

IN UNISON WITH THE TRADITION

The foregoing shows that the theonomous way of speaking about the Unspeakable does coincide with the Christian message about God. It goes far beyond the affirmation of the existence of a personal and creating Higher Being named God. Such an affirmation is not more than Deism. The Christian message rests on the experiences of Israel and even more on those of Jesus, and as a result it teaches that this mysterious God has been enamored by humanity from the beginning, that He wants to bring it to completion and, to realize this, He draws it unto himself long before it turns itself towards him, and that He will fulfill its deepest yearnings in as much as it will turn itself towards him. If theonomy confesses that the essence of this all-generating evolutionary force is Love, who says 'you' to us and in whose glow we live, what, then, is still missing from the ultimate Good News that is proclaimed in Scripture and Tradition?

Admittedly, this theonomous language, which is, by the way, also biblical language as testified by the well know adage 'God is Love', must evoke critical questions. How can God be love, loving humanity without limits and wishing its perfection, if one sees all the suffering that tortures humanity without him lifting a finger to prevent this or to heal this? A large part of this suffering may be due to the humans' bad will and preventable errors. But why this sea of suffering for which people are not responsible? And then there is the question that drives our mind even more into a corner: whence this bad will and all the other evil, if everything is the self-expression of a perfect Goodness? To this question, theonomy has no more satisfying an answer than heteronomy. Heteronomy tries to pass the buck to the devil, but in that way it only shifts the problem to a different spot. Because whence does evil originate in a spirit that, as the expression of God's perfection, can only be good? What cannot be demanded of heteronomous thought should also not be expected from theonomy. Together they have to endure this contradiction, and, in doing so, affirm their faithful surrender to this mysterious, paradoxical God. And amazingly enough, this worshipping surrender reveals itself as meaningful, liberating and consoling. The heart finds peace in this very surrender. It apparently experiences existentially the inner unity of the two opposites, without being able to grasp this unity intellectually, in a way that would also satisfy the mind.

CHAPTER 8

PRIMEVAL STONE OF OUR DOCTRINE OF FAITH?

"JESUS CHRIST, TRULY GOD AND TRULY HUMAN"

One who has confessed the above as something self-evident about Jesus of Nazareth from childhood, and who calls Jesus' mother 'the mother of God' without problems, will be surprised as well as offended when he notices that modern faithful have difficulties with this 'truly God'. He would prefer to deny those people the right to call themselves true Christians any longer. For is this confession not a piece of primeval stone of our doctrine of faith? At least it appears to be so. Indeed, at the Council of Chalcedon of 451 it was solemnly proclaimed that the one person Jesus of Nazareth unites without confusion as well as without separation two natures in himself, a divine and a human nature. Is it possible, then, for someone to ignore this confession and yet consider himself a sincere and true member of our large Christian community, which uses this confession as a touchstone for one's adherence to its beliefs? Strangely enough, maybe this is possible. One does not exclude the other. But to understand this and assent to this, one needs to be willing to follow the road of an honest inquiry into the origins, the development, and the scope of this formulation.

THE PRIMEVAL STONE OF OUR CONFESSION OF FAITH?

Speaking about primeval stones: what can truly be considered the primeval stone of our faith as Christians? Indeed, it must be what Jesus' disciples 'saw' and experienced in their encounter with him and what they later proclaimed as good news for all people, as a message of existential salvation. Christianity is not a philosophy; it is an attitude of faith in this man Jesus of Nazareth, who appeared to be much more than a man from Nazareth, even more than a prophet. And this connection with him has generated a connection between those who believe *in* him, and they have become a community of its own unique kind, the Church. Connection with this Jesus is the criterion for belonging to that church. And this relationship is one of total readiness to listen, to follow, to abandon one's own opinions and value scales, adopting his instead. Not the titles that one gives to him are the criterion for truly belonging to him and in this way to this group. The criterion is the honesty and the depth of the veneration one has for him; the titles are only expressions of this, and like all words, they are colored by the personal psychology of the confessor and of the cultural milieu to which he belongs.

For that which the followers of Jesus have seen in him with admiring eyes we are completely dependent on testimonies, and second-hand testimonies at that, dating back, moreover, almost two-thousand years. That is not so bad in itself. We are in the same situation regarding the history of the Roman Empire and that does not undermine our certainty about what happened there. But in that case, of course, we have to do with inner-worldly, historical facts, apart from the apotheoses of the emperors, that is, their entrance into the divine pantheon. As to the latter, we modern people no longer read these apotheoses as facts, but as mythological magnifications of a successful reign—successful, at least, for its beneficiaries. In a mythologically thinking culture, such a successful reign was enough to establish the certainty that those emperors had descended to earth from the world of the gods and later ascended again to the realm to which they belonged. That's were the shoe starts to pinch. Would it not be a similar magnification when we hear that Jesus of Nazareth is a divine being who descended from Heaven to the village of Bethlehem about 30 years after the sea battle at Actium, and ascended back to Heaven about 33 years later from a hilltop near Bethany?

The problem, of course, is not the assertion of Jesus' humanity and of the exceptional impression he made on his contemporaries, but rather the confession that this 'truly human' was also 'truly divine', appearing on earth in human form.

THE ORIGIN OF THIS CONFESSION

Where did this confession originate? Let's start with denouncing Jesus' miracles as the proof for his divine status: Elijah is a match for him in the Old Testament. And what is written about the life of Apollonius of Tyana, the pagan miracle worker from the end of the first century CE, is not far removed from what is found in the Gospels. But apart from this, miracles presuppose a world of thought which does not know of binding laws of nature. A story that mocks these laws is considered to be part of our mythological heritage, and is therefore obsolete in modernity.

Now that the miracles have been denounced as an argument or proof for Jesus divinity, we can proceed. If we base ourselves on the sources that are closest in time to Jesus' public appearance and tragic death, then we can be assured that he did not conceive of himself as a divine being, let alone as the 'second person of the Trinity' which was an utterly foreign way of thinking in that time. And further that the confession of Jesus' divine nature neither surfaced during his life, nor in the first decades after his death, but only 60 or 70 years later. It very much appears that such a confession is an interpretation by the church community of the end of the first century. This community was no longer identical with that of the first years. In 70 CE, the Romans had dealt the final blow to Jerusalem as the center of Judaism, which also resulted in the disappearance of the local Judeo-Christian community that had played a dominant role in the larger Church. This, together with the influx of pagans into Christianity, had considerably watered down the Jewish character of the Church by the end of the first century. In the Jewish religion with its stress on the absolute and infinite transcendence of God, there was no place for a godly man, but at the most for a metaphorical Son of God, besides a Servant of God, a Lamb of God, or an Anointed of God, which are all time-bound and unsatisfying attempts to get some sort of a grip on the divine aura of the saving human figure of Jesus. In pagan culture, on the other hand, there was plenty of space for human demigods and the distance between those and the actual gods of the Greco-Roman pantheon, which were also characterized as humans, was negligible. And the Church thinks and speaks out of necessity in the frameworks of the culture to which it belongs, because it consists of people from that culture.

The distinction between the Jewish concept of God and that of the Hellenistic culture to which the Church belonged after 100 CE can be captured with this simple grammatical formula: for a Jew, 'God' was always the subject of a sentence, whereas for a pagan, 'god' was always a predicate, and this predicate could be attributed to many different subjects. To say about Jesus that he was god—'god' being the predicate of the subject Jesus—was unthinkable for a Jew. It could only said about Yahweh that he was God. Yahweh and God meant the same thing. But for a converted pagan it was not at all unthinkable to make 'god' the predicate of Jesus because what the former pagan meant with 'god' was not at all the 'creator of Heaven and earth' of the Jewish Bible, but an exponent of a higher world, with the characteristics of power and immortality (in the Iliad another name for the gods is 'the immortals') and the capacity to move about freely and sovereignly in the human realm, manipulating it at will. All this fits perfectly with the exalted Jesus. The more so because, if Hercules, the slayer of monsters, or Asclepius, the healer, could be revered as gods, and if even emperors such as Augustus or Vespasian could be reckoned among the gods after their death, why would a Christian who was born into paganism not recognize and venerate as god the saving figure Jesus of Nazareth who had 'come from God' and returned after his death to this God-Yahweh? He deserved this title a thousand times more than all the gods and demigods of the Hellenistic Olympus together.

Jesus' first disciples, as well as Paul, and even the synopticians who came after him, would probably have been flabbergasted at hearing someone speak about Jesus in this way. To call Jesus 'God' sounded audacious, even blasphemous in their Jewish ears: only Yahweh was God and could be called God and no one else. Thus all speaking about Jesus as god was impossible in the first half of the first century. Furthermore, those pagans were newcomers in the Church and they had no right to think they knew better than the Jews, who were the original owners of the Church home.

Only after the triumphant breakthrough of the Hellenistic element in the Church, and the fast waning of the previously dominant Jewish tradition after 70, it became possible and soon plausible and eventually even normal to call Jesus 'god'. This explains why the confession of Jesus' divinity does not turn up in the New Testament before the end of the first century, and then only with the necessary restrictions and nuances. For the author of the Fourth Gospel, the Father is still greater than Jesus (John 14:28), and the words he puts in the mouth of Thomas when he addresses the Risen are not 'Lord and God', but rather 'My Lord and my God' (John 20:28). These words sound as the correcting echo of the title 'lord and god' with which Emperor Domitian demanded to be addressed in the same period, and they express that not the emperor, but rather Jesus, was the real 'Lord and God' for the Christians. This warrants also the supposition that 'god' is used here in the same Hellenistic sense as in the title of honor which Domitian claimed for himself, and not in the Jewish sense.

Already in the first quarter of the second century, it was no longer unusual to call Jesus 'god': the letters of Ignatius of Antioch demonstrate this clearly; and the Roman governor of the province of Bithynia, the writer Pliny the Younger, infers in the year 115 from the judicial interrogation of arrested Christians that in their congregations 'they sing hymns to Christ as to a god'. Calling Jesus 'god' was for those Christians the expression of their personal reverence and their total devotion to him and not a theological statement about his unity of substance with the Father as this would be decreed in 325 at the Council of Nicea.

THE PROBLEM WITH GOD-YAHWEH AND GOD-JESUS

It took a while before people started to reckon with the theological implications of a confession that, despite its stress on monotheism, revered Jesus as a god next to Yahweh. For in Scripture, that is, in the Old Testament and the authoritative letters of Paul and the somewhat later Gospels, the title 'God' remained strictly reserved for Yahweh. How could they reconcile this with the pious practice of 'singing hymns to Christ as to a god'? For a century, no one lost any sleep over this. They believed *in* God and they believed *in* Jesus. That was enough. Not until the third century did efforts to harmonize these two titles start to get under way. But then, for lack of historical perspective, they did not realize they were uncritically mingling two different worlds of images and their respective language systems. They were apparently not aware that the one word 'god' labeled two very different ideas, a Jewish one and a Hellenistic one, and that every attempt to harmonize those two was doomed to fail. Besides, their philosophically oriented minds could not even rightfully refer to Scripture in their theological attempts of harmonization. The amount of texts that seem to call Jesus God is indeed very limited and for a good part of it a different grammatical explanation can be brought up. It is a golden rule in text interpretation that a meaning that contradicts what is obvious everywhere else, should adapt itself to the other instances, rather than the other way around. And everywhere in Scripture Jesus appears as a human who looks up to God, who prays to God for help, who directs himself to God's will, who recognizes God as someone greater. The texts that could be interpreted differently, such as the prologue of the fourth gospel, only surfaced later, that is, further removed from Jesus' historical appearance. But these late texts of Scripture were ranked as literal revelations of God and therefore as incontestable certainties. Thus, in the third century, the theologians thought that they had a safe foundation to rest upon. But even more than on these few texts, they rested upon the meanwhile increased ecclesiastical habit of calling Jesus 'God'. In the third century, this title was automatically read in terms of the Jewish notion of God, because, for contemporary Christian readers, there was no longer another god. Yahweh's being God therefore seemed to them to be applicable to Jesus too, in one way or another. But how could they confess Jesus as God without contradicting the oneness of God-Yahweh that is affirmed on every page of Scripture?

The groping and searching to solve this problem took a century and was evidently the work of thinkers rather than prayers. Indeed, the latter had venerated Jesus for a hundred years without brain-wracking as to how exactly they should understand the title 'god' with which they invoked him. This Christian groping and searching led at the same time to very unchristian slandering-matches, intrigues and mutual condemnations and anathemas. The catalyst of this process had been the appearance of the ascetic presbyter Arius (260–336) and his doctrine of the twofold Logos, the twofold Word of God: the Logos that is with God, is an attribute of God, eternal and uncreated just like Him; and, on the other hand, the Logos that became human, appearing in Jesus of Nazareth, is a being that is created by God, his first creation, a kind of Demiurge, who was in his turn in charge of the rest of the work of creation. Strangely enough, this abstruse attempt to unite Jewish and Hellenistic speaking about God met with a lot of response and following. But at the same time it aroused fierce resistance from the so-called orthodox. And these won suit. In 325 the Council of

Nicea confessed Jesus as 'of one substance with the Father, very God of very God', and in this way tried to render the 'unconceivable and unthinkable', as it would be called in the Council of Ephesus in 431, somewhat conceivable and thinkable. What they declared there so solemnly, of course, missed every foundation in human experience. How could those theologians have known about the inner life of the Mystery that we call God? But they felt challenged by texts from Scripture, which they considered as words of God himself, fallen from Heaven, and which yet seemed to contradict each other: Yahweh was God and Jesus was God. And yet Jesus was not Yahweh. And God could not contradict himself, could he? With this formulation, the Council of Nicea offered a beautiful sample of philosophical craftsmanship in the service of a way of reading Scripture that is no longer tenable for us. And it deemed to have solved a problem that in fact did not exist. The solution of Nicea therefore carried the seeds of its demise within itself. And that is what is happening now.

We can only admire the toughness with which the theologians of that time tried to reconcile Jewish monotheism with Hellenistic polytheism—something that comes close to the squaring of a circle—and for the geniality of what they considered to be the definitive solution for the problem. But modern insight into the origins and the development of these proposals, and at the same time into their time- and culture-bound philosophical character, mercilessly bares the relativity of their results and induces us to find out how the authentic experiences of faith of the first and the later disciples of Jesus can be voiced into the ways of contemporary thinking. Indispensable for this modern way of thinking is giving up the scheme of the two worlds, and this necessarily leads to giving up the formulations about Jesus that are based on this two-fold division and to replace those with new and inner-worldly formulations which, however, incorporate the same experience of faith. No less important is a different way of approaching the texts of Scripture, which should no longer be read as the Koran is still read today, but as the reflection of the groping and the searching of a faith community to say something meaningful about the unspeakable.

IN SEARCH OF A MODERN FORMULATION

To find such a modern formulation we first need to return to the origins of the practice of calling Jesus 'god' and attributing to him the corresponding nature and characteristics. What did the Christians of the beginning of the second century intend to say with this title? They thus confessed his transcendence, conceived of as a feature that applied to all beings that were revered as gods in that time. Words are like coins: they have a fixed value in the society in which they circulate. The same holds for the word 'god'. One needs to keep in mind that the Christians at the end of the first century had no longer known Jesus personally. When they gave him the title 'god', this was no longer the reflection of an historical encounter with him, which would have brought them to the sudden insight that they stood eye to eye with the one, eternal, almighty, dazzling, thrice-holy Yahweh which Isaiah had seen in his calling vision. With this title, they rather gave a contemporary name to the image that they made of him, as the fruit of the proclamation about him and of the resulting experience of existential salvation and inner rebirth. As much as he was human, he clearly did not belong to this disappointing world; he surpassed it and was in this sense transcendent, and in so far he fully deserved the name 'god'. In giving him this name, the faithful of the second century stressed the fact that he, like the gods of the Hellenistic pantheon, transcended our human limitations: he did not age, he no longer suffered, he was immortal, no longer bound to the limitation of the earthly domain, he could appear and disappear at will, or take on different forms, he heard and saw what happened here, could intervene with punishments and rewards, could save and destroy, was entitled to veneration, and took care of those who venerated him and begged for his help. And to those who relied on him, who 'believed' *in* him, he gave eternal life after their deaths, that is, he had them take part in his own immortality, that is, in his own (Hellenistically conceived) divinity. In concrete terms, this meant Heaven, conceived of as a life like that of the Olympic gods, a paradisiacal existence in undisturbed, eternal happiness.

Most of the characteristics that were connected with the notion of the transcendence of God in Hellenism, and first of all the other world to which this notion referred, are bound to die in a modern sphere of thinking. In our encounter with the living Jesus we can still have the same experience of transcendence as the Hellenistic Christian of the second century, but, unlike them, we can no longer take recourse to the title 'god' to express this. Because of our Jewish-Christian way of thinking, we immediately hear in that word the name of Yahweh. And Jesus was precisely *not* Yahweh. This means that we can no longer unproblematically call him 'god', but that we have to express in a different way what those Hellenistic Christians meant: that he is a transcendent, that is, all-surpassing, source of salvation and renewal. Therefore, this does not mean a new content of faith, the price of which has been reduced so as not to scare away modern customers, but only a new language for an enduring experience, and this change of language does not need to take anything away from the authenticity of our being a Christian. But what then should we call Jesus?

We can start with returning to the language of the first witnesses, used before the time when Hellenism in the Church started to give Jesus a divine position. In fact this is not a new language, not even for us: it is the language of the major part of Scripture, and we constantly fall back on it in the liturgy and the creed. The first witnesses called on Jesus with the Old Testament as their background: Lord, Savior, Christ—that is, Messiah—, Son of Man, Servant of the Lord, Lamb of God, and above all Son of God—that is, God's human counterpart and representative and elected. We can do the same without impediments. Sure, in the title 'Son of God' we automatically hear the later Trinitarian creed, but we can learn to tune out this association. Nothing keeps us from understanding this title as did its original users in the pre-Trinitarian time. Further, we also have the formulations of the transitional time, that of the fourth Gospel, written around 100 CE and the key witness to the hesitant beginnings of the practice of calling Jesus 'god'. The fourth Gospel calls Jesus the Way, the Truth (in the sense of truthfulness, reality, genuineness) and the Life, the Word of God, the Light of the World, the True Grapevine, the Shepherd, the Living Bread, and it has created the genial formula that one who sees Jesus, sees in him and through him the Father, who is greater than he. With all these, the faithful of that time expressed in a multiform way the unique place that he took up in their existence, and we too can still speak in that way. This multi-sidedness also demonstrates that no single image and no single title can exhaust the richness which they recognized in his personality. Therefore it was eventually easier for them to take recourse to the all-encompassing and all-surpassing title 'god'.

We don't need to follow them in the latter. We can remain believing Christians without this. If the creed is the sign of recognition that we are members of the community of faith of those who believe *in* Jesus as the Christ, then the shorter Western form of the creed which is recited each Sunday after the reading of the Gospel should suffice. It warrants the 'orthodoxy' of those who no longer feel at home in the Hellenistic way of speaking about Jesus. In this Western creed, Jesus only receives the titles: 'Only Son of God', and 'Lord', and neither of these requires an interpretation in the sense of the four great Councils of the fourth and fifth centuries: Nicea (325), Constantinople (381), Ephesus (431) and Chalcedon (451). These titles of the Western creed still breathe the spirit of the time in which they gradually originated and that is the time before the Christological and Trinitarian disputes.

TREASON TO THE TRADITION?

But can we, as Christians, permit ourselves to say farewell to those Councils and to abandon a creed that has belonged to the central content of faith of all the Christian churches and denominations for more than fifteen centuries? Certainly we can, if we have insight in the time- and culture-bound origins of the formulation of this creed and retain its essence. This essence does not exist in the attribution of the category 'god' to Jesus, but in the confession that we expect our salvation to come totally from our faith in him, because in him we recognize God's saving approach to us and because we effectively experience that salvation. Further, we should not forget that the practice of calling Jesus 'god' does not make sense for modern people, because the world-view in which this title offered no problem, that is, Hellenism, has long gone by. Someone who recognizes this may safely swap this title for a more contemporary one. He will even profit from doing so. Admittedly, Jesus may appear as greater and more super-human when dressed in the philosophical garb of the 'second person of the holy Trinity', but does this make him more of a savior than when one sees him and believes in him in the way his first disciples and the Church of the first decades did? Certain formulations may increase faith in him. One can assume that the decrees of the four decisive Christological councils did this and have continued to do so until yesterday. But today they apparently no longer do. The entire climate of thinking in which they were born has been completely washed away. In this case, it does not make sense to stick to them at any price. One is better off replacing them with others that seem more promising.

With this being said, those who are still afraid to give up the traditional creed should ask themselves this question. What is more important: to call Jesus 'god' (often a stick to beat someone who is no longer able to do so), or not to call him so but to let oneself be completely determined by him, by giving up one's own freedom of choice and opinion and taking over Jesus' choices and opinions instead? Not what one thinks and says can make a claim to reality and validity, but what one does. We only may give up the absolute good of our freedom if we do so for something or somebody that is even more absolute. To say about Jesus in words that he is god, while not directing oneself towards him in everything, is showing with deeds that he is not. Sure, one should not look down conceitedly on those past formulations: what is condensed in them is the fruit of sharp-witted thinking and testifies to a deep allegiance to Jesus Christ. And it betrays the intense concern for leading the 'living water' which is Jesus through the channels of that time towards the people of that time. 'Of that time', indeed.

The authority of the four Councils as the main witnesses to the theological insights of the fourth and fifth centuries remains uncontested. But the question of principle remains: does something belong to the perennial Christian message because the majority of the bishops that took part in a given council were of that opinion? Don't forget: they lived in a culture of two worlds in which it was very well conceivable (but nevertheless astonishing) that God descended graciously from his world to earth to take up human nature; and their lack of historical insight in the pious practice of venerating Jesus as (a) 'god' puts their insights and convictions in perspective and with them also their anathemas. Moreover, they read Scripture as a book of oracles that offered infallible arguments for a theological position. But as has already been argued: Scripture is no such thing.

Historical circumstances have also played a role in the genesis of the dogmatic formulations of the fourth and fifth centuries. This shows, among other things, from the fact that the Council of Nicea in 325 was convened and presided over by the autocratic head-of-state, Constantine the Great, who wasn't even a Christian at that time and who was more motivated by his concern for the unity of the Empire than by a quest for the truth. Not to accept the formulation of Nicea against the Emperor's will entailed for the participating bishops the risk of deposition and banishment. How would we judge today a Council convened and presided over by Vladimir Putin? And the Council of Ephesus in 431 was not only convened by the then emperor, but it degenerated, moreover, into a bitter struggle between the majority and the minority, who mutually excommunicated each other diligently, the winner, Cyril of Alexandria, calling the loser, the pious Nestorius, a new Judas. In such a climate finding the truth is much less important than steamrollering one's own right.

CHAPTER 9

EQUAL IN ALL THINGS

CONSTANTINOPLE'S DOCTRINE OF THE TRINITY

The previous chapter must have been like an earthquake for traditional believers. And earthquakes cause panic. We can appeal, then, to stay calm, and repeat in all keys that there is no reason to panic; that our existential attitude of belief in Jesus does not need to suffer from the translation of the formulas; that for us he remains the alpha and omega as the manifestation of the transcendent God; that the amazing formula of the Gospel of John stays in place unwaveringly: one who sees him, sees the Father; that we don't deviate from the original tradition—the question is whether this reassuring really helps. Anyway, we will have to leave the philosophically colored formulations of the fourth and the fifth centuries behind. In the theonomous world of thought there is no longer a place for a God who, at a certain moment, descended from his heavenly realm to pitch his tent on earth and 'take on the flesh' that he did not yet have. With this, the central pillar of the Christian doctrine of faith seems to collapse with a heavy boom. And in its fall it inevitably takes two other ancient pillars of the traditional orthodoxy along: the classical doctrine of the Trinity, and the attribution of the title 'mother of God' to the mother of Jesus. What will remain then of the holy banners under which Christianity marched in closed ranks through history? It is absolutely necessary that we scrutinize this question seriously. Because, as things look now, it appears as if theonomous thinking inevitably announces the funeral of the transmitted Christian faith.

INCARNATION IN A DIFFERENT LIGHT

'Came down from Heaven', says the creed. Originally, this may have been imagined as an actual descent from a Heaven located above the earth. Pious medieval painters even managed to depict this literally: on a ray of light that proceeds from a bearded God-Father, a tiny baby descends towards Mary at the time of the annunciation by the angel. Even if we leave such a literal image behind, a heteronomous division between two worlds remains the precondition for endorsing the classical doctrine of the incarnation. And theonomy, which is a form of autonomous thinking, therefore cannot affirm such a doctrine. If this other world is nowhere to be found anymore, the classical idea of the incarnation becomes yet another sparkling chandelier that falls down to pieces from the heavenly dome.

Fortunately, the previous chapter taught us that the doctrine of natures and persons, to which the classical doctrine of the incarnation is related, was in fact only a makeshift contrivance constructed by the Fathers of the Church in order to solve, by means of philosophical high technology, a problem that they had unwittingly created for themselves. Moreover, this construction of hypostases (or persons) and natures may have been 'good news' for the Greek-speaking and -thinking intellectuals of the late-classical world; it cannot be such for all of humanity in the East and the West, the past and the future. If something is entitled to be called 'good news', then it is, rather, the fact that the all-generating Mystery reveals itself in Jesus as God-with-us, that this Mystery cares with infinite and active loyalty for us all and for our salvation; that this God reveals through Jesus that he is Love, that one who sees Jesus will recognize in him God's active presence more than anywhere else; and that one who follows him will find a fulfilled existence, or to use a biblical term: salvation. This indeed was the message from the start. For this, we do not need the subtle philosophical language about natures and persons, so subtle that it is incomprehensible and therefore irrelevant even for the faithful. This confession of God's unconditional love for humanity and of Jesus' crucial role in our encounter with that all-creating Love is what matters for the Christian. And theonomy stays unconditionally faithful to this. It merely gives up the language of Athanasius and Cyril of Alexandria and formulates its faith in the language of our time. If we want to continue to speak about the incarnation of

God, we will have to fill this in differently. Process Theology can help us with this.

In its vision, an incredible and creating Wonder takes shape in the amazing process of the development of the cosmos, from the Big Bang until the human of the present. Our encounter with Jesus of Nazareth assures us that the essence of this Wonder is something that in human language we can call 'Love'. For the Christian the entire cosmic history becomes in this perspective the gradual self-expression of that Love. The cosmos is, as it were, the astonishing word in which this Love expresses itself. And since this self-expression appears to be directed towards the generation and the perfection of the human, we can say that God wants to take shape in the human. And in this way we have returned to the 'incarnation' of God, even though in a different way than before. In the past, this vision referred to the execution of God's eternal plan at a certain moment in time, about 30 years after the sea battle at Actium. But in theonomous thinking the sacred Mystery has was already incarnating itself in the cosmos from the beginning, resulting in the human. It does not do this by adding, as it were from the outside, the biological factor of the 'flesh' to its unknowable secret essence but by gradually revealing its secret essence in the genesis and the evolution of humanity.

CHRISTMAS OBSOLETE, BUT THEN AGAIN NOT

So what remains of Christmas? What remains is Jesus' birth, the beginning of the decisive phase in the ascent of humankind towards perfection and thus of God's gradual incarnation. But we can no longer sing about this good news in the way the Fathers of the Church did, who felt at home as fish in the water in classical rhetoric with its preference for parallelism and contrasts, and who never passed over a chance to let off fireworks of pointed (though sometimes empty) paradoxes in their Christmas sermons and meditations: God and human, infinity and smallness, eternity and time, omnipotence and powerlessness, king and child, palace and stable, darkness and light, and so on. We also can no longer celebrate it like the medieval people and their spiritual offspring, with Christmas carols that are often musical pearls, but equally often theological miscarriages, because they deal tenderly and sometimes compassionately with a baby, while the real reason for celebrating Christmas is the appearance of him who realizes God's merciful plan with us. Francis of Assisi's first Christmas crèche in the village of Greccio was a huge success, in that his example has received a billion-fold following. But, when an important person, a president, a state-hero, or the founder of an institution is celebrated, will one ever honor him by displaying his baby-pictures on walls and bulletin-boards? Two things should make us even more skeptical towards this ill-oriented cult of Christmas and its winter romanticism. First, that Jesus was not at all born on December 25. In fact we know nothing about his birthday. In the fourth century, the Church of Rome chose that day, in an effort to 'baptize' the then still widely celebrated pagan feast of the 'Birth of the Immortal Sun'. And second, that despite the testimony of the two infancy gospels (Matthew and Luke) Jesus was probably not even born in Bethlehem, but rather in Nazareth—Bethlehem, the birth place of David, being merely the codeword for his identity as the Messiah. Moreover, the huge commercialization of that holiday in recent decades has turned Chrismas into a straight mockery of what should actually be celebrated.

TRINITARIAN DOGMA OBSOLETE, BUT THEN AGAIN NOT

To skip over Chalcedon (451), Ephesus (431), Constantinople (381) and Nicea (325) back to the time before those councils (with all respect for the conciliar efforts to explain Jesus' relationship to God), and thus to stop professing Jesus as the 'second person of the holy Trinity', is in fact dealing the final blow to the traditional Trinitarian doctrine. If we do so, what remains of the essence and uniqueness of actual Christianity? Don't we reach the point where the distinction from Judaism or Islam lies only in the fact that our prophet is not called Moses or Mohammed, but Jesus, and the rest is six of one and half a dozen of the other? These are many questions at once, and not easy questions at that.

Even some Church leaders dare to say that most Christians are in fact worshipping three gods. This is probably not far from the truth. Certainly the way medieval painters sometimes depicted the Trinity—of course inspired and paid by their ecclesiastical commissioners—points in this direction: the three 'persons' are depicted as three identical characters, brotherly seated next to each other on one single wide throne. Church authorities eventually reacted, rightfully, and prohibited the making of such images any longer. But they reaped what they had sown 1000 years earlier. Too bad for the hard work of the theologians of the fourth and fifth centuries! Their subtle distinctions have proven to be gibberish for the average faithful. These docilely confess that abstruse doctrine of natures and persons and of the perfect unity and equality of the three in perfect distinction, but they don't understand a thing of what they confess. Nor do they care about it at all. Or they turn it into a doctrine of three gods. In fourth- and fifth-century Constantinople, the milkman and the grocer could fiercely discuss at the barber's whether the correct specification of the relationship between Father and Son was 'equality of essence' or 'identity of essence', but these times have passed. The Christian of modernity stands again where the first Christians stood, who were evidently good Christians themselves and for whom the revelation of God in Jesus existed in the message of God's fidelity and mercy, and not in an abstruse doctrine, however ingenuous it might be.

BACK TO THE BEGINNING

We therefore do the right thing to return once again to the time of Jesus and the early Church. If Jesus was indeed not worshipped as a god until about 100 CE, then all this time there was no talk of the (later) doctrine of the Trinity, which is characterized by the confession of the complete identity of essence of three clearly distinguished persons. For the early Church this would have been abracadabra. Paul, in any case, cannot be called in as a witness to the classical Trinitarian doctrine, even though he mentions the Father very often, sometimes with the Son, sometimes also with the Spirit. But nowhere does he put Jesus or the Spirit on a par with God. There is no talk of 'identity of essence' anywhere in his writings. Not even in the pre-Pauline hymn included in his Letter to the Philippians, in which it is sung that Jesus 'did not regard equality with God as something to be exploited' (Phil. 2:6). Moreover, hymnal language is poetical language, which is something very different from theological language. Neither can it be found in Matthew, who wrote a few years later. When Matthew quotes Jesus, saying that his disciples have to baptize in the name of the Father and the Son and the Holy Spirit, he was not even close to thinking like the Church Fathers at the Council of Constantinople in 381, where the Trinitarian dogma was definitively settled. For Matthew and his contemporary Church, the Father is still the almighty creator and the infinitely merciful; and the Son is still the Son of Man Jesus,

God's image and symbol, through whom we get to know God; and the Spirit is still the dynamic force with which God creates life and liberates the faithful and leads them towards perfection. In their 'name', that is, embedded in their saving presence, new members are added to the community they assemble.

Although the formula 'Glory to the Father' may from the beginning have been understood in a Trinitarian sense, we can continue to pray it in a pre-Trinitarian sense, glorifying God for what he is and does, and glorifying Jesus, through whom we have access to Him, and glorifying the Spirit of God, whose salutary activity we perceive in history and in our life.

Our modern inability to warm to philosophical speculation about God has as its positive side a deeper awareness of what the 'good news' is really about. It is not about philosophy and not about the ingenuously cut diamonds of confessional formulas. It is exclusively about the salvation of humanity. Sure, the Trinitarian doctrine is not at all mere scholarly abracadabra and it has inspired many pious people and helped them to raise their heart towards God and to live as Christians. But one should not be reckoned as an inferior Christian because he finds this doctrine a maze rather than an inviting path towards God; and because he rather sticks to the beliefs of the time before the Christological and Trinitarian disputes.

THE HOLY SPIRIT

The following is not a tractate about the Holy Spirit. It rather tries to answer the question as to how the Council of Constantinople arrived at a confession of God's Spirit as a divine 'person' in addition to the Father and the Son. In the Old Testament (and the New Testament does not suddenly think very differently), the Spirit is the creating force with which God wants to bring Israel, and through Israel the whole of humanity, to its desired completion. They had derived the notion of a 'spirit' from the human domain, where it refers to the breath of life. Someone who lives breathes. God lives and hence he has breath of life. He breathes life, power, and energy. This breath of life can be noticed in a thousand ways in the cosmos. No pious Jew in Jesus' time would have asked himself how this Spirit should be determined and described further. It was simply God's energy, which inspired, protected, and sanctified Israel. Such a pious Jew would never have thought of turning Yahweh's Spirit into an equal person next to Yahweh, 'equal in all things', as the Baltimore Catechism taught. But towards the end of the fourth century the world had changed. In 325, the Council of Nicea had taken place and it had recognized Jesus as God-of-God, a divine person next to God himself. The active role attributed to the Spirit in the New Testament apparently raised the question as to whether one should not say the same about the Spirit as they did about Jesus. In 381 in Constantinople they finally knew the answer. It was 'yes'.

For their affirmation that Jesus is God-of-God, the bishops at Nicea could refer to a few late texts from Scripture, but still more to the liturgical practice of worshiping Jesus as (a) God. But neither Scripture nor liturgical practice urged the recognition of Spirit of God as a yet another separate hypostasis, as a third 'divine person'. The traditional reason for this affirmation is the activity of the Spirit himself. He allegedly did what He had promised the Church in the Fourth Gospel (John 16:13): to guide them into the full truth. This chief argument for the development of the dogma has, however, already been weighed above and found wanting.

The more one thinks about it, the more one becomes surprised at the decrees of the Council of Constantinople. How could the assembled bishops have known that the holy Being of the unknown Mystery had, apart from one *ousia* or essence, also three *hypostases* or persons? Certainly not on the basis of a direct vision of God. No, again on the basis of biblical texts about the Spirit of God which they read in this way, despite the fact that these texts had been read differently for three centuries, namely as an expression for God's breath of life and creative energy. The now newly explained texts consequently served as irrefutable arguments for their conviction. But we have long left this way of reading and understanding Scripture behind.

Anyway, in Constantinople, the great credo of the late Latin High Mass was born, and in the sixth century it gradually became also the official creed of the churches of the West. Compared with the Nicean creed, it is characterized by the addition of clauses about the Spirit in which its divine nature is stressed: 'who is Lord and gives life, who emanates from the Father and the Son; who is worshipped and glorified with the Father and the Son'. This confession was intended to restore the unity of the Church in the struggle against the Pneumatomachi, who wanted to turn the Spirit into a creation of the Son. But alas, a few centuries later it became one of the causes of the schism between the Eastern and the Western Church. In the early Middle Ages, the West had started to add 'and the Son' to the original formulation 'who proceeds from the Father'. And the East did not at all agree with this. Leaving behind the question as to where they got this knowledge about the subject in the East as well as in the West, in 1054 this triggered the break-up between Rome and Constantinople.

Despite the solemn clause in the Creed that raises the Spirit up to the same dogmatic level as the Son, the Spirit only plays a very modest role in actual Catholic life. He is only invoked when the liturgical time of the year demands it: at Pentecost. After that, He again recedes to its modest place. His name is often heard, but only in formulas such as the sign of the cross or the 'Glory to the Father'. And formulas are dry twigs, the remains of what was once a vital confession. Fortunately the time has also passed that the Spirit was evoked for the 'illumination of the mind', in classes, at homework, and at tests. He must be a very small god, if He is only deemed necessary for such insignificant things.

A very important remark to conclude. It might seem that in this and in the previous chapter some central articles of the Christian faith are brutally run down. It should have become clear that only their heteronomous formulations are run down, because they no longer have a place in believing modernity. The same holds for a third holy pillar that is dragged along in the fall of the other two, namely the title 'Mother of God' that was solemnly attributed to Mary of Nazareth in the Council of Ephesus in 431. This is the topic of the following chapter.

CHAPTER 10

A REVERSED PYRAMID

"THE MOST HOLY VIRGIN MOTHER OF GOD, MARY"

Quotation marks say that something is quoted. The title between the quotation marks makes tangible the exalting style employed by the Catholic community to speak about Mary. This style in itself already reveals something of the bewildering flight of fancy the cult of Jesus' mother has taken in this (and the Orthodox) community. But this title is no more than the tip of an iceberg. It is not exaggerated to speak about the nearly idolatrous veneration Christendom has shown towards Jesus' mother since the very early Middle Ages, and which it—with the exception of the Churches of the Reformation—still shows. And this holds not only for the popular church with its pilgrim sites for the Virgin Mary, its litanies, icons, medals, holy statues, chapels, scapulars and rosaries, but also for the hierarchy from the lowest to the highest ranks. The universality and the intensity of this reverence can only be the fruit, so it is said, of the so-called *sensus fidelium*, the sense of the faithful. And this sense would be the hallmark of Tradition with capital T; it is supposed to be correct and reliable and to guarantee that the Church doesn't make mistakes, because it would reflect the workings of the Holy Spirit in the Church community. For its defenders, the praiseworthiness and the importance, yes, the indispensability of this veneration for all who want to call themselves Christians, is therefore beyond dispute. Consequently, reluctance towards this veneration is identical with a questionable lack of faith.

But it is also beyond dispute that this veneration isn't based on Scripture. It is not there that one will find the sources from which the mighty stream of the veneration of Mary, and the dogmas about her that are linked with it, have sprung. The Reformation with its campaign-cry of *sola scriptura*—Scripture only—therefore reacted against the cult of Mary. Especially since this veneration often came close to idolatry, and often overshadowed Jesus himself. As a result, the counter-reformation made extra efforts to propagate the contested cult of Mary and tried to justify it theologically. And later when the concept of a 'dogmatic evolution' arose, it didn't take long before the veneration of Mary became the showcase of such an evolution. But it has already been demonstrated in Chapter 2 that we can only speak about an actual dogmatic evolution, sanctioned by the Spirit of God, when the result can be recognized as the further development of an original tradition, that is, when its origin can be found in the testimony of Scripture. Before discussing briefly the scant Scriptural material with which the defense of the cult of Mary has to do, it is useful to explain the purpose and the structure of this chapter.

The aim of this chapter is to justify theonomy's view on the veneration of Mary. Indeed, this view clashes with four dogmas: the title *theotokos*, 'mother of God', attributed to Mary in Ephesus; her virginity during the conception of Jesus, with the ecclesiastical extension of this to *in partu*, during childbirth, and *post partum*, after childbirth; her 'immaculate conception'; and her assumption into Heaven 'with body and soul'. Despite their limited importance with respect to the Good News of God's eternal fidelity towards all people (and no longer towards Israel only), made visible and active in Jesus, they serve in fact as the hallmark of real Catholicity. Therefore this is an important chapter, despite any impression to the contrary. It should prove that theonomy is indeed 'orthodox', despite these (and other) apparent heterodox statements; that it continues to sail in the delta of the original tradition, even though its fairway may be different from the one that already took shape in patristic times and that meanwhile has become infinitely wide and deep. This chapter therefore attempts to show that medieval Mariology and Christian confession can very well be disconnected. Of course they don't contradict each other. But neither are they conjoined twins and it is quite possible to be a true Christian without being a devout worshipper of Mary. This defensive chapter will contribute the necessary arguments to prove this. But it endeavors to do even more. It wants to draw attention to the dark side of this veneration, thereby hoping to enhance our healthy development as Christians.

To do so, it will first be asked from which sources this veneration has arisen and still arises; and it will be shown that most of these are not as Christian as they are usually thought to be. Thereafter, each of the four dogmas will be investigated so as to show why one can stop affirming these without becoming a heretic.

SCRIPTURE AS SOURCE

It is evident that at least some useful verses should be found in Scripture. Because without scriptural backing, even popular piety cannot manage very long and liturgy even less. But, as has already been said, this source flows too scarcely to explain the width and the depth of the river that the veneration of Mary has become. In fact, the Biblical material that one can collect is limited to two passages from the first chapter of the Gospel of Luke: the annunciation by the angel, and the Magnificat. Are these two texts sufficient to found the litany of Mary's honorary titles?

Unfortunately they are not. To start with, they belong to the most mythological and therefore historically least reliable part of Luke's Gospel. Moreover, modern exegesis has taught us that Luke draws Mary in his story of the annunciation with the traits of the 'Virgin Israel' and therefore barely teaches us anything about the historical Mary. The Magnificat, on the other hand, which is put in Mary's mouth by Luke, has all the characteristics of a Psalm of triumph from the time of the Maccabees. And even to the extent that it goes back to the Song of Hannah in 1 Samuel 2, it does not fit in the mouth of a young girl from Nazareth who has just discovered that she is pregnant. Moreover, if one wants to connect it to this pregnancy, one has to take the message of the angel, with which the Magnificat is closely related, for an historical event. And for a modern mind that is, alas, impossible.

Doesn't Mary appear in historically more reliable texts? Yes she does, very incidentally, but those texts are of no avail, they even take us out of the frying pan into the fire. Take the exclamation of the woman who 'blessed the womb that bore' Jesus, as rendered in Luke 11:27–28. It is hard to come up with a positive reading of Jesus' reaction: 'Blessed rather are those who hear the word of God and obey it!' For this seems to mean, rather, that others deserve to be praised more than she. Nor is Jesus' answer in Matthew 12:48–

49, when he is told that his mother stands at the door and wants to see him, a stimulation to venerate her. Quite to the contrary. He claims there that his real mother can rather be found in 'whoever does the will of my Father in Heaven'. The Marian liturgy barely uses those texts. It prefers to exploit the wine miracle at Cana (John 2:1–11). But wine miracles hardly count as historical facts and, moreover, the unbiased reader of that story does not at all get the impression that Jesus wants to stimulate the veneration of his mother with his answer that means as much as 'Lady, do not try to tell me what I should do!' Jesus' words at the cross (in John 19:26–27) seem to offer more helpful material. However, Mary's presence at the site of the cross not only clashes with what the historically more reliable synoptic gospels (Mark, Matthew and Luke) teach us, but more than that, in modern exegesis, these verses are no longer regarded as a call to venerate her as 'our mother'. They are, rather, regarded as the affirmation that she is finally accepted in the circle of the disciples, as opposed to the above quoted texts in Luke 11 and Matthew 13, which clearly left her out. This seems to be confirmed by Acts 1:14 that indicates that after Jesus' death, his mother, and also his initially skeptical brothers, became part of the circle of his followers. Finally, it should be noticed that in the 21 letters that constitute the second half of the New Testament, nothing whatsoever can be found that would support the veneration of Mary.

The liturgy therefore prefers to find its much-needed scriptural material in texts that do not deal with Mary at all, but rather with Esther, Judith, God's Wisdom, Eve or an unknown young woman who is about to bear a child. A fine example of such a text is the reading from the book of Revelation at the holiday of Mary's Assumption (Rev. 12:1–6). The woman, 'clothed with the sun', is clearly not Mary but rather the threatened Church, being protected by God. Because of its evocative power, this text nevertheless supports the veneration of Mary in an authoritative way. The following process seems to have taken place. Searching for passages in Scripture that could be applied to Mary—something that in itself already bespeaks a developing veneration of her—her faithful came across this and similarly lofty and inspiring texts. Those were laid as transparencies over the figure of Mary, so that one gets the impression that, already in Scripture, those words of praise apply to her rather than to other figures. The new meaning those texts thus received took a share in the infallibility that was attributed to Scripture, authenticating what was apparently said in them about Mary. Thus, it was taken for granted that the Holy Spirit had inspired those texts precisely with Jesus' mother in mind. Moreover, a biblical author—be it the visionary John of the Book of Revelation or the author of historical novels such as Judith or Esther—was supposed to utter only infallible statements. However, Scripture is not a book of oracles, as has already been said, but rather the crown witness to what the Tradition confessed and meant at the time when the texts were written down. And when these texts were written down, the authors did not even come close to confessing anything about Jesus' mother.

The Influence of the Theotokos of Ephesus

It follows that other things than scriptural tradition alone must have played a decisive role in the unstoppable growth of the cult of Mary. To start with, there is the title 'Mother of God' that had already been in use for several decades in the East before it was solemnly attributed to Mary at the Council of Ephesus in 431. But the actual veneration of Mary has much more to do with emotions and feelings than with theological insight and dogmatic precision. In the case of the title 'Mother of God' it rather received its driving power from the combination of two psychologically forceful concepts that merge in this one title: the concept of a mother, which suggests care, tenderness, comfort and help; and the concept 'God', which suggests omnipotence. Medieval people did not understand this formula as a dogma, but rather as an answer to their own fears and needs. In the medieval vale of tears (we do not realize how lucky we are living in the twenty-first century Western world) the heart needed such an answer a hundred times more than today. Medieval piety saw Mary in the first place as the caring mother and comforter and guardian, without which life on earth would be unbearable.

Her veneration as mother of God had therefore barely anything to do with the dogmatic intentions of Cyril of Alexandria and his supporters. Indeed, these intentions concerned Jesus rather than Mary. Cyril used the title 'Mother of God', which had been in use as early as the third century, to settle scores with Nestorius, who held that Jesus, although being identical with the eternal Word of God, yet as a human was distinct from that Word of God, so that Mary could not be called 'Mother of the Word', neither *theotokos*, 'giving birth to God', but only the mother of the man Jesus. According to Nestorius, the two natures of Jesus should correspond to two distinct persons, otherwise we would have to say that the perfect and immortal Word of God had increased in wisdom and years, that it had had been hungry and thirsty, and that it had known fear and eventually had died. *Theotokos* was the banner under which Cyril battled in Ephesus against the two-person doctrine of his opponent Nestorius. The unholy atmosphere at this dogmatic battle can be inferred from the fate of the defeated party: Nestorius himself and the bishops that continued to support him, were banished to a desert town in Libya, a most inhospitable place at the far southwestern border of the Byzantine Empire.

Modernity does not recognize itself in the slandering-matches and the intrigues that were the order of the day at the Council of Ephesus, or in the content of the discussions. The subtle arsenal of philosophical terms that was called into play has become totally foreign to us, as much as the idea that expressions of the author of the fourth Gospel ('The Word was God; and the Word became flesh') are like meteorites fallen from Heaven, eternal truths, and therefore useful as uncontestable arguments in discussions.

Note moreover that in that era the word *theotokos* evoked the lofty image of a Byzantine empress. Was she not the mother of the real emperor Jesus Christ? Thus she is depicted in the fifth century mosaics in the Santa Maria Maggiore in Rome, which were completed shortly after, and influenced by, the Council of Ephesus. But in the Western Church this suggestion of a Byzantine *Augusta* was soon driven out by the image of the Madonna with the Child. These motherly Madonnas demonstrate that the 'Mother of God' of our Hail Mary may be the literal translation of the *theotokos* of 431, but that it has a very different emotional value. That is another reason why the title 'Mother of God' has little in common with the dogmatic formula of Ephesus, to which the worship of Mary nevertheless incessantly refers.

OTHER SOURCES

The formula 'Mother of God' was, however, only one of the booster rockets that propelled the Marian cult into its earth orbit, where it follows its lofty trajectory, undisturbed and unassailable ever since its launch. There are many indications that another major influence is to be found in the veneration of the ancient female goddesses Artemis-Diana, Athena-Minerva, Isis, Ceres, the Magna Mater and even Aphrodite, whose temples were transformed into Marian sanctuaries. In South America a similar thing happened with the cult of the Pacha Mama, 'Mother Earth'. The violent abolition of the cult of these goddesses by Christianity could not stop their veneration, living on in disguise in the Marian cult. Centuries old, deeply rooted religious needs and experiences are not easily eradicated. But even where Mary is clearly not venerated as a goddess, but as Jesus' mother, and where her veneration does not go beyond the *hyperdoulia*, that is, 'super-slavery', sanctioned by the Church authorities, a form of veneration clearly distinct from the strict adoration of God, many other things that can hardly be ascribed to the Spirit of God seem to play a role. Mary was apparently felt to be the female counterpart of God the Father, who was perceived as too one-sidedly male, strict and fearsome. This is evidently a distortion of the Christian image of God, and certainly not the work of God's Spirit. It is, rather, the result of the understandable and forgivable human deficiency. When people are in need, they automatically relapse into the state of a threatened child that cannot save itself and seeks help. And in such situations a child seeks refuge with his mother rather than with his father. This escape towards 'Mother Mary' instead of towards God, and the search for safety and cover under her cloak is, therefore, rather a distortion of the original revelation than a further development thereof.

This collective flight of popular piety towards Mary very soon also had impact on the official liturgy, and not only on Roman Catholic liturgy. One of the most beloved prayers in the Byzantine liturgy is the wonderful *Akathistos*, a pure Marian hymn. In its turn, the official liturgy reinforced the cult of the 'most Holy Virgin and Mother of God' by introducing ever more Marian holidays, with their own prayer services, prefaces, antiphons, litanies and hymns. Already in the Middle Ages, theologians had distilled out of this *lex orandi*, this practice of prayer, a *lex credendi*, a rule of belief. But because the scriptural arguments for this rule of belief were quite poor, and the best of those belonged moreover to the realm of poetry rather than theology, they also sought to come up with purely rational arguments in support of the veneration of Jesus' mother. For example, that her Son would certainly have done what every good son would do for his mother: to give her all the privileges that he could give her. Well, since it was within his power to grant her an immaculate conception and an assumption into Heaven with soul and body, he certainly must have done so. This kind of reasoning does not sound very convincing. Besides, in his public life, at least according to the synoptic gospels, Jesus did not show his mother all the kindness he could show her. But this, the theologians wisely preferred to ignore.

A last powerful source of Marian devotion seems to be found, not in the highlands of theology, but in the chasms of Depth Psychology, where it is indebted to a stubborn ecclesiastical structural element, namely the fact that the Church has been governed for centuries by male celibates with at least an unconscious need for a female object of veneration. Since because of forced celibacy the way to a woman of flesh and blood remained closed to them, they had to find another outlet. The sublimated female figure they found in the 'virgin Mary' filled this void without burdening them with guilt feelings, and could even make them feel elevated to holy heights.

When the deep emotional attachment of hearts to Mary became a self-evident virtue among the church leaders, these reinforced the already flourishing cult of Mary in the hearts of their flock through their proclamation. Also among certain clerics, a surviving mother-bond can have found a pious disguise in their affection towards 'Mother Mary', thus becoming a not so scriptural source for the widening and deepening of the stream of Marian devotion in Catholic communities.

Most Holy Virgin

This is the other recurring title for Jesus' mother. The emphasis on her virginity is based on the narratives in the infancy gospels of Matthew and Luke that Jesus' conception was the Holy Spirit's work, not Joseph's. If so, this emphasis seems to be part of the original tradition, albeit not of the most ancient one. For neither the oldest gospel, Mark's, nor the even earlier letters of Paul mention anything about a singular conception. For a theonomous mind it is even more striking that the infancy gospels teem with mythological elements, such as angels with messages or singing carols or warning in good time, or the sudden emergence of a star showing the way and staying put above a house. And the more mythology, the lesser historicity. Moreover, the two infancy gospels contradict each other more than once. In Chapter 4 it has been mentioned already that in Matthew, Joseph flees with his wife and child to Egypt immediately after the visit of the magicians and remains there for several years, whereas in Luke, they already return to Nazareth six weeks after Jesus' birth. Moreover, in Matthew, Joseph clearly lives in Bethlehem, whereas in Luke he lives in Nazareth, which forces Luke to come up with a reason (or a pretext) to have Jesus' birth take place in Bethlehem. Therefore the two infancy gospels cannot be adduced as historically reliable sources. And the same holds for what they say about a virginal conception.

But that is not the real reason why modernity should think differently from the tradition. The real reason is the heteronomous, that is, highly mythological character of the idea of a virginal conception. This mythological character clearly shows from the following. For human beings, copulation is a *conditio sine qua non* for fertilization, because male sperm has to be directed to a female egg cell. Luke may have the angel say that for God nothing is impossible, because in his traditional way of thinking the 'other world' would do for once without the necessity of copulation. But in modernity there is no longer a world that can interfere powerfully from the outside to make the male contribution to conception superfluous. And this necessary male contribution cannot help but make an end to the state that is indicated by the word 'virgin'. To say it more clearly: for the modern faithful, Joseph of Nazareth is Jesus of Nazareth's biological father. For some this may be shocking and irritating. Probably because in their eyes it means a deadly menace to Jesus' divinity, to which they are so attached. And probably also because of the 'mother-virgin' only the 'mother' will remain.

But with regard to the divinity of Jesus: those who are shocked or vexed would do better to reread Chapter 8. Moreover they should consider this: that Jesus would have received his total genetic code from the human Mary does not seem to hurt his alleged divine nature for them. Why then would that nature be endangered if half of this code came from her and half of it from another human, namely Joseph? Moreover, conception without sperm would result in a form of parthenogenesis, with the surprising outcome that Jesus for lack of a Y-chromosome would have been a girl. Modern science and biblical stories are sometimes quite a bit at odds with each other.

And as to Mary's being a mother and not being a virgin, why would that be such a disaster? Because celibacy and monastic life would then lose a banner under which they can gather? But if experience has not taught that this type of unmarried life in itself constitutes a real enrichment, then that banner is no more than a fig leaf. Moreover, beneath this resistance to accept a non-virginal Mary a remainder of ecclesiastical uneasiness with sexuality might be hidden, perhaps even a straight rejection of sexuality. Indeed, for fifteen centuries such a rejection was considered a virtue in the Church.

But why do the two infancy gospels, while at other points often disagreeing with each other, fully agree where it comes to presenting Jesus' conception as a direct intervention on the part of God that suspended for once the normal course of nature? Just as Jesus' birth in Bethlehem, this has everything to do with proclamation. Evangelists are not journalists; they are preachers of the good news. What they proclaimed unanimously was Jesus' unique greatness: they said in this indirect way that whoever saw him in action or heard him speak, received a glimpse or an idea of how God himself must be. According to the biology of their time, the child was considered exclusively as the product of the father. He was the hopefully improved new version of his father, his 'likeness and image' as said in Genesis 5:3 about Seth, the son of Adam. But for the faithful of the early Church, Joseph was a few sizes too small to be Jesus' prototype in view of the latter's messianic greatness. They saw Jesus as the unique image and likeness, and thus as the son of the invisible God and savior of Israel. Moreover, those were times without knowledge of egg cells, chromosomes and genes but with a deep existential conviction that for God everything is possible, such as causing to conceive against all odds. For one who thinks heteronomously, there is nothing problematic in this. Besides, until two or three decades ago, none of us had any question or doubt about Mary's virginity. Now many have. The breakthrough of modernity, that in the Church dates actually from the times of the Second Vatican Council, has opened our eyes to the fact that we have to do here with a piece of ancient Christian mythology. However, a mythological story is less an impossible story than a story with a message. If Mary is called 'virgin', then the message is identical to the message that Jesus has been conceived of the Holy Spirit, and doesn't have much to do with physiology either.

Strangely enough, in later centuries precisely this physiology rather than the symbolism has been stressed by confessing Mary's *virginitas in partu*, that is, that even her delivery of Jesus did not harm her virginity. But in this way virginity is reduced to an intact hymen; and which message of salvation for humanity could possibly be included in this physiology elevated to dogmatic heights?

One remark to conclude. Praise for Mary's virginity is all too often based on very doubtful Christian factors. Think for example of the litany of Our Lady of Loreto (ecclesiastically sanctioned and blessed with indulgences). The accumulation of adjectives, added to mark the idea of the virginity of Mary as a mother, such as 'most pure, most chaste, inviolate, undefiled', suggests that sexual intercourse renders a woman unchaste and impure, defiles and violates her. This is no praise for marital love nor for motherhood. Such ideas are at variance with our message of faith rather than based on it. They are unconsciously Manichean rather than consciously Christian. And what hides beneath the obsession of liturgical texts to emphasize Mary's virginity each and every time she is mentioned? Is her real greatness not to be found in her attitude as a 'maidservant of God' rather than in her physical condition? Why then, does the latter always get all that emphasis? Isn't there indeed a subtly disapproving attitude towards everything that has to do with sexuality?

THE MARIAN DOGMAS OF 1854 AND 1950

The above described combination of popular piety, liturgy and biased theology, significantly furthered by mostly hidden psychological influences rather than by the testimony of the early Church, has gradually paved the way to the Marian dogmas of 1854 and 1950. The previous paragraphs explain why we may rightfully ask what percentage of the dogmatic final product has really been affected by God's Spirit. The final decisive criticism, however, concerns its heteronomous character. Let's start with the dogma of 1854 that proclaims Mary's 'immaculate conception', which means that she did not inherit original sin when her father impregnated her mother.

It has already been demonstrated extensively in Chapter 3 that it is impossible for modern people to affirm this dogma; that in doing so, they would subscribe to a doctrine of original sin that stems from the brilliant Augustine of Hippo, but for which there is no longer a place in our world-view since Darwin. This is all the more true if we have, despite the encyclical *Humani generis* of Pius XII, simultaneously said farewell to monogenism and thus accepted that humanity started with more than one pair. The dogma moreover implies that original sin causes a blemish from which Mary would have been spared, again by extraordinary divine intervention. The term 'divine intervention' is already enough to sound all the theonomous alarm-bells. How, then, could a theonomous Christian celebrate Mary's immaculate conception as something very joyful, let alone as a dogma?

The heteronomous character of the second dogma, that of Mary's assumption, promulgated by Pope Pius XII in 1950, is, if possible, even more conspicuous. Its formulation presupposes a Heaven to which Mary was transported (by angels?), and corporally at that. The latter presupposes a previous resurrection, which is an equally disturbing foreign concept in the theonomous world-view, as will be demonstrated in the following chapter. Evidently, there is not a bit of support for this dogma in Scripture, which contains even less about Mary's death than about her life, namely nothing at all. The dogma of Mary's ascension to Heaven developed from legends that can be called flowery, to say the least, or bizarre if we are honest, and which date from the fourth century. If from these legends finally in 1950, the declaration of the dogma has emerged as the crowning of that Holy Year, then we owe it in the first place to the stream of Marian devotion, growing century after century and carrying all along. In need of a more rational foundation, the declaration of the dogma found support in the alliance clever theologians managed to forge between this and the other heteronomous dogmas of her immaculate conception and her virginity at the conception and birth of Jesus. The result of this close bond, however, is that one dogma shares in the discredit of the others.

MARIAN DEVOTION AND MODERNITY

The following is indeed a strange phenomenon. The further the Church is forced by modernity into a defensive strategy without any prospects, the more strongly its leadership emphasizes and propagates Marian devotion. Not only did the two Marian dogmas of her Immaculate Conception and her bodily Assumption originate in exactly that period, but also towards the end of the nineteenth century the first Roman documents emerged that sought to attribute her two supplementary honorary titles: 'Mediatrix of all Graces' and even 'Coredemptrix'. However (and fortunately) regarding the latter title, it is safely added that she is so only in a lesser and very analogical sense. That means, not really—in other words not at all. This non-committal proviso is an absolute necessity. For not only are these honorary titles not founded in Scripture, but to the contrary, Scripture points in the opposite direction as there Jesus is clearly considered the sole mediator. That the concept of a mediatrix is moreover a very heteronomous one will become clear in the last chapter, where intercession and supplicating prayer are treated. Indeed, according to the Roman documents Mary's being the mediatrix stands exactly in her role of intercessor.

Despite all the efforts on the part of the Church's leadership, Marian devotion among the modern faithful is clearly on the way down. The traditional church remains faithful to its Marian past. Pilgrimages to Marian sanctuaries are still popular; the rosary is still being prayed, at least by older people. But who among younger people still prays the rosary? And what remains of the once-flowering Marian congregations, of the many Marian fraternities, of her cult of the Seven Dolors or the 'Immaculate Heart of Mary', of the wearing of her scapular, and of so many other expressions of former Marian piety? And where August 15 is still a holiday, people don't rejoice because Mary has 'ascended into Heaven with soul and body', but rather because they enjoy an extra summer vacation day.

Just as modern atheists, so modern church-goers too become noticeably estranged from the Catholic Marian past. They apparently find the center of gravity of their faith elsewhere. In doing so, they have Scripture on their side and that remains the most important form of the Catholic tradition. Moreover, they feel that Marian devotion is an inclined plane from which one easily slides off into side issues, because it has to do more with feelings and emotions than with biblical belief. Think about the sad spectacle of the hordes of credulous pious that come running up at the umpteenth rumor of a Marian apparition, as if the salvation that is promised by God is to be found there. The real message with its scriptural foundation threatens to disappear behind blue Marian clouds of incense.

Part of the rejection of the modern faithful might also be due to the fact that the Roman glorification of Mary, the 'maidservant of the Lord' forms the invariable overture to a glorification of male priority in the Church, Mary presented as the idealized but unrealistic picture of the woman who, following Paul's directions, keeps her mouth shut in church. And modern femininity is far from pleased with such an ideal.

SO WHAT?

So what remains standing, after all this, of the amazing skyscraper of Marian devotion in the Catholic and Orthodox tradition? This building is not only bewildering because of its size, but also because of its shape. It looks like a nuclear mushroom cloud, or a reversed pyramid. For in Scripture it finds hardly any support, but nevertheless it has gradually filled all but the entire ecclesiastical sky. Moreover, one who ventures to revert to the Gospel is immediately suspected of heresy or lack of faith.

If we nevertheless go on a quest in the Gospel for the so revered Mary, who will we eventually find? Simply the mother of the Messiah, not the *theotokos* of 431. But, if this Messiah is the alpha and omega of our lives, our gladness and thankfulness for his appearance will overflow to the one through whom he has come to us. And she is much more than just the biological source of his existence. Jesus did not descend from Heaven booted and spurred, like Athena from the head of Zeus. He was born as a drooling and crying baby and had to learn everything, really everything. And his mother has played an irreplaceable role in this learning process. The result of this process reveals something of how she has been herself. The apple never falls far from the tree. The Magnificat may not have sprung from her; it nevertheless expresses how she thought and felt, so that Jesus learned to think and feel in the same way.

Among the Marian prayers that still can appeal to modern people, the Magnificat therefore retains its full value. Among the other liturgical prayers, the most useful are those that glorify her, not because she is queen of all and everyone, or because she is the immaculate, inviolate, most pure, most chaste, etc. virgin-mother, but because from her 'the sun of righteousness' has risen. Or those that praise her as the morning star who announces the day; or other prayers that do not detach her from her vital bond with Jesus and his being the Messiah. And also those prayers that praise her attitude of being the 'maidservant of the Lord', despite the fact that those alleged Marian words are derived from the story of the message of the angel, and can therefore not make any claims to historicity. But something doesn't need to be the exact account of actual facts or authentic words in order to be genuine. Neither has the Hail Mary had its day, at least not its biblical first half, even though it goes back to the same mythologically colored chapter. Everything that is put in the angel's and in Elisabeth's mouth there, retains its value and richness for the veneration of Mary as the mother of the Messiah.

CHAPTER 11

BEWARE OF THE ARTISTS!

BELIEF IN THE LIVING JESUS OR BELIEF IN HIS RESURRECTION

The two parts of this formulation hide more than they express! To begin with, the modest conjunction 'or' is already important. It doesn't serve as a mere link between two more or less synonymous terms, the latter only clarifying the former. No, it opposes the two concepts and demands a choice. One who thinks theonomously will have to choose the first half, as will soon become clear. Also the preposition *in* is important. In the second half it refers to an actual believing, on the authority of others, that something is true—in this case that Jesus has risen bodily from the grave. Such belief supposes that one trusts their knowledge and truthfulness. Depending on this trust, it certainly includes some grades of existential depth. Nevertheless, this kind of belief is essentially a rational process, a matter of the brain, not of the heart. It deals exclusively with the acceptance that something is correct. It corresponds to the use in classical Latin of the verb *credo*, 'I believe', followed by an infinitive sentence. Such belief can range from having an opinion or hesitantly accepting something, to being so convinced of the truth of something that one would bet his head on it.

In the first half of the title, however, the preposition *in* refers to a totally different content, to an attitude of trust in somebody, of having faith in someone and only secondarily of believing his words. It means an existential commitment that has much more to do with the heart than with the intellect, much more to do with love than with truth. And it is only this first kind of 'belief in' that fully deserves to be called 'faith'. Only this faith connects one with the God who reveals himself in Jesus of Nazareth.

To express this attitude, the classical Latin verb *credo* was not adequate. *Credo* could only be used with either a dative to express that one trusts somebody enough to take his sayings as credible, or with an infinitive sentence to express what was accepted or agreed upon. The language of faith of the disciples of Jesus needed other means to express their relation of total devotion to God and to Jesus. Therefore they had to develop a new grammatical construction, namely the use of *credo* with the preposition *in* with the accusative case, an expression unknown in classical Latin. In fact they adopted this construction from New Testament Greek, which had faced the same problem. But when this construction is translated into English with 'to believe in', it blurs the distinction with the other meaning of 'to believe in', which has no existential value and which merely refers to accepting the truth of what is said, or to take for granted that something exists. If we want to specify that the existential 'belief in' is meant, we can either use a different word such as 'trust' or 'faith', or we can stick to 'belief in', hoping that it will be clear from the context which form of 'belief' is meant. In the following, when the expressions 'belief in' or 'believe in' refer to the existential disposition of trust and commitment [*credo in*], the preposition *in* will be italicized as a help for the reader.

Consequently, belief *in* will always refer to a dynamic process that rises up from deep inside ourselves, that has to do with being touched and with commitment, with dedication and devotion. It surpasses the domain of the purely rational and implies a movement of the heart. One does believe, for example, *in* human nature, *in* love, *in* Marxism or *in* the holy *jihad* (at least in its sense of effort or dedication). And the faithful believe *in* God and *in* Jesus of Nazareth, which includes surrender and discipleship. Whereas believing in God is static and uncommitted, believing *in* God touches our existence. It is something that glows and that changes our life. Only believing *in* can be said to have saving power; to bring about salvation. Or to say it with a traditional ecclesiastical term: to redeem us. One can believe in the devil, but only Satanists can believe *in* the devil. If the devil were to exist, he wouldn't have a hard time believing in the existence of God, and he would in that sense have more belief than agnostics or atheists, but it wouldn't help him one bit: he would remain what he is, a poor devil, and it would not turn him into an angel. To have belief *in* God would, however, be a mission impossible for him, because it would make him stop being a devil. Of course it is not possible to have belief *in* God without believing in His existence. But the opposite is very well possible: to believe in (the existence of a) God and stick to it, without approaching and meeting God and being changed and saved.

Because this distinction is blurred in daily English, countless surveys about believing are worthless, because the subjects of the survey don't know whether the question concerns the innocent conviction that there exists somewhere a powerful Being, which controls the course of events, a supreme watchmaker, or rather the risky readiness to go through fire and water for God. Precisely because of this existential, saving character, the traditional Latin Credo opens with *Credo in Deum*, 'I believe *in* God' and not with *Credo esse Deum*. 'I believe in (the existence of) God'.

Despite this important difference, and maybe because the English translation features an indistinct 'I believe in God', we are wide off the mark, when we think that our creed is a compendium only of intellectual affirmations, like the purely intellectual affirmation of the existence of God, of the virginity of Mary, of the historicity of Jesus and of his resurrection from the grave on the third day. In short: when we think our creed merely affirms our belief that these are not fairy tales, but truths. And that this belief is all we need to be a Christian. On the contrary, that's only the beginning. Indeed, to be a Christian involves that we believe *in* God (and *in* Jesus, and *in* the Holy Spirit) and that means that we adjust our entire thinking and acting to the Wonder we call 'God', as it appears in Jesus, even if that cuts across our own inclinations or social trends.

In this book, this distinction is consciously and consistently made. Hence the distinction in the title of this chapter between belief in the resurrection, or belief that Jesus has risen, and belief *in* the Living. Why not belief *in* the Resurrected? Because the imagery of a resurrection from the grave on the third day is so heteronomous that a modern believer doesn't know what to do with it. He has to find a different language to describe the magnitude of what happened at that moment. This has to be a symbolic language, because that is the only way to reach the deeper level of existence we are talking about. And that symbolic language has to be freed as much as possible from the influence of the heteronomous culture, in order to fend off the danger that the actual liberating message be veiled rather than revealed for the modern believer. It will be made clear in the following that the language of 'life' fulfills these requirements. That is why the title mentions belief *in* the Living.

Those who anxiously defend Jesus' literal rising from the grave, making it a shibboleth of true Christian faith, are entirely wrong if they think that those who reject this bodily resurrection, deny in essence the Christian message itself and belong to the guild of the grave-diggers of the Christian faith. But modern believers, who want to express what happened with Jesus of Nazareth after (or in) his death, can no longer do so in the language of the Gospels. For that language, including the term 'resurrection', is the residue of a different view of humankind and of the world than ours. To express the good news that the execution of their Messiah Jesus was by no means his final defeat, but to the contrary his real victorious coming and the birth of a new world, the Christians of the first century could not but use the framework of their own worldview, which is no longer ours. A formulation that is authentic and revealing to us has to spring from our contemporary worldview. The language that was authentic in the past, and that was able to open theeyes to the light hidden in the darkness of Jesus' death, is no longer convincing today. It provokes resistance rather than endorsement.

A SECOND-CHANCE LIFE?

A preliminary word about the views of humankind and of the world in the ancient Church is due. As long as the Jerusalem Church was still setting the tone, these views were still basically those of the Old Testament, which portrays the human being as an animated body. Speaking about the soul and speaking about the body was the same thing. 'My body' meant as much as 'me', and 'my soul' as well, but also 'my heart', and 'my mind', and 'my flesh', and even 'my kidneys' and 'my innards'. For the Old Testament, these all referred to the same person, merely seen in different lights. To die meant, therefore, the end of the person. Unlike other cultures in the Middle East, Israel didn't know life after death, but at the most a void existence as a shadow in the depth of Sheol, the underworld. However, such a pale and bloodless state did not deserve the rich name of 'life' in their eyes.

Not until the second half of the second century BCE did they start to realize that death isn't necessarily equal to the irrevocable end. This initially faltering confession was not based, as in Socrates and Plato, on the metaphysical foundation of an immortal soul that inhabits the body, but purely on their faith in God's promise. Part of the ABC of the Jewish doctrine of the Covenant was the certainty that someone who honored this Covenant would find life. Scripture is full of this promise of God. God is indeed a God of life and of the living. But what they experienced during persecution by Antiochus Epiphanes in the middle of the second century BCE seemed to contradict this. At that time, especially the most devout worshippers of God, some still very young, had to give their life for their fidelity to the Covenant. On the basis of his promise, God owed it to himself, so they thought, to compensate the loss of lives that his enemies had made them suffer, by offering them the chance of a second life. This second-chance life would not take place in the heavenly domain, as Christian thought would later see it, but on earth. For Heaven was the inaccessible abode of God, whereas humans have their residence on earth. It is interesting to see that the message of 'life after death' that originated in ancient Judaism was neither born from fear of disappearing forever, nor that it is the result of a daydream, as atheist criticism often presents it, but the fruit of a theological logic, be it the logic from another era than ours.

SLEEPING, WAKING UP, RISING

Therefore a pious individual who did not reach his full share in life, had the right to reach that full life as yet. This did not necessary mean 'eternal' life, but at least a life that surpassed by far the regular expectations, for God is God of abundance. And it could be expected to be a corporeal life, because a human being is an animated body. This is important for our topic. For in ancient Israel the dead were not cremated but buried, that is, laid down in the earth. The idea that the just and devout person that lies there would come to life again some day, entailed the idea that he was sleeping in the meantime. In later Christian Greek, a cemetery would be called a *koimèterion*, a place to sleep. In Latin this became *coemeterium*, which in English became 'cemetry' and in French *cimetière*. If the Old and the New Testament speak about 'waking up' the dead, then this way of speaking originates from the same imagery of sleeping and waking up, of lying down and rising. Therefore we speak about 'rising' from the dead and 'resurrection', derived from the Latin term *resurrectio* that means 'rising up again'.

These images soon merged with the much older conviction that God, who abhors injustice, would judge the world in His time, on 'the last day', and make the ever-trampled righteousness prevail. For this purpose, he would call the entirety of humanity to court. And this gave rise to the idea that his angels would announce this ordeal with the forceful sound of trumpets to wake up all the sleepers at once and call them to God's judgment seat.

The normal Jewish way of disposing of the dead was interment, not cremation. This practice was a culturally determined fact, not an inevitable necessity or an eternal disposition of God. By the same token it could have been cremation. But had cremation been the case, it would have been difficult to speak of the 'rising' of the dead. A lying body may rise. A handful of dust and ashes cannot. And 'to rise up' is precisely the translation of the Greek verb *anastènai*, which is used in the New Testament to describe what Jesus did 'on the third day'. Resurrection, therefore, is only a culturally conditioned image, depending on the way in which the Jewish people traditionally dealt with their deceased.

To ask someone whether he or she believes in Jesus' resurrection is often used as a sly way to test the orthodoxy of the person questioned. In fact, one should answer this question with a counter-question: 'Do you mean to say that death is merely a state of sleep from which one will eventually be woken up, whether or not by the sound of the Trumpets of Judgment'? The fact that this may have to wait a few thousand years should not be a problem: as everyone knows, for God a thousand years—and then probably also ten thousand or a hundred thousand years—only last one day. Whether the answer to this question is 'yes' or 'no', the good news about Jesus cannot exist in the fact that he 'fell asleep' on Friday night and 'woke up' before dawn on Sunday morning, and rose and left his tomb.

GREEK THOUGHT NOT MUCH BETTER

Whereas the ancient Church spoke and thought in these images, and gave shape to its testimony in the Gospels (and Paul in his letters), another way of thinking and speaking about humankind developed among the Christians of the next generations, most of whom had come from paganism: a Hellenistic way, this time characterized by the ideas of Socrates and Plato. In their world of thought a human is a dual being consisting of an immortal soul and a mortal body, and obviously the soul is by far the most important of the two, in fact the only important part, and even the human's essence. The body, on the other hand, is often more a burden than a pleasure. Dying is no longer the end of the human being, but rather the end of a cumbersome connection. In this view, resurrection would be the reunification of the two, something the meanwhile liberated soul could hardly wish for. Indeed, what kind of good news would that be for the soul? To be stuck with this confining body once again? And how would this reunion take place, if from that body not even the dust has remained? These and similar problems should be solved by those who believe in it…

DID JESUS REALLY DIE?

For modern people it is even harder to appreciate this ancient Jewish imagery of waking up from a centuries-long sleep. A dead body that comes to life again, after all its organs, and in the first place its brain, have died off, requires no less than miraculous supernatural intervention to make this organism immediately and completely functional again notwithstanding this 'total loss'. Moreover, such a miracle would mean the total reversal of the law of entropy, a law to which matter is bound as much as it is to the law of gravity. To escape from this contradiction between physics and a mythologically expressed message of faith, Reimarus, an evangelical theologian and philosopher from the beginning of the Enlightenment era stated against the unanimous testimony of the Gospels, that Jesus did not really die on the cross, but that his so-called death by crucifixion was only an apparent death. After some time, the coolness of the stone on which he was laid in the tomb would have woken him up from this state of apparent death. No single historian or exegete today still takes this seriously. But Reimarus saw no other way out but this clumsy stratagem. Just as everyone else in his time, he still took Scripture for reliable historical information, but his already modern-critical mind stubbornly resisted the idea that a dead person could live again and rise from the grave.

ON THE THIRD DAY, ACCORDING TO THE SCRIPTURES

These stories about rising from the grave, however, don't feature historical accounts and the language of facts; they feature the language of imagery. A first indication of this can be found in Paul's words in 1 Corinthians 15:4 'raised on the third day in accordance with the Scriptures'. With 'the Scriptures' Paul obviously means the Old or First Testament. The New Testament had not even started to exist. But, alas, nowhere in those Scriptures is it mentioned that the Messiah—or whatever name or shape one would look for to find Jesus there—will rise from death, not even that he would die. Only about the 'servant of the Lord' in Isaiah 53 is it said that God will save him from death. This Servant of the Lord probably refers to the People of Israel, not to the Messiah. The application of the text to Jesus of Nazareth makes the Christian heart feel good. But this application is an entirely free choice. Moreover, that text does not mention the 'third day'. A couple of raisings from death can indeed be found in 'the Scriptures', but again, without a trace of a 'third day'; moreover, in these stories, the 'resuscitated' person simply resumes his daily routine. This is miles away from what the Church intends to say with Jesus' resurrection. Moreover, those texts do not deal with a messenger of God, a prophet, or somebody else in which one could see the prefiguration of Jesus-Messiah. Finally, there is the famous chapter (37) in Ezekiel in which the prophet sees how a valley filled with dead bones changes into a nation of living people, but he explicitly says that this is visionary imagery, dealing with the People of Israel as a whole. And this instance of resuscitation is, again, not related to the third day. So what remains of Paul's claim that Jesus' resurrection on the third day can already be found in the Old Testament?

Something does. What is found more than once in the Bible—so that Paul can speak of 'Scriptures' in the plural—is the importance of the third day. The third day is, time and again, the day of decisive events, and often such a decisive event is a case of God's saving intervention. For the notion of the third day shares in the symbolic power of the number three. What are we still doing when we want to move something heavy together? We count 'one, two, three!' and on 'three!' it happens. That Jesus rises on the third day in the biblical tradition needs therefore not to be taken literally. This third day is not a day on the calendar but a symbol of the fact that God intervened in a saving way at the moment of Jesus' defeat. So, if Paul connects the resurrection explicitly with this symbolic third day, the resurrection itself may probably also be understood in a symbolic way. So far this has never happened, for even before the Gospels were written down, some 40 years after the facts, this third day was already conceived of realistically, as a day on the calendar. And this prepared the way for dating the resurrection on Sunday, as a literal understanding of what counted as the third day from Good Friday on, and it consequently served as the background of the stories about the apparitions that would have happened on that day.

CREDO QUIA ABSURDUM?

Modern faithful are no longer capable of accepting the corporeality of Jesus' resurrection. To their relief, they find strong backing in the clearly unhistorical character of the stories about the apparitions of Jesus on which the belief in his corporeal resurrection has always been based. If these stories were the reliable rendering of proven historical facts, we would have no choice: willy-nilly, we would have to reconcile ourselves to the facts and 'believe in the resurrection', against the grain of our entire world of thought. This would be a very typical case of *credo, quia absurdum*, that is, a flight into blind belief, because to accept the reality of such a belief in the resurrection would radically cut across the rest of our thinking. Against all the laws of an autonomous world, someone who has bled to death would appear healthy and well among his followers after two days, despite the fact that an enormous stone had been rolled in front of the entrance to his grave, and the doors of the room in which his followers congregated had been locked. And nevertheless he would be as corporeal and as spatial as before: capable of hearing, seeing, feeling, capable of walking miles, and displaying normal digestion, which he proved by consuming a piece of fish. And as if this were not enough, he would be able to disappear as surprisingly as he had arrived. In short, that would be equal to a continuous act of magic. In that case, belief in the resurrection would mean accepting what is totally foreign to our way of thinking, saying 'no' to reason and 'yes' to the inconceivable. And that borders on schizophrenia.

But are these texts indeed the unadulterated representation of historical facts? The evolution in the way the apparitions are related, and the contradictions between the authors, lead to the suspicion that this is not the case. What can a brief investigation of the four Gospels teach us? The oldest, Mark, does not yet relate any apparition stories; he mentions only a messenger angel, who evidently doubles as the evangelist in disguise. The catalogue of apparitions at the end of his Gospel is, as is well known, a later added summary of the apparition stories from the other Gospels. Some years after Mark, Matthew knows already of two apparitions: one to the women at the tomb, with the message that the disciples should go to the Galilee to see Jesus there, and a second one, a few days later, because of the distance they needed to cover, indeed in the Galilee. Again a few years later, Luke already knows of three apparitions, now all three on Easter Sunday, and all three in or near Jerusalem. But Luke has Jesus neither appear to the women, nor in the Galilee. In his account, there is moreover no time left for an apparition in the Galilee, because the third apparition in Jerusalem ends with the Ascension. Although there is no indication for this in the story, this ascension, however strangely, must have taken place in the dark. For the two men who went to Emmaus had already returned to Jerusalem, and it was already dark when they started their journey of seven miles back. Again several years later, the Acts of the Apostles mention forty days of apparitions, which at least gives the impression that there were more than three. And finally, around 100 CE there is the account of John. He mentions four apparitions, the last of which happened in the Galilee, several days after the third one which already happened eight days after Easter in Jerusalem. But already twenty years before the Gospel of Mark, Paul mentions a series of apparitions of Jesus in chapter 15 of his First Epistle to the Corinthians. He only mentions them, without any details. And of the four apparitions that he mentions, apart from the vision of the risen Christ he has had himself, at least two do not concur with those related in the Gospels.

No wonder historical criticism doesn't leave a trace of those stories standing. The defenders of corporeal resurrection try to play down the many contradictions, arguing that they would only concern minor details and that, on the other hand, the scriptural authors unanimously confirm the reality of the apparitions, this unanimity being more important than the differences. This may be true. But historicity does not allow contradictions. Saying that they will see him in the Galilee (so Mark and Matthew) and then mentioning only apparitions in Jerusalem (so Luke) do not go together.

Nor does disappearing forever (what else could ascension mean?) in Bethany on Easter day, according to Luke, or a few days later in the Galilee, according to Matthew, and yet, according to Acts, continuing to show up for another forty days and on the last day even eating with his disciples. And the stone has either been rolled away before the arrival of the women (in Mark), or while they were present (in Matthew), but not both. To agree with one evangelist is to disagree with the other. Whom of the two should we believe? Another possibility, the most plausible one, is that they are both off the mark. Rather than accounts, these are rumors, things that they heard and passed on, without being able to verify them. Is that a problem? Not at all. We only need to understand how the first disciples came to telling such stories, most of them contradicting each other, but all of them agreeing on one important point: we have 'seen' him.

No Facts, but Images

The question at hand here is not yet how to speak in theonomous language about what happened to Jesus. We first need to find out what Jesus' followers experienced, because that is what they tried to express in ancient Jewish and hence heteronomous images. We need to try to understand their messages and reformulate these in the language of modernity.

A preliminary remark is due. Paul, the authors of the synoptic Gospels, and the author of Acts use yet other terms beside 'resurrection', some of which do not remind at all of standing up from a grave, such as: to sit at the right hand of God, to be glorified, to be installed as Lord and Messiah, to receive the Name that is above all names. These don't refer to just as many phases in a chronological process that would have started with Jesus' waking up from the sleep of death in a tomb. Rather, they all refer to one and the same event that is elsewhere indicated with the very heteronomous term 'resurrection'. Similarly, 'ascension' is only one way of speaking of what happened to Jesus when he died, namely that he 'went to the Father'. In the past, when space travel and astronauts were unknown, and miracles were unproblematic, ascension to Heaven was indeed conceived of in a very literal way, as something that could have been filmed, as it were. We only have to look at the iconographic renderings and literary descriptions of the event. But people of the twenty-first century can no longer accept this. Moreover, we have learned meanwhile that ascension is a very ancient mythological motif, known in pre-Christian literature. Just a few examples: the prophet Elijah rides up into Heaven in a fiery chariot; on the outer wall of the San Marco in Venice, Alexander the Great is represented riding into the sky in a carriage drawn by flying griffins; and according to Ancient Roman mythology, Rome's founder Romulus was translated to Heaven during a thunderstorm. But together with this ancient mythology the conviction that these ascensions should be taken literally has also died out. Today we understand that the same holds for Jesus' ascension: It did not take place; he did not ascend into Heaven, not on the first day and not on the fortieth day. However, ascension says in a different way the same as resurrection, as is demonstrated by the usage of Scripture. If the literal interpretation of ascension is given up, why not do the same with resurrection? Because orthodoxy vetoes this position? But the factuality of a dead body coming to life again, followed by its leaving the grave is as unthinkable for a modern mind as an ascension conceived of in astronautic terms. How can theonomy sail safely between the Charybdis of inconceivability and the Scylla of heterodoxy?

About Apparitions

To start with, we have to stop speaking about 'resurrection stories'. Scripture only knows of apparition stories. Therefore, it is first necessary to investigate the phenomenon of apparitions. In the past few centuries in that part of the Western world that has remained Catholic, scores of faithful souls, especially children, have declared that Mary appeared to them. In some of these cases it is unlikely that these little seers came up with fabrications. They must have seen something, or as they say it, have 'seen Mary'. The quotation marks are an evident sign of reserve. Why? Because when we see something, a ray of light falls onto our retina, inducing a chemical reaction that stimulates the optic nerve which, in turn (however difficult this is to understand) converts these stimuli into images. If this chemical reaction occurs on the retina, then it should also occur on film. Well, for example, in Medjugorje no single photographer or camera man has ever seen anything appear on his negative plate or film, even with the most light-sensitive camera, no matter how carefully he had directed his lens towards the point that was suddenly fixated ecstatically by the group of seers. This means: no light stimuli, and therefore no images on the retina. Thus nothing to be seen. And yet these children saw something. More specifically, they saw Mary. And they heard her voice. Something could also be said about this voice, for example that the air vibrations caused by the voice (because that is what speaking means) would also reach other eardrums. But, alas, they never seem to do. We have to accept that the seers are honest. So what does this seeing and hearing mean to them? Possibly something like this: It happens that one wakes up in the dark and sees things or people that appear not to be there when one turns on the light. This is the psychologists' fare. They know the answer: projection. Someone can experience something inwardly with such intensity that he or she thinks to see it outwardly. The shape that the projection will take depends on our psyche, which in turn depends on the culture in which we live. It is plausible that these seers had an intense experience of transcendence. And in their psyche this has been translated by the above mentioned phenomenon of projection into seeing and hearing Mary. Seeing and hearing Mary, because Roman-Catholic piety is impregnated with her.

Back to the apparitions in the Gospels. After Jesus' death, the disciples went through a deep valley of panic and disappointment and hopelessness. But after a while (for the third day is not a chronological fact), they had an exceptional experience of transcendence: the overwhelming awareness that the Jesus they revered so much was 'alive', despite his pitiful end. This experience made them aware that his death was not the senseless end of their expectations. Quite to the contrary, what could be read everywhere in the Scriptures had happened to him: that God is a God of the living, that he is faithful in his divine way to everyone who turns himself towards him, and especially to the righteous person who is persecuted because of his devotion to Him. This was therefore not primarily an intellectual process, a conclusion after arguments, discussions and Bible study, but an intense experience of Jesus' being alive, even so intense that it projected itself outwardly, and took visible and audible form in the shape of the Jesus that they venerated. From the New Testament we can gather that this experience started with Peter. And his experience aroused or strengthened the experience of the others, for deep experiences are contagious. The shape of this experience differed corresponding to everyone's own psyche and the concrete circumstances. This can probably explain some of the differences between the stories.

FROM SEEING TO PROCLAIMING

The next phase existed in their urge to proclaim the good news and its enriching implications to their people. If the executed Jesus was living and present, this meant against the background of Jewish portrayal of mankind that he must have awoken from the sleep of death, and consequently risen, in other words: that he had been resurrected. For they had 'seen' him themselves. And then this message started an unstoppable process of growth in the oral tradition. In 1 Corinthians 15, the oldest account of the apparitions, Paul says only that Jesus 'made himself visible' (Gr. *oophthè*: literally: 'was seen'). He does not distinguish between Jesus' appearance to the disciples and his appearance to himself, with which he refers to his experience near Damascus. But there he only saw a light and heard a voice. This likewise puts the 'seeing' of the other apparitions that he mentions in perspective. In the Gospels, written several years later, the original testimony that Jesus had made himself visible, will become more and more colored with catechetical motives, enriched with new details and expanded with symbolical stories. As a result, the proclamation gradually lost that unique, precious quality of immediate and shared experience. Precisely these catechetical motives explain the colorful and often contradictory image of the apparitions that has reached us. Among these symbolic stories, apart from the Emmaus Road Story, especially that of the Miraculous Draught of Fishes is worthy to be mentioned. In the many apocryphal gospels that have been rejected by the churches, this growth process borders on the phantasmagorical.

THE COUNTER-ARGUMENT

Okay. So there is no body that appears from a grave. And no need to roll away a two thousand pound rock. But here come the supporters of physical resurrection with what in their eyes is the conclusive counter-argument: if the body were still in the tomb, then it would have been child's play for Jesus' Jewish opponents to expose the proclamation of his 'resurrection' as pure humbug. But nothing is known of such exposure. This looks like a good argument. But it is less good than it seems. First of all because the priestly caste had to avoid at all costs touching a grave or handling a corpse, because that would make them ritually impure. Secondly because in the Acts of the Apostles, the proclamation of Jesus' resurrection only starts seven weeks after Easter, at Pentecost. Is it imaginable that Jesus' opponents would go and exhume a corpse two months after his execution only because part of his previous supporters stubbornly hold that they have seen him living and well? They themselves had seen well enough that he was dead. They would rather have shrugged their shoulders at so much naivety. And thirdly, because this argument supposes the historical correctness of what the Gospels say about Jesus' burial. And a thing or two raises doubt, such as a certain Joseph of Arimatea suddenly turning up, coincidentally a secret disciple of Jesus, even though he was a member of the High Court, and equally coincidentally on good terms with Pilate; in short, too good to be true. Or the impossibility to fit all the narrated events into the available timeframe. Or the Roman custom of throwing the bodies of the crucified into mass graves.

But can a Christian afford to think and to say that the body of Jesus remained in the grave after Easter as cold and rigid as the day before and that it started to decompose after that? Is someone who thinks and speaks like that still a Christian? Why not? The essence of the good news is not concerned with what happened with Jesus' corpse, is it? The classical presentation of the resurrection nevertheless gives that impression. And it leaves the modern thinking faithful with a lot of discomfort. Only someone who thinks in a two-world scheme, with miracles as a bonus, does not stumble over this presentation. The real good news, on the contrary, proclaims on the basis of experience, that a life-giving power goes out from the encounter with Jesus, now freed from the limitations imposed by time and space to which he was subjected before his death. And that this power changes all who turn themselves towards him and tune themselves in to him for the good; that it is a source of human fulfillment and salvation for them. For this, must Jesus' corpse have disappeared from his grave without leaving a trace? Did the remains of Francis of Assisi need to disappear in order to uphold the world-wide influence of this charismatic man? To argue that only his soul remains active from Heaven (whatever that may mean) is a heteronomous eyewash. No one deals with the Poverello's soul, but rather with the Poverello himself. And to speak in terms of an immortal soul and a mortal body, with death as the separation of the two, presupposes a view of humankind that is not founded in Scripture. To try to explain this Jewish-inspired message with Greek reasoning can only result in disastrous chaos. Scripture deals with the whole person of Jesus. Jesus' followers have seen him die or have heard about it and have later experienced that he lives. Period. The experience that he lives, should therefore be the point of departure of a theonomous approach of what was called 'resurrection' in ancient mythical language.

HE LIVES

But saying that Jesus lives is mythical language as well. Living is indissolubly connected with biochemistry. Without biochemical processes there is no life. And death makes an end to these processes once and for all. But life is at the same time an ambiguous term. It has a much richer content in an animal than in a plant (where it is nevertheless already an amazing wonder), and in the human the term life has again a much richer meaning than in the animal: it now also refers to spiritual experiences of creativity and charisma, of selfless love and inner light, that just as a the life processes of a fungus cannot occur without a biochemical foundation, but that transcends this level endlessly. This transcendence is the beginning of a way towards a yet more endless transcendence, which brings us to the all transcending Wonder that we call God. For if we speak about the 'Living God', the word 'life' receives a meaning that surpasses the biochemical level by far. If we may call the divine Wonder a self-effacing Love that takes form in every love, the loving human will become more united with that Love the more he loves, and he will share in the same amount of its creative richness. In his death, Jesus has become the pre-eminent loving human, and thus our most pure and vital model, for there he went to the extremes of self-effacing, and thus of love. This brings us to the limits of what we are able to say about the 'resurrected' or the 'glorified'. Here we reach also the limits of what we are able to conceive and to express, which is normal for all speaking about God.

This is exactly what makes 'resurrection' as a way of speaking about what happened to Jesus a bit suspicious. It is all too easily imaginable. It even owed its success to its imaginability, fast food for uncritical artists. They took advantage of the available possibilities and with their creations they stiffly enforced the self-evidence of this image. One should therefore be careful with their depiction of the resurrection. Because in the way they depict it, the resurrection becomes a one-time, divine, unworldly intervention in the natural course of events, an all-surpassing miracle. In a time when miracles were part of the general world-view, it was possible to think and speak in this way without evoking critical reactions or unbelief in the listeners or readers. But that time lies behind us. Since Reimarus.

But this heteronomously conceived confession would not have enjoyed such a long life, if the readers or listeners had not personally experienced something of the reality of the good news that it proclaimed. The apparitions to the disciples were peak moments of this experience. But it made itself felt in other and more common ways too: in experiences of peace, light, hope, gladness, joy, courage, and transformation as the result of the belief *in* Jesus as the living Messiah. Paul speaks in this regard about 'fruits of the Spirit'. In essence, these are ways of participating in the richness of life that has become part of Jesus, because of his love until death. The Fourth Gospel beatifies those who have not seen him, yet existentially believe *in* him. For it is possible to experience him as fully alive without having seen him in the manner of the first disciples. On the condition that one has not merely belief in the resurrection or in the Jesus of history, but belief *in* the Living. The story of the Road to Emmaus illustrates this. It has taken a long time before it became clear that the author does not intend to tell what happened on Easter day between Jerusalem and Emmaus, but rather that he intends to demonstrate by means of this story that all the faithful can experience Jesus as the Living one. This happens, says this story, each time their hearts become warm at the proclamation of the good news about him. And when they gather in friendship to remember with bread and wine his victory over death, they become aware of his beneficent and enlightening presence,. Belief *in* the Living rests on this experience. And on that belief the Church is built, so strongly that neither death nor the underworld can destroy it.

Chapter 12

Better Coarse but Wholesome Bread

Is There Life after Death?

In this chapter, theonomy enters completely unexplored terrain. It is like walking on ice that creaks at each step. This creaking might be frightening and alarming to many that venture to come along, but there is no return. One who has said 'a' has to say 'b'. As soon as one has left the image of a second world behind, only this cosmos remains, and God as another name for the transcendent Depth of this cosmos, which is not cold and lifeless, but knowing and loving. So what happens to the human who dies, since there is no longer a second world in which he can enter, having passed the borders of this existence? Does heteronomy know? It thinks it knows because it possesses an ancient, piously preserved map of that unexplored country, made by people who have never set foot there, but who have drawn that map with good faith in Holy Scripture, convinced that its language is an eternal, infallible and descriptive language. But it is a temporal and mythical language. And to supplement what was lacking, they called in their human imagination and granted it the necessary freedom. The result of all this is the following.

When he dies, the human—or in any case his soul, which presupposes a historically defined philosophical view of humankind—crosses the border between life and death, and arrives in another world. There awaits him on the spot the judgment of the righteous God which exposes even his most hidden flaws, whereupon he receives his due punishment or reward. Punishment can be temporary (in which it is automatically assumed that there is something like time in that other world) or eternal; and the punishment is quite terrible as it consists of torture with fire—one of the cruelest forms of torture that the human has devised for his fellow men. Eternal torture is due, if one has perpetrated at least one mortal sin, such as staying away from mass one Sunday, remarrying after a divorce, or using contraception, without repenting of this crime. Tradition did not see anything wrong in calling this a righteous punishment, but a sober comparison of the seriousness of the crime with the heaviness of the punishment makes it very hard to see the righteous character of this sentence. Conversely, the reward also surpasses all earthly measures and proportions: for some years of faithful keeping of God's commandments, one will enjoy (though, as a rule, after the said barbaric time in Purgatory) so complete a state of bliss that compared to it, all earthly pleasures pale into insignificance—and this for all eternity. Nevertheless this notion still allows for a brief intermezzo in the punishment or the reward: there will be a second judgment, not an appeal against the first sentence, with a second chance of acquittal or a new risk of conviction, but a pure confirmation. For this trial the entirety of the already judged human family will gather again somewhere (they apparently knew where: in the Valley of Josaphat) before God's judgment seat, each one with his or her restored body, which will from now on join in the eternal punishment or reward. And this time the judge will be the Son. We have been raised with these images. Not knowing that they are a concoction of figuratively meant, but literally read words of Scripture, we have accepted them uncritically, for they correspond to our innate sense of justice. Otherwise so much evil would remain unpunished and so much good unrewarded, and that would be contradictory to the idea of a righteous God. Strangely enough, as a rule, we think that this punishing righteousness applies in the first place to others, while the rewarding righteousness would be reserved for us.

There is no single other area of Christian doctrine in which the disappearance of the second world and all the related certainties entails so many problems and meets so much resistance as here. Because, if the journey needs, alas, to be canceled for lack of such a world, what are we to do with the entire Tradition? For that Tradition repeats in all keys that there is really a different and eternal life after this life, with judgment, punishment and reward.

THE ROLE OF THE ENLIGHTENMENT

It is no coincidence that the denial of a life after this life only arose during the Enlightenment. Leaving aside Epicureanism, in the entire classical era, and even more in medieval culture, it had been self-evident that life continues in one or the other way after death. Death was a border but not a terminal station. What was the origin of this conviction? For in neither of those centuries did anyone have the slightest personal experience of a life hereafter. The dead disappeared forever behind the doors of death and never returned. Survivors saw no more traces of an eternal life in that time than after the Enlightenment. Yet they remained convinced that something new started at the other side of that door. And this conviction was strong enough to determine their behavior: they built tombs that looked like houses as a surrogate for the lost human dwelling; they organized ceremonies and rituals to secure the journey of the dead to the other side; and they designed their actions in view of the punishments and rewards they expected there.

What happened, then, that caused this certainty to wane in the eighteenth century in the West, and even so fast that a few centuries later half of the Europeans became convinced of the opposite certainty, namely that there is, alas, nothing at all after this life? Simply a kind of cultural mutation had happened. Modern Western culture indeed implies a real mutation in the development of humankind, and not only in the domain of technology. Ours is the only culture that has hatched from the egg of a pre-scientific vision of the world, has recognized the autonomy of the cosmos and, related to that, has said farewell to an extra-cosmic world and a God that inhabits it. Precisely therefore, it is also the only culture that has given up belief in an ongoing life of the dead in another world. For it does not know of any other world.

Is it blind, then, to what the past saw or claimed to see? To the contrary, it started to see something in a much sharper way, namely that it is impossible for our consciousness to survive death. Indeed, our consciousness is the 'interiority' (so Teilhard de Chardin) of unimaginably complex chemical processes. And these inevitably come to an end when we die. To speak about eternal life, happiness or sadness, reward or punishment, loses its meaning when there is no longer any consciousness.

To the Medieval Christian, this was fully different. What thinks and feels inside of us, in his conviction, is an immortal soul that will continue to think and feel when it escapes the body. Because that was death in his eyes: the liberation of the soul from the bothersome yet necessary body. Medieval Christians did not know where these convictions came from, that they owed them much more to pagan antiquity than to Holy Scripture. Yet such was reality. In that matter they were docile pupils of pre-Christian Greek philosophers. It was from them that they had inherited the idea that soul and body belong to two different worlds and that they each go their own way at death: the body back to the earth from which it was taken, to decay there; and the immortal soul to the other world. This is how medieval people thought, but modern people can no longer think this way. They see themselves as a further stage in the development of mammals, endowed with a higher intelligence, but no less than the other mammals a biochemical compound that is born and dies. Forever.

How, then, is it still possible for a modern person who thinks that consciousness after death is unthinkable, to believe in Jesus Christ, as a living and conscious being? Will belief in this Jesus become the umpteenth case of *credo, quia absurdum*, to believe because thinking has to give in? No, because it is possible to reconcile the two, and to stay in the intention of the Tradition despite the disappearance of the second world and the end of the biochemical substrate of consciousness. But for that purpose the Tradition will need to be formulated very differently. The foundation of this new way of understanding has already been laid in the chapter about Jesus as the eternally living.

PREAMBLE TO A NEW PERSPECTIVE: WE CAN LIVE WITHOUT

As a run-up to this new formulation of the Tradition of life after death two important remarks are due. The first one is that we should free ourselves from the idea that it is infinitely important for our own little ego to survive death. There are other things in Heaven and on earth that are much more important than staying alive and being happy forever. Such as the realization of God's dream of mankind as a world-wide community of people, freed from all its miseries and calamities and evil. If we could buy this future at the price of disappearing forever, would we not on the spot say yes? This proves that at least one thing is more important than staying alive forever: namely 'the Kingdom of God', which coincides with the welfare of humankind. It should be our first concern to seek and to fulfill God's will, with or without the prospect of an eternal life. Then we are back where ancient Israel stood, because neither Abraham, nor Isaac, Jacob, Moses or any of the other prophets, psalmists or authors of the Old Testament, at least until the second century BCE, had knowledge of a life after death; and this did not keep them from 'walking before God' in joy. Belief in immortality is apparently not a condition for belief *in* God, neither for being happy in it, nor for leading an ethically high-principled life. Israel achieved this for a thousand years while all the surrounding cultures believed in some form of immortality. That too puts the importance of life after death in perspective. In other words, we should be ready to live without life after death and to let go of all claims or expectations on that subject. Only then will we have the correct attitude to receive it as a gift, in whatever form it will be offered to us.

No Pacifier

A second remark is this. In the eyes of modern criticism, belief in a form of life after death, especially in its Christian form, that is, belief in eternal bliss, is a pacifier with which people try to soothe their pain over the fact that they have to die. The prospect that we are granted but a relatively short and often disappointing portion of life is indeed not very joyful. But this explanation doesn't do justice to the reason why belief in resurrection arose in Israel. Israel had no urgent need for a pacifier. It had proven for a thousand years that it could do without. Its late-born confession that life does not stop with death, despite the convictions of the forefathers and disregarding what the eyes see, had its origins elsewhere, namely in the religious conviction that our relation with God promises 'life'. Israel had always understood this in an inner-worldly way, as a long and happy life on earth. In the second century, persecution by the Greek ruler King Antiochus IV taught them the hard way that there must be a flaw somewhere in this view, that fidelity to the Torah could entail suffering and death. That persecution brought about the conviction that pious victims would be resurrected sometime. This vague 'sometime' became gradually more concrete: this resurrection would take place on the day that God would inaugurate his kingship on earth through the coming of his Messiah. This image is the source of the remark in Matthew that at the moment of Jesus-Messiah's death, the graves opened and many of the pious deceased rose up. Matthew apparently understood the hour of Jesus' death as the beginning of his messianic kingship. To resurrect before the advent of the Messiah would bear the danger that one would become for a second time the victim of the anger of God's opponents. First, these should be definitively eradicated. The Jews did not agonize over the question whether this second life was forever or just for a very long time. What God would do would be good, and in any case they wouldn't have to complain. 'Going to Heaven' was obviously out of the question. Heaven was God's domain, not theirs; their home was the earth. The happy hunting grounds were not located in another world: they would return to *these* hunting grounds, to catch up here on what they had missed out on here; this is another sign that the Jews did not borrow their belief in resurrection from their neighbors. Resurrection was of course reserved for the pious who, through the fault of God's enemies, had missed out on their full share of earthly happiness to which they were entitled because of their loyalty to Torah. Some 150 years later this idea of resurrection, even with adaptations, was still unacceptable for certain groups within Judaism. The keepers of the tradition, the Sadducees, still rejected it (Matt. 22:23), while for the Pharisees and for Jesus resurrection had become a certainty.

The fear of disappearing forever is therefore clearly not the ground from which Christian belief in the resurrection sprouted. This fear rather explains the success of the doctrine of reincarnation with modern Westerners, imported from the East and distorted during this import. Why distorted? Because in Hinduism and Buddhism, reincarnation is the inevitable long way towards Nirvana—the dispersion of the ego—whereas in the West it serves the exact opposite. For in the West incarnation promises a new chance for that ever unsatisfied and death-threatened ego.

THE AMALGAM OF THE TRADITIONAL IMAGE

If we want to present a modern interpretation of the ancient Christian myths about life after death, we need to understand their basic meaning. And this in its turn presupposes that we recognize the components of that complex message. It is indeed complex, and not without internal contradictions, since it is a mixture of Jewish and Greek thought, of mythological and philosophical images.

The personal experience that Jesus as the symbol of God was living and creative despite his death, forms the unshakeable foundation. But because he had disappeared from this world, the young Church had to relocate his resurrected existence to another world, that is, with God in Heaven. The same held for all those who died, belonging to him through their belief in him. At least at this point, they abandoned the ancient Jewish notion of the resurrection which imagined an ideal existence on earth. Gradually, this so far ancient Jewish notion of the young Church became mixed up with Greek ideas about the immortality of the soul. The latter already surfaced in the late book of the Wisdom of Solomon. It became more and more dominant as Hellenism gradually replaced Jewish influence in the Church, since more and more pagans entered it. But, as in Judaism, the 'when' of the resurrection still remained hidden behind the horizon of time. It would occur at the coming of God's Messiah, which was now conceived of as the second coming of the glorified Jesus on the clouds of Heaven, to judge mankind. And the day or the hour of this coming was unknown even to the earthly Jesus himself. Meanwhile, however, the deceased faithful would already be sharing in his heavenly glory. An equally purely Jewish ingredient was the certainty that God would call all humanity before his judgment seat and as a righteous judge would reward the good and punish the bad. Already in the Old Testament, this had had consequences for the presentation of the resurrection. The Book of Daniel, for example, betrays the conception that resurrection would no longer be reserved for the pious, as a compensation for their suffering, but would also include the 'bad'. For them, judgment would result in verdict and punishment. A last ingredient in this mental concoction was made up by the texts of Scripture that deal with 'the End', announced by the promised coming of the Messiah as the judge of the End. This End became gradually understood as the end of the world. In fact it meant the end of times of evil in the world, from which the pious had so far suffered. On that day the wheat would be sifted from the chaff, the rams from the sheep, the tares from the corn, and everything found to be no good would fall prey to the fire—an eternal fire, Gehenna, Hell. And God would be all in all for the saved.

This heterogeneous and sometimes contradictory matter was diligently and uncritically stirred and further enriched with medieval ingredients, such as the well-known Purgatory and the lesser-known Limbo. This was a copy of the Jewish *Sheol* and at the same time of the related Hellenistic Hades. Already in the New Testament there were rumors of such a subterranean place, where the souls of the saints from the Old Testament would await their salvation. In the Middle Ages, a similar place was thought up for the souls of children that had died before they were baptized. This confusing alchemy resulted in the above described medieval representations: the immortal soul would be judged after its departure from the body to be rewarded in the other world with paradisiacal pleasures, or punished with the fire of Purgatory or Hell. And at the end of this world, everyone would be resurrected (this time not conceived of as waking up from a long sleep but rather as the reunification of the soul with its previous body) to be definitively judged. The recuperated body would then participate in the reward or punishment of the soul, and this time forever. Jesus would no doubt have been utterly dumbfounded, when hearing about this theological concoction.

For 1500 years the faithful have been nursed with the mother's milk of Tradition thus formulated. And however mythological this amalgam may sound in our ears, we cannot just say farewell to such a continuous tradition without further ado. It does betray a hunch of God's plan with humankind and reveals at least a part of it. But we can and should say farewell to the mythology in which these representations are steeped. What kind of reality will show up after this farewell? And in what contemporary language can we formulate it?

A NEW INTERPRETATION OF THE OLD MYTHS

The master key that fits all of these locks is certainty of belief *in* God's fidelity to humankind. This certainty is not at all the same as mathematical cogency. It is a matter of good faith, which presupposes that we see something of the invisible Wonder behind things. And that we venture to rely on Israel's and Jesus of Nazareth's experience of God and learn from them. In the course of this we can also call on the thoughts of philosophers like Lévinas or Whitehead. This modernly formulated certainty teaches that God's Love, which is another name for his essence, does not pass over us, but takes form and shape in us. Our love is the imprint of his essence in our depth and this imprint shares in his eternity. Nothing that comes down on us from the outside can separate us from Him, that is, can slow down or smother the active growth of love inside us. Not even death can change anything about the reality of our being more or less unified with the eternal Wonder. From this perspective we can now scrutinize and re-interpret all the elements of the medieval doctrine.

Belief in eternal life is another name for belief *in* God. And belief *in* God is another name for the movement of unification with the divine Wonder; for 'believing *in*', which is etymologically related to 'loving', is a dynamic process of drawing near, surrendering, and abandoning oneself. One who confesses in the Jewish-Christian tradition that the essence of the absolute Mystery can best be named with the term 'love', will also have to confess that growing in love means gradually becoming more divine, and therefore participating in God's eternity despite biological death. But here ends our ability to describe. We do not know God. Everything we say about him is counterfeit, as has been argued in Chapter 7. Everything we say about eternal life is counterfeit too. The only correct thing we can say about it is that we should and may surrender ourselves to the Mystery; that it is good, and maybe the only thing that is really good, to fuse with him, to become love. That it is good and therefore indispensable to let our existence be inspired by love, whatever may befall us, even if it is horrible.

All well and good, but how does this answer the criticism of modernity, that the end of biochemistry means the end of consciousness, and that it does not make any sense to speak about happiness or sadness across the border of death? Or about life, because that too is a biological term?

Modernity has it right, of course, that biochemical consciousness ends with death. Yet it does not necessary follow from this that it does not make any sense to transcend this border by speaking even there about peace, light, comfort and happiness. When applied to the process of fusing with God, these words no longer refer to the psychological categories they seem to apply to. They are only translations into our language of the absolute meaningfulness and desirability of unification with God. The comparison of speaking to blind people about light and colors can put us on the right track here. It is possible to teach blind people that what we call light and color is a matter of vibrations, of longer or shorter wavelengths. 'Vibrations' is an accessible term for someone who is blind. And so are waves and wavelengths. In this sense, a blind person can speak meaningfully about, for example, the color red. In doing so he speaks about something that is, on the one hand, completely unknown to him (because he has never had an experience of 'red'), yet on the other hand somehow familiar, because he knows its equivalent: a certain length of waves. Red means something else than yellow for him, and not only another word, another sound, other signs in Braille, but a different reality, namely a different wavelength. In a similar way we can talk about eternal bliss without any experiential knowledge of its real content, and yet say something that is not content-less. For in this way we translate that it is good to love. Which in its turn means that love is the law of our essence and that it should govern our entire behavior.

This clarifies one thing. It is an internal contradiction to detach that hoped-for eternal bliss from unification with God, understood as the transformation of our being into love, or to turn 'Heaven' into an isolated state of bliss, in the sense of an eternal vacation in the Caribbean. If unification with God is not the alpha and omega of what we consider eternal bliss, then there simply is no eternal bliss. The more we project our childlike or childish dreams beyond death, all the more do we misunderstand and deny real eternal life, which is nothing else than identification with God. In everything we say about eternal life, we have to remain aware that we are just making clumsy references to the completely unknown, but completely good, desirable and indispensable unity with God, and thus to the fulfillment of love in ourselves. In this way, modernity and tradition can be reconciled. The price for this is giving up the mythology of old; the profit is an orientation towards the essential, which was often overlooked in that mythology.

But if this is so, eternal life is already happening. Occasionally, its goodness and richness already break through into our psyches in the experiences of inner peace, meaningfulness and the joy of unselfishness. But what its goodness and its richness are in reality, not in the prism of our psyche, still remains veiled, inaccessible. We feel the vibrations, but we don't see the colors yet. We only know that it is goodness and richness.

GOD IN EVERYTHING AND EVERYONE

The previous reasoning began with the idea that our essence is not a spiritual soul that lives in a body, but a spark of God's own cosmic self-expression. It is certainly more convenient to conceive of a person as a soul in a body. That is something on which we can get a grip. But a spark of God's self-expression? What are we supposed to do with that? It can teach us something that escapes us in the familiar representations. That we have to see ourselves from God's side; that God is part of the definition of our being. We exist to the extent of his presence in our depth, thus to the extent of our love. This brings us to the following two, maybe disconcerting, thoughts.

Because God is everything in everything and everybody—and not just something in everything and everybody—all things form a complete unity. Also the human and the cosmos are one and not two. The human is the cosmos in so far as it has developed itself after billions of years of trial and error up to this level. Therefore the human is a richer self-expression of God than everything that originated in the previous stages of evolution, not only because its intelligence and ingenuity reveal more of the intelligence and ingenuity of the all-generating Mystery, but even more because he is capable of real love. Everything that preceded this—the cohesion of the parts of matter, the connection of cells into a living organism, the mating and caring instincts of animals—is only a preliminary stage, an onset. Only in humankind does the cosmos reach the level of selfless love, way beyond love as instinct. The more we love, the more we allow God to take shape and to express himself and the more we become one being together with Him. And that is what we denote with 'eternal life'. That is not an empty, but a full concept, and a concept full of promise. 'Life' stands for everything that is desirable; and 'eternal' liberates it from something that is unacceptable here: the end.

However, we are this highest self-expression of God not as individuals, only as humankind. Although we experience ourselves as individuals, as one among the many, in our depth we form a unity, one human being. The sperm cell and the egg cell, from which every individual is the amazing development, are only cells of a pre-existing human organism, which in its turn has originated from the fusion of a sperm cell and an egg cell, in their turns cells of pre-existing organisms. The more than six billion individuals of the present generation are nothing else than the inconceivable self-duplication of a few human egg and sperm cells, which themselves came forth from the will to live of the first living cells in the course of hundreds of millions of years of evolution and they will always remain one with those. In this perspective, all of us together are still those first cells that have duplicated and developed in an increasingly richer way under the impulse of evolution. Like a tree that continuously produces new leaves to obtain its intended shape, every human originates to further the cosmos's process of becoming God. Because of physical limitations, one succeeds better in this than the other. And also the mystery of human freedom, suspended between gravity and grace, has a hand in this. But we all reap what each individual sows. And dying doesn't mean that one drops from the whole. We cannot do that. We are part of it forever and participate forever in the goodness of the whole. And also our contribution to humanity's process of becoming God, that is, becoming love, is utterly indestructible, remains forever.

THE ANSWER TO A PRESSING QUESTION

As united humanity we form the increasingly perfect self-expression of God and in this we find our fulfillment. This is a liberating view for those who struggle with the question that cannot be answered in the traditional pattern of thought, namely what entrance to God will open at the moment of death for severely mentally handicapped persons, who were never capable of moral discernment. In the classical representation, they would all need to be judged and rewarded or punished. For what? Or what will be the fate of the millions of human beings that die before they have gained any conscience: aborted or stillborn or crib death. In the now disconcerting view of Augustine of Hippo, which has marked Western thought for many centuries, these deserved to be punished for the sin of Adam, together with the *massa damnata* of all the other unbaptized, and with eternal damnation at that. Fortunately, in the course of time the Church, at first hesitantly, at last clearly, has made a clean sweep with the doctrine of its church doctor. But also the hypothesis of a decisive choice for (or against) God at the moment of dying, which has been put forward by modern theologians, does not satisfy, even if only because it is a pure hypothesis, without the slightest support in human experience. Moreover, there is no need for it, if the human being is a leaf on the one divine tree of humankind, and if together we form one human being and together we grow into the Mystery that is God and that is good. Everybody will inherit from all the others and the problem will be solved automatically. In the language of first naivety we can say that the infant after SIDS is an angel in God's Heaven and that we will find it back there, just as death has snatched it away from us here below. This is a comforting thought, which is already something. And within heteronomous language, this isn't even entirely false. It expresses in its own way the belief that God has only blessing in mind for humankind, including babies and fetuses. How could it be otherwise, if humanity is His most advanced endeavor to give shape to His own goodness?

FAREWELL TO HELL AND PURGATORY

Consequently, Hell as the antagonist of Heaven disappears automatically from the stage. It already had a difficult position in the modern sense of faith. In less than half a century, however, it has become completely discredited. Which minister today would still try to make his congregants obey the commandments of God by means of this threat, like the missionary preachers of the past did, and with great success? They themselves feel so ill at ease with this point of belief, that it cannot cross their lips. Only those who regard Scripture as a book of oracles, its descriptions of eternal fire as a description of reality, and the catechism as the definitive formulation of truth, panic at the farewell to Hell. Because in their view cutting loose such a heavy block from the dome of the traditional Church doctrine threatens to make the entire dome come down.

Whatever applies to Hell, applies in its own way to Purgatory. Admittedly, the latter does not have the same impressive credentials as Hell, because there is no trace of it in Scripture. The few passages that are often referred to are clearly dragged in by the head and shoulders. Their authors would rub their eyes if they could see for what purpose they are now used. What is called 'Purgatory' appears as a compromise that slowly crystallized. Indeed, the theologians faced the problem that there is guilt in every life, but not such a heavy guilt that it would need to be punished with eternal damnation. Such a punishment would be mockery of the righteousness that characterizes God's judgment. There had to be a middle course between getting out without punishment and being punished eternally with Hell, such as being sentenced to a time of expiation. Even in human courts, the death sentence is not the only alternative to acquittal. And apparently this solution fully complied with the expectations of pre-modern religiosity. For since the early Middle Ages the non-biblical Purgatory made an unstoppable triumphal procession through the popular church, and from there through scholastic theology. And on its way it caused a lot of mischief. For it is the basis, among other things, of the dubious success of indulgences, of the distortion of the Eucharist into a means to save the deceased (for a fee) from that place of punishment, of self-affliction as a means to escape from it oneself, and of the fact that the holiday of All Saints became overrun by All Souls' Day. In theonomous thought, Hell *has to* give in, and therefore also Purgatory and its doubtful consequences. Because punishment is not necessary. Indeed, as will be demonstrated in depth in Chapter 16, punishment is born from the need to create some order in the course of events here below, and from our incapacity to arrive at this in another way than by means of sanctions. In fact, punishment is a primitive procedure that reminds one of the training of animals. But even today we cannot do without it, because of the still primitive level of humankind, which deems technical knowledge more important than growing in love, and the preservation of the self as more desirable than unification with the Whole. But exactly because of its primitive character, punishment is utterly unsuitable as a term to denote the relationship between God and the human. As is already remarked in the First Letter of John: love drives out fear (of punishment).

THE PLACE OF THE PUNISHING GOD IN THE GOOD NEWS

A farewell to Hell and Purgatory does not excuse us from the task of trying to find out what those mythological images tried to mediate to us about God. Something that has such deep and strong roots in Tradition cannot be eradicated without maiming Tradition. The path of reformulation starts with a new interpretation of what are, in essence, evil (also called sin) and punishable acts. They are not transgressions of a law (because that would lead us back to pre-modern categories), but they are our resistance against what God pursues: the growth of love, which is His self-expression in us. We are obstructive to God's urge for richer self-expression by refusing to act in love. But damaging the growth of God's self expression is akin to damaging ourselves in our deepest kernel. For we *are* His self-expression. It is in essence this damage that we can call our punishment, just as our enrichment is the essence of our reward. Neither of these two is therefore added from the outside as a belated answer of God to our 'yes' or 'no' to his admonitions. Speaking about punishment is therefore no more than a clumsy way, borrowed from our inner-worldly experiences, to say that resistance against the growth of love (because that is the essence of evil or sin) is a disaster that has to be prevented at any price; it is purely symbolic imagery for the reprehensibility and harmfulness of that refusal. But is our refusal a real and free refusal? Is it not as much inability, incompleteness, immaturity? Whatever it may be, the more it is free refusal, all the more frightening is the disaster that one calls upon oneself. Hell is just the image of what an absolute refusal would mean, namely the absolute catastrophe.

The opposite holds for eternal reward, also known as Heaven. Likewise that term is a rickety way to say something else, namely that love, the supreme manifestation of all that we call good, is the only advantageous and desirable thing. But it will become pure mythology if we turn it into descriptive language and transfer it unrefined to whatever befalls us in our relationship with the Mystery.

Three more brief reflections to conclude this section. First again about Hell. If 'Heaven' refers to our complete participation in God's fullness and hence to our transformation into pure love, then Hell would mean that there could be a human individual without the least bit of love. But this is impossible because we are all part of the one large body of humankind, which is the already developed self-expression of Love. Also therefore we had better forget about the traditional Hell.

Secondly about what happens to an individual after death. Maybe it is something in this sense, even though this image can evoke many objections. We originate from God like raindrops that originate through evaporation from the ocean. As we die, we fall back into that Ocean, enriching it by the love that has taken shape in us during our life. But in that Ocean we fully remain the drops of water which we have become. Nothing of our essence gets lost, only our separateness, our individuality. And like the whole grows through each additional individual, all together participate collectively in the common result. Images and comparisons should not be burdened inadequately by insisting on full congruity with that which they try to illustrate. They don't survive such ill-treatment.

Their function is to open our eyes to a notion which cannot be encompassed by conceptual categories. The above mentioned image, derived from Dorothee Sölle, opens our eyes for two things of essential importance for our life as Christians. First, that the primeval miracle, "God", is the first and the last word in our existence and that its elimination will make that existence meaningless and contradictory. That makes God infinitely more important than in heteronomous thought, and our private immortality infinitely less important. Is this a loss? Secondly that the way we live is determinant. The image says: give love all opportunities in life, don't retire into yourself, but turn to your fellow human being and to the world.

Finally about the 'resurrection of the flesh', as this article of the creed had it in the past; now it is called 'the resurrection of the dead'. It has been made clear above that this is the historically determined and fully mythological form in which ancient Judaism had molded its certainty that God is a God who gives life, even across the borders of this life. We retain this faithful certainty. But we give up its mythological dress without any pain.

IN RETROSPECT

Whatever our mythologically formulated Tradition teaches about what happens to us at our death, has therefore to be conserved and at the same time completely changed. What has to be conserved is the very vague intuition of the Christian community, aroused in its midst through its intimacy with God, that everything has been created towards the better, because God means 'life'. What has to change is the mythical formulation of this intuition. This mythical and therefore heteronomous formulation implies that dying is the transition towards a similar but better existence in a different world, called Heaven, freed from all the limitations and disappointing sides of our existence here below. Parts of these disappointing aspects are evil and injustice, suffering and death. An absolutely righteous judgment will punish evil and injustice, and in that way rectify and amend it, whereas the trampled and despised good will ultimately reap its reward. Suffering and death on the other hand will make way for salvation and immortality. These ancient Christian myths have to be translated into new, but equally Christian, myths. This has been attempted in the foregoing, on the basis of a view of the cosmos as the self-expression, culminating in humanity, of a Wonder that is love. This modern view may sound less comforting than that of heteronomous times. But children also prefer to eat ice cream instead of coarse but wholesome bread.

CHAPTER 13

THE HOLY SEVEN

SACRAMENTS AS RITUAL SIGNS

The saying goes that in Protestant churches the pulpit is the center, and in Catholic churches the altar. This acknowledges the fact that for Catholics the focus of attention is on the sacraments, and for Protestants it is on Scripture. The preponderance of the sacraments in Catholicism is betrayed in its language and practice. 'To go to mass' has become the terribly watered-down synonym of belonging to the faithful. Parents are unhappy when their dear sons or daughters stop showing up for mass on Sundays. But that their children never pray or read anything religious, and certainly not the Bible, or that they are above all concerned with money and their careers, or, worse, participate the popular animosity against asylum seekers or foreign workers, does not keep them awake at night. Because all too often, their children only follow their examples in these matters. Nevertheless, personal piety and social action and concern are at least as essential for a Christian life as participating in the sacramental rituals. Confirmation, and even already First Communion are blown up into great events, but that communion without following Christ is not even half an egg, but only an empty shell, even more: just downright illusion—to this the majority of parents turn a blind eye. In the past it was pardonable ('only' a daily sin), if one stayed away from mass until after the sermon, because the service of the Word was not a sacrament; but woe if one stayed away longer, because that was the beginning of mortal sin, and along with that, the way to certain damnation.

QUESTIONS EVOKED BY THE CURRENT PRACTICE

Turning the sacraments into a key part of the belief system is a woeful mistake. It amounts to setting the Catholic cart before the horse. Indeed, faith transcends taking part in rituals by far. Catholic rituals make someone at most a member of the Roman Catholic cultic community, a performer of religious observances, but not a true disciple of Jesus. Discipleship is a continuous and existential process, which marks and changes our existence, and this process is the only path towards lasting salvation. Even daily participation in rituals such as mass and communion will not bring this salvation about, and even less the sociologically heavily stressed one-time rituals such as Baptism, First Communion, Confirmation, and Matrimony. This is also Paul's vision in 1 Corinthians 10:1–5: that Israel passed through the Red Sea, ate manna in the desert, drank water from the rock—in the eyes of Paul a foreshadowing of Baptism and Eucharist—was ultimately of no avail to them. The overestimation of the importance of the sacraments is especially noticeable in rituals where any existential experience is evidently lacking, such as in child baptism or in administering the Anointing of the Sick to patients who are already unconscious.

The more one looks at the phenomenon of these seven so highly regarded rituals, the more questions it evokes. For example, why are they exactly seven, and not two or twelve or twenty? And why precisely these seven and not seven others? Why, for example, is the washing of feet (a rich symbol and clearly established by Jesus) not a sacrament, whereas the Anointing of the Sick, clearly not established by Jesus, but based on the Letter of James, is? Why are the consecration of virgins, or the monastic vows not sacraments, but Matrimony is? That the Church has decided this one day is as equally unsatisfying an answer as the 'because I say so!' with which hard-pressed parents react in irritation to the obnoxious but persistent 'why?' of their child.

SACRAMENTS IN HETERONOMOUS PERSPECTIVE

The success of the seven sacraments is no doubt related to the very human need for rituals. But an at least equally important role in that success is played by the heteronomous presentation of their function. For in that presentation it is a human ritual that opens the floodgates of divine grace, which really means a small investment of time and effort to reap a thousand-fold profit. Who would not take advantage of such an investment offer? But how does this human investment bring about that divine result? Certainly not on its own. For the effect surpasses by far every human capability. Apparently, a well-oiled cooperation between Heaven and Earth is at play here. Once and forever, God-on-High would have decided that he would let certain workings of grace correspond to certain acts of certain (male) members of the Church, hereto mandated by yet other (male) members of the Church, in an uninterrupted process initiated approximately the year 30 CE.

The similarity to magic is remarkable. A first resemblance is that in both magic and sacraments, the effect depends on the correct execution of the rules. One who doesn't know the password can spare his efforts. The sorcerer's apprentice of the well-known oriental fairy tale knows everything about this: the broom remains deaf to his incantations and supplications and drags on more and more buckets of water until the boy almost drowns in the flood. Saying 'Sesame open!' even a hundred times is of no avail if the correct magic formula is 'Open Sesame!'. For many a priest this magical connotation made the pronunciation of the Latin words of consecration: *Hoc est enim corpus meum*, a real nightmare, because the correctness of each syllable and sound demanded the utmost from his pronunciation abilities, and often a two- or three-fold running start was necessary to bring the operation to a successful end—a painful performance for those present and a caricature of what a sacrament is supposed to be.

A second resemblance between the sacrament and magic is the lack of any obvious proportion or logical relationship between the task to be performed and its result. The magician sticks a needle into the heart of a wax doll and strangely enough (or so it is thought), a person dies far away. The baptist pours water over an infant's head and says the correct words and strangely enough (or so it is thought), original sin disappears and the child receives the right to eternal and endless bliss.

Exactly because of this dubious resemblance it is very important for heteronomous theology to strictly mark off sacramentality from magic. This is done with the help of the following two-fold distinction. In magic, the correctly executed ritual automatically effects the desired result. This is not the case with sacraments. Even the often adduced *ex opere operato*: 'through the performing itself of the rite', doesn't imply this. The effect of the ritual depends entirely on God's free intervention. God pours out his grace (however one may understand this expression) where, when, over whom and in the way he wants it, but apparently He has committed himself to do this, when the sacramental rites are correctly executed. He has made this commitment through Jesus. For the latter is, as true God and true human, the keystone of the two worlds that meet in the sacrament: that of the invisible divine grace and that of the human ritual. Therefore, it is an indispensable part of the classical definition of the sacraments that all seven of them have been established by Christ. This formula entails that the God-man establishes and guarantees an intimate connection between this specific trivial activity in the earthly domain and its infinite effect in the supernatural world.

The second difference is that the effect of magic can in principle be noticed, for it takes place in our world; but that of the sacrament does not at all. Of course it can always happen that the magician has bad luck. The formula was maybe not entirely correct this time or an even more powerful magician with a more powerful formula has foiled his plans. But a magician who always has bad luck should look for another job. Conversely, in the case of the sacraments, the effect in principle can not be noticed, it is utterly imperceptible. This does not take anything away from its reality. The eucharistic bread has really been transformed into the body of Christ, but no one is able to notice the difference. And the newly baptized baby has really been reborn in sanctity, whereas the unbaptized baby in the adjoining crib is still wholly in Satan's claws, submitted to original sin and excluded from Heaven; but no one notices the difference. The difference, for that matter, will be no more visible forty years later, except if one child will be raised as a Christian and the other not. But to raise children so or otherwise belongs to the inner-wordly domain of human relationships and their creative workings, not to the supernatural domain of pure grace. In the traditional and thus heteronomous presentation, the effect of the sacrament resides so fully in that supernatural order that it is nowhere to be noticed in the natural order, with the result that one cannot help thinking of Andersen's tale 'The Emperor's New Clothes'.

In the traditional presentation, Jesus Christ has not only established the seven sacraments, but he has also granted the right to his so-called Vicar and his successors to further implement these rites and occasionally change them in accidental details. That Vicar usually delegates his right to do so to the Vatican Congregation for the Sacraments, which ascertains grudgingly these last decades that the people of God shrink less and less from usurping this right for themselves. In fact this Congregation hereby puts the center of gravity where is situated in magic: in the correct execution of prescriptions and not in the creative power of gestures and material symbols. This way they slide off inadvertently from the existential domain into the juridical, if not already into the magical. The Eucharist is called with good reason 'the breaking of the bread', but what is being broken is in reality something that barely reminds of real bread. However, that does not take away from the efficiency of the sacrament. And baptizing might mean 'immersing', like a pen in ink or bread in coffee, and baptism was originally a real immersion; but now a baptism is 'valid' (note that purely juridical term to qualify the efficiency of the rite) if a few drops of water flow over the head of the baby.

This familiar doctrine of the sacraments is automatically arrived at when starting from the axiom of two parallel, but totally different realms. Only in that world of thought is it meaningful to state that an earthly and thus imperfect rite could bind or dissolve anything in a heavenly, eternal, and perfect domain. This result is not produced automatically as in magic, but only thanks to a mercifully promised divine intervention. For earthly business of its own accord is completely unsuitable to produce a heavenly effect. But if certain conditions are fulfilled, this effect is still guaranteed, because God has committed himself through the God-man Jesus to produce that result if the rite is performed correctly and with at least a minimum of faith. From this world of thought also originates the unfortunate expression 'sacramental grace', as if grace were not so much God's kindness, his merciful care, his undeserved offer of salvation, but rather a certain amount of divine energy, which he allows to flow through our spiritual ducts to charge our spiritual batteries.

The Sacramental Sign in Theonomous Perspective

But how do things look when we start from the other axiom, namely that God is the creating and sustaining Depth of the Universe and does not belong to a parallel, externally interfering order?

The effect of the sacraments will then become the result of the innate creativity of the signs, established by the Church community, the body of Jesus Christ. For signs do not only reveal something, they are creative as well, they bring about something. Think about the interpersonal relations of love and hatred. Signs of love will make love grow, make it stronger. An embrace connects also the hearts. A smile unbends, clears, relaxes the interpersonal atmosphere. To put a rings on the other's finger touches something very deep inside the bride and groom. The more honest and existential the sign of friendship, the more it will it recreate and enrich the existing relationship. A formal handshake as a sign of non-hostility nurtures at the most a climate of non-hostility, whereas a handshake out of joy at the unexpected meeting with a friend, communicates that joy and strengthens the friendship. Conversely, expressions of hatred, aggression or contempt raise similar feelings in those who are the targets of such signs. And to slam a door behind oneself seals the end, at least temporarily, of the relationship. All this is the result of the intimate unity between matter and mind in the human. That unity is so strong and reaches so deep that the human mind can only grow and become itself by expressing itself, by taking shape in the material world.

In the same vein the sacraments are essentially material signs, which is precisely the cause of their spiritual effect. The latter is not obtained because God-in-Heaven executes a promised intervention as a result of specific signs and words, but because signs are creative by themselves, to the extent that the effect is proportional to the expressive power of the sign. This is different from magic. What the sorcerer does is not much more than some hocus pocus; on the other hand, what he effects or thinks to effect with it, is disproportionate to his actions. Something similar holds for the traditional vision of the sacrament: in that view, a few words or signs can decide between eternal bliss or eternal damnation. This is in line with the fact that in the traditional practice words, gestures, and the use of materials only theoretically serve as signs. In reality, they serve as signals. Their role is restricted to giving the necessary signal from the human world to the divine world, so that the latter can come into action and bring about a specific result. If that result is indeed brought about, then this is not the effect of the rite, but exclusively of God's free intervention, who does on the spot what He has promised.

This is of course fully different in theonomous perspective. When a person expresses his inner approach towards the saving God in a sacramental sign, that inner approach will gain in power the more that sign embodies existential depth. At the same time this existential change produced by the sacramental sign is identical with God's workings in the faithful. Of everything that is good, God is the source. Our personal human growth as the fruit of our taking part in the sacramental sign is only our side of God's making us grow in humanity. And because this human growth is purely the result of God's kindness, to which no human can lay a claim, we call it 'grace'; because grace in reality means God's freely offered, completely undeserved love.

Thus it becomes clear that, in theonomous thought, the truthfulness of the sign determines the measure of the change it brings about. And that change is itself identical with God's working in us. There is no need for a divine decision or for an establishment by Christ. Fortunately so, because the former makes no sense in theonomous thinking, and the second is not tenable in historical thinking. In heteronomous thought, on the contrary, a sign, even one that can barely be called a sign, but rather a faithfully given signal, can make sacramental grace shower down. In theonomous perspective it cannot, because it has barely any existential value or creative efficacy.

CONSEQUENCES FOR THE PRACTICE

As to the view of the sacrament as a sign, the two basic assumptions are consequently very different. And that is not without practical consequences. In heteronomous thought, God's works of grace are dependent on the correct execution of the ritual, not on existential sincerity; and consequently the multiplication of multipliable signs is a good thing indeed: daily mass and communion bring more blessings and grace than when these are performed only weekly, and there is nothing wrong with forcing pupils to participate in them, even with the aid of pedagogical sanctions: seven times a week yields more than once. To be sure, it is often overlooked that it yields often a seven-fold aversion rather than a seven-fold joy. And if a young person is being confirmed because of the family tradition and the festivity that accompanies the event, without the slightest intention of performing what they make him promise there, even then the traditional view nurtures the illusion that he will at least receive the Holy Spirit, and that the sacrament will in any case let the flood of grace come down on him. Only, it will glide off like water from a duck's back.

In a theonomous view, this doesn't make any sense. Signs are only creative, humanly as well as divinely, in as far as they are sincere. If I promise faith without meaning it, I will not grow in faith and I will not experience the existential change that a true promise of faith would bring about. And that change, as it is said above, is identical to God's grace. This subject will come up again in the discussion of Baptism and Confirmation.

But first this needs to be said: Sacraments are the ritual signs of an encounter with the divine Depth that draws our hearts, and for a Christian, this encounter always involves Jesus of Nazareth, the Christ. But there are other ways as well to arrive at this encounter. Not only non-Christian ways, such as that of Socrates or Buddha or a Zen Master who has reached enlightenment, but also other Christian ways. This qualifies the indispensability of the sacraments. They remain precious and useful, but usefulness is not the same as indispensability. And their usefulness varies, depending on the appeal a sign has for someone. The past emphasis on the indispensability of the sacraments had more to do with the need for a social identity as a Christian (and after the Reformation: as a Roman Catholic), than with their alleged necessity. Without an individual profile, defined by particular practices, forms, demands, and style, the internal bond of a group, *in casu* the Church, evaporates, so that it can not continue to exist in the long run.

This view is obviously based on the theonomous principle that the sacraments did not descend from Heaven, unassailable, complete and eternal, like Athena emerged in full dress from the head of Zeus, but have risen from the divine depth within the Church, often after long groping and searching for the right form, and even so they are not necessarily meant to stay forever as they are, and even not necessarily to stay forever at all.

The 'necessity of the means' that was ascribed to the sacraments in the past is therefore a fiction. And to measure the degree of Christianity from the place the traditional sacraments take in someone's life is therefore a dangerous distortion. It should, rather, be measured from the place and influence Jesus has there. That encounter with him can be furthered by means of rituals is indisputable. But again, it is not the ritual in itself that is important here, and even less its correct execution or repetition (such as the prescribed daily mass for clergy), but its result: the encounter that is sought through it. And someone who feels that a ritual, even if it is one of the holy seven, doesn't help him or her, will have to seek encounter with Jesus Christ in a different way. Saul's armory was no doubt of excellent quality but for the young David it was no help.

CHAPTER 14

FIVE ONCE-IN-A-LIFETIME CATHOLIC RITUALS

1. BAPTISM

If we are looking to this sacrament for the creative sign and the existential change it brings about, we had better put child baptism between parentheses for a while, for there can be no question of existential change here. We have to return, therefore, to what baptism was originally: the sign with which someone expressed that he freely chose Jesus Christ and wanted to enter into the latter's fullness of life; that he wanted to be submerged, cleansed, refreshed and recreated by belonging to him. Initially, baptism made this visible as well as real. The person to be baptized descended into the bath in which he experienced a kind of rebirth, in which his past was symbolically, yet also really rinsed from him; in which he was renewed for a new future. And that process of change was brought about by the expressive power of the symbolic immersion that he underwent.

This desire to associate oneself with Jesus Christ is, however, preceded by something else, something decisive, without which the person would never have made the step towards baptism: the attraction, the workings of God's Spirit inside him, which aroused the desire in him to grow spiritually and opened his eyes to the way in which that could happen: the way of unity with Jesus of Nazareth. To agree to be baptized is to say 'yes' to that invitation. That becomes visible in the sign as well: a person doesn't baptize himself. He doesn't descend into the bath of rebirth on his own initiative: he *is* baptized. This passive form indicates that one doesn't so much join a community as much as one is accepted into it. And that community is not just any organization or society or club, but it is the ever farther twining grapevine that is called Jesus Christ. One can only belong to this community if one is engrafted onto it as a new tendril. And this is done by the pastor in the name of the community: he baptizes.

Two Different Ways to Say the Same Thing

In heteronomous language, the consequences of the sign of baptism are expressed in non-existential terms such as: removal of original sin, pardon and remittal of punishment for other sins, infusion of sanctifying grace and of the three theological virtues—all non-verifiable forms of intervention by another world into ours. In existential translation this becomes: a real bond with Jesus Christ, whose power of attraction has been felt and whom one has sought to join. Or also: the confirmation of the way that one was already going, a humanly renewing way, a style of living clearly distinct from the style that one practiced before believing *in* Jesus and his God, a style of living inspired by Jesus' Sermon on the Mount. This way also includes a conscious bond with the receiving Church community in which the neophyte is incorporated, because Jesus is to be found only there, and only through him do we find the Father. All this is verifiable to a certain degree. At the same time it is an inner-worldly translation of the same gift of God that is formulated in the non-verifiable language of the Tradition and called 'sanctifying grace'. Because what does 'sanctifying grace' mean? The biblical 'grace' translates the Greek *charis*: kindness, mercy, favor, and also attractiveness and charm. It is another name for God's kindness and approach and his attraction: God approaches humankind through the person of Jesus and attracts everyone, and the faithful respond to him by allowing themselves to be penetrated by His Spirit, transformed into his own image and made 'sanctified, holy', that is: made loving, because God is Love. But now this no longer occurs as the divine response to the human gesture that baptism is; no, baptism brings this about by symbolizing it, and the more effectively so, the more that sign is sincere and is truly experienced. Baptism symbolizes this in more than one way: the person participates in a refreshing and renewing bath; or in a purifying bath; or in a passage through death (water representing the possibility of drowning), in which death refers to leaving behind one's old ways of life, the 'old' person, in order to become a new person; or (for those who are sensitive to these biblical symbols), participates in a symbolic manner in the crossing of the Red Sea or the Jordan River and the entry into the Promised Land.

For many, baptism has become a purely formal rite of entry that guarantees their enrollment in the Church by their inscription in the register of baptisms and entitles them to participate in the other rituals of the Church. The symbolic value does not play a role for them. But in that case we can no longer call it a sacrament in the true sense of the word, a sacrament being essentially a sign. Maybe one can still call it so in a heteronomous world of thought, in which it is sufficient that the rite is executed correctly to cause the floodgates of heavenly grace to open. But this is no longer possible in existential thought, the only kind of thought that can still guarantee any future for the Church in a modern world.

The Problem of Child Baptism

Here the problem of child baptism rises in its full proportions. *The argument in favor of it is Tradition.* But this is a Tradition impregnated with heteronomy, which saw the threat of eternal damnation hanging above the child as a Sword of Damocles in the event that it would die without baptism—a not so glorious theological mistake with which Augustine and Jerome infected the entirety of medieval culture. The Church has needed many centuries to free itself from this mistake: first, in the twelfth century, by hesitatingly accepting the idea of Limbo, and later by stretching and eroding the notion of baptism until nothing reminded of actual baptism (with water), such as in the 'baptism of blood' (even if no bloodshed was involved), or the 'baptism of desire' (someone wished to be baptized but did not have the chance) and even of implicit desire: 'if one would have known that baptism was absolutely necessary for salvation, and that he then would have desired and asked to be baptized, he would be saved'—an example of unreality. The heteronomous bias of such ideas is so obvious that modern people can't do anything with it.

In addition, it should be noted that in the time when child baptism originated, very different views of the family and of personal freedom prevailed. In that time, a child was part of the family clan. When the head of the clan decided to become a Christian, everybody had to follow him, which meant: they had to be baptized. A good example is the baptism of the Frankish king Chlodowech, better known as Clovis I, which occurred a little before the year 500 in Reims: together with him all his Frankish army chiefs were baptized. It is doubtful whether that changed anything in their lives. The conversion to which first John the Baptist, and later Jesus, had called out, a conversion identical with the existential renewal God works inside of us, was obviously marginal. For Chlodowech himself, baptism was primarily a political act, by which he could count on the recognition and support of the Catholic South. For his followers, it was a declaration of loyalty to their leader. In a sacramental doctrine of the heteronomous kind, such a practice of baptism does not cause a problem. Even then, all the graces enumerated above were believed to be poured out over the Frankish chiefs with the water of baptism—even though the effect must have been like water flowing over a duck.

Is there still a place for child baptism in theonomous thought? Very little. Indeed, in that thought the redeeming encounter between God and humanity occurs in the existential domain, and the baby is far from ready for existential acts, let alone that he would be able to experience this encounter in the expressive sign of a purifying and renewing bath. But the weakness of child baptism is not in the first place due to the fact that it is a product of heteronomy. In the ancient Church adult baptism—which was very meaningful—was also conceived heteronomously, just as anything else in the past. Worse is that child baptism is a remainder of a theology that drew its vital fluids from a different time and culture. The dying out of that culture has caused a considerable withering and shriveling of the sacramental rite, too. What remains is the liturgical rite of registration of new Church members, usually paper members, in the registry of baptism in which they gradually dry out into archival dead bodies. Another problem is this. Because a purely pious registration rite leaves most people unsatisfied—our innate need for depth and transcendence is felt also there—baptism has shifted to a religiously colored celebration of birth. Even if such a celebration is very laudable, baptism means something very different, and to identify it with, or reduce it to, such a celebration would be dishonest. The name and the wrapping are saved, but the content has changed entirely. Moreover, a religious celebration of birth can be shaped in different ways, and many rituals can be thought up for this, even without water and chrism and without a Christian confession of faith, and thus without baptism. Summoned by the autonomous world-view of modern culture, child baptism can only be defended with reference to its venerable age. But it has already been demonstrated that it owes its survival to two things that have meanwhile disappeared: a different view of the relation between family or clan and person, and the early medieval fear that the child might otherwise be doomed. This fear has at first coagulated into the mold of baptism of newborns, and this process of coagulation has later turned into petrifaction. Infant baptism, too, is part of the statue of Nebuchadnezzar, which in modernity clashes with autonomous thought and will collapse and be pulverized. Its survival is mostly due to the need for a ritual with which we can celebrate the wonder of birth, and to the lack of any other appropriate ritual for this. But in how many of the spectators (to call them participants would be a lie), does the ritual of baptism still evoke the bath of rebirth in Jesus that baptism originally was?

Adult Baptism
So much about child baptism. But adult baptism has its problems too. Not only is its liturgical language incurably heteronomous, but the sign has become all but empty—and the sign is the essence of the sacrament. For how far does water still play its symbolic role here? Can the pouring of a handful of that element over someone's head be experienced honestly as a 'bath of rebirth by the Holy Spirit'? A bath is clearly something else. And experience is clearly something else than intellectual connection. Also from the original adult baptism, hardly anything more than an initiation rite remains.

And this is not all that is wrong with baptism. Its character as a creative sign is closely related to the climatologic circumstances in which it originated. In a hot and dry region such as the Jordan River area, submersion in a river was the ideal way of evoking the experience of rebirth, thus serving as the eloquent sign for the renewal that follows from joining Jesus Christ. But in large parts of North America this is almost impossible, especially in the wet and cold months. And for the Eskimos it becomes totally impossible. In cold and rainy regions, entry to the salvation that comes through Jesus requires a different sign, insofar as a ritual sign is necessary. Maybe a warm bath or a hot shower could serve the purpose. Such experiments can be noticed in religious movements that have returned to adult baptism. But our modern Western culture seems to lack the sensitivity that is required to read the meaning of holy signs in general, and to experience in the baptismal rite in particular, rebirth through Jesus Christ. Mostly, adult baptism is merely seen as the obligatory and somewhat strange rite through which one is accepted in that cultic community.

This lays bare the culture-bound roots of this first and most important of the seven sacraments, and at the same time also its relativity. What is culture-bound is bound to place and time, and cannot make any claims to absoluteness, universality, and necessity.

2. Confirmation

As with baptism, also here the sign, originally the imposition of hands, later an anointing, should constitute the creative power of the sacramental event and be the measure of the desired and effective result. Otherwise we fall back into the system of heteronomy and the rite becomes a signal for which God-in-Heaven waits to take action with his grace. As for the anointing, we have to admit that it is little more than a far memory of real anointing, the reduction to the absolute minimum that permits to give it that name. Comparison with the anointings in the Old and New Testament clearly demonstrates the shriveling of this sacrament: think of the oil that according to Psalm 133 dripped down over the head of Aaron onto his beard; or of the anointing of the kings of Israel, who were installed by pouring a horn full of balm over their head; or of the anointing of Jesus by the sinner or by Mary of Bethany. But it would be anachronistic to try to reestablish the sign in its fullness. Because then the same problem as with baptism would pop up: the original anointing is completely rooted in a different culture. There no further explanation was required to understand it as a religious sign. In our culture, anointing is no longer customary, so it doesn't have a spontaneous symbolic value. But loss of symbolic value means loss of sacramental value and power, because a sacrament is really a symbolic action. People that don't know the handshake cannot experience it as a rite of friendship, not even if it is explained that this gesture means friendship and peace—those people will know it in their minds, but in their hearts this gesture will remain something foreign and strange, and that cripples its creative (here: binding) power. Moreover, an important function of ointment in antiquity was that of perfume. In the anointing of Jesus by Mary of Bethany the exquisite smell of the nard perfume filled the whole house. But no one will make the connection with perfume when being anointed (more exactly, smeared) with the (not at all good smelling) chrism. And finally, oil was used in antiquity (as it is now) to massage muscles, but the distance between the rubbing of a pinch of ointment on the forehead and a (spiritual) massage is a bit too large.

But there is something else that devalues the sacrament even more and that can also be charged to the account of a heteronomous thought that has turned juridical: that confirmation is invariably given to young people, half children still, for whom, due to the secular climate in which they grow up, the Holy Spirit is an empty word, and Jesus is much less important than any pop star. Many of them are not at all eager to become active members of the Church and don't have the slightest intention to do what they promise: to live as Christians. If they want to be confirmed, they do so because all their friends (still) do so and even more because it means a party and presents, and they will be the center of attention for one day. So confirmation has become folklore, and can no longer be called a sacrament, being nothing more than a show, a solemn ceremony of lies, performed again each year with great pomp by the Church of Jesus. And that gives youngsters the impression that being a Christian is a piece of cake.

Confirmation in a Theonomous Setting

What positive shape can confirmation take in the light of theonomy? Originally, it was so closely related to (adult) baptism that together with the latter it formed one initiation sacrament. This could remain so. Baptism (or another initiation rite, see above) could remain the symbolic action by which one becomes a member of the community around Jesus; confirmation the symbolic action by which one is filled with a new spirit by this membership, the spirit of Jesus and hence with God's Spirit. Originally also, anointing was not the ritual sign, but imposition of hands. Anointing only surfaces in the third century next to imposition of hands. The influence of the liturgical texts, speaking in a symbolic sense of an 'anointing by the Holy Spirit' must have played a role here. And possibly imposition of hands was no longer found an expressive enough sign. Now the situation is, rather, reversed, especially when one sees what remains of anointing. It would be a good idea to return to the original rite. Imposition of hands is a much more accessible sign, today still used by healers, and also meaningful without explanation. It is spontaneously experienced as the creative sign of the transmission of vitality and health, and as the connection with a higher source of power. And the direct meaningfulness of the sign is decisive for the value and fertility of that sacrament and hence for its future, if one doesn't want it to wither into a ritual signal.

3. ANOINTING OF THE SICK

Because the Eucharist evokes many questions it will be treated separately in Chapter 15. The same holds for Confession, because the latter is inseparably connected with notions of sin, pardon, penance and the like, which require a longer explanation (Chapter 16). Therefore this chapter will further treat only the Anointment of the Sick, Holy Orders, and Matrimony.

The Anointing of the Sick thanks its origins to a healthy principle of ancient times: that (olive) oil is good for everything. Moreover, in the time of the Letter of James 5:13, where it is first mentioned, most healers were charlatans rather than physicians. In these circumstances one did better to trust the power of healing that Jesus had attributed to his disciples than the often inadequate human competence. Finally, in a heteronomous culture it was self-evident that in times of trouble one could better turn towards the other world, for this had the last word in everything on earth anyway. And because in that time in the Jewish world sickness was associated with guilt and punishment, it was taken for granted that the fight against bodily ailments should be connected with the repair of the spiritual order, the so-called 'remission of sins' that will be treated in Chapter 16.

What role is there still for the anointing of the sick in a culture of modern medical care? How does theonomy look at this sacrament? It reads this rite as the beneficial encounter with the caring and healing Jesus. Being always present and active in his community, he comes to the sick in the shape of the mandated representative of this community, who imposes his hands on him (just as Jesus did) and anoints him with oil (as Jesus didn't do). The latter suggests that the anointing, despite the name 'Anointing of the Sick' (or Unction) is less essential than the imposition of hands. That anointing has meanwhile, as in the Confirmation, been reduced to minimal proportions and its symbolic value has evaporated accordingly. But to be touched by loving hands (also with little ointment or even without ointment) could mean for the sick the tactile experience of Jesus' saving presence that can bring him physical healing or at least an internal revival.

In the Letter of James, the said representatives are the *presbyters*, literally the elders, which means: the leading council of the parish. In later developments those *presbyters* have been changed etymologically and liturgically into priests, that is, consecrated ones. But consecration is part of heteronomous thought. In theonomous thought it is meaningless. If every faithful, consecrated or not, may baptize, at least in times of need, thus accepting new members into the community, it follows that, in principle, everyone may act in the name of the Church. Why, then, is only a priest permitted to do so? Should this sacrament cease to exist when the last of these Mohicans dies? If so, heteronomy is more important than life. Alas, the Church authorities will continue to reserve this sacrament for the priests (for not even a deacon may anoint the sick) as long as their heteronomous way of thinking prevails. And they will brandish the threat of invalidity of an anointing administered by somebody who is not a priest. But invalidity is a purely juridical term, which seldom covers the existential truth. Therefore, there is not much to be objected to if hospital pastors, men and women alike, do not care a straw for this threat and this prohibition from another world. But then the local Church, which is the parish rather than the diocese, should mandate these pastors formally to act as his representatives.

4. HOLY ORDERS

What about the ordination of priests, so-called Holy Orders? Two things have to be noted first: that not the priesthood is the sacrament, but the ordination of the priests (or deacons or bishops), and that the Latin name of that sacrament is *ordo*. *Ordo* in later Latin means as much as social class. Social classes in that time were as fixed then as castes are still in India. It was not possible to rise to a higher class on one's own: one had to be accepted into it. *Ordinatio*, ordination, originally only referred to acceptance in that class and did not contain any reference to our sacred notion of consecration. Ordination meant only elevating someone above the level of the so-called lay people, thus creating an unbridgeable gap. Only in the fifth century did ordination become a consecration in the present sense of the word and receive the meaning that through an intervention of God-on-High, a man (women were formally excluded by God) received miraculous powers. He could change bread and wine into the body and blood of the glorified Jesus of Nazareth, and forgive sins.

For a theonomously thinking person, such far-reaching heteronomy is completely inaccessible. This doesn't mean that this sacrament should be erased from the list, as was done in the Reformation, albeit on different grounds. But it should receive another meaning: it should no longer mean that a ritual consecration from another world turns a man (never a woman) into some kind of magician, but rather that a man, and a woman as well, is invested with the pastoral care of a community. And this community is not a club or organization: it is the concrete body of Christ, animated by the Spirit of God, the Church as a fertile vine, which is the image the Gospel of John uses for the glorified Jesus. Just as any other living organism and every other organization, also the living Church produces the organs that it needs to function appropriately. And one of these organs or functions is leadership. But there is something very particular about this leading role. In contradistinction to what is often the case in human organizations, the pastor, as head of the congregation, should not consider himself as a master: he is the servant of the whole community, and his right of speech and decision making is solely due to his participation in the leading role that Jesus' Spirit plays in the congregation. It would be a good thing, if the Church established a ritual for the appointment of such pastors with which it expresses that this appointment does not come from God-on-High, but from the living Jesus, present in the Church community. That ritual could consist concretely in the sign of the imposition of hands by (representatives of) the whole local Church, and not only by other priests, as is done now.

Because of the incurably heteronomous sound of the words priest and ordination, both should better disappear from theonomous language. Moreover, they cannot but evoke an ecclesiastical world of two classes, which was foreign to the early Church and which only settled in after a few centuries under the influence of not-so-Christian ideas. That Jesus, who was himself a (Jewish) lay person, was not enthusiastic about the (Jewish) priestsly cast and their sacrificial cult, is nothing new. Nor is the fact that nowhere in the New Testament the leaders of the communities are called *hiereis*, priests. When the author of the Letter to the Hebrews calls Jesus 'High Priest', not only does he mean this purely metaphorically (as to the usefulness of the metaphor in modern times we might have some doubts), but he explicitly excludes a real priesthood in the Church. As to the use of the Greek term *hiereus* or the Latin *sacerdos*, it only shows up in the third century when the Eucharist starts to be understood as a cultic sacrifice, for cultic sacrifice calls for priests. And it initially became understood in this way out of an apologetic urge, because in the public opinion of those times a religion without sacrifices could not be a true religion. But after Jesus' death, there is no more need of sacrifices, says the Letter to the Hebrews. Therefore we don't need priests either. In Chapter 15 it will be explained why modern people have to bid farewell to this sacrificial theology. In its further development the priesthood even poached on the preserves of magic, judging by the etymological derivation of *hocus pocus* from the Latin formula *hoc est enim corpus (meum)* with which the priest was thought to effect the great miracle of transubstantiation. And together with the word 'priest' also the misbegotten term 'lay' will have served its term.

For those who think all this through in a logical way, including the new view on the doctrine of transubstantiation (see Chapter 15), conducting a Eucharist service will no longer be a matter of consecration from on high, but of appointment or delegation by the community, which is indeed the living body of Christ. That the pope and the bishops strongly condemn this conclusion and its practical consequences should not surprise or impress us. One who assumes a heteronomous point of view cannot subscribe to theonomous conclusions, especially if those threaten to uproot deeply anchored certainties and traditions.

The Priesthood of the Faithful and the Ordination of Women

Nowadays it is tried to grant the lay person some right of speech in the Church by brandishing the general priesthood of the faithful. This is a misconception for two reasons. The first is exegetical: the texts that are referred to for this, almost without exception, come from two passages from the First Letter of Peter and only mean to say with this term that God sets Christians, as the continuation of Israel, apart from the other nations, protects them in a special way and also sets particular requirements for them. This so-called priesthood has nothing to do with a cultic task. If so, we should not use it to extend the cultic priesthood, which in the traditional Church is restricted to a select number of consecrated and divinely chosen persons of the male sex, to every Tom, Dick and Mary. Further, because with this metaphor from the First Letter of Peter we again end up in heteronomous shallows. For the notion of a priest suggests the image of a mediator between Heaven and earth. Such a figure has no foothold after this dichotomy has been abandoned. And this makes all talk about a general priesthood of the faithful meaningless. Unless one likes to use 'a royal priesthood' (1 Pet. 2:9) as a Biblical metaphor for the community that has entered into a very specific relationship with God through Jesus. But it is doubtful whether such a metaphor can still be useful.

A theonomous approach to that sacrament, which turns the mythological priest again into the existential spiritual leader he was in the early Church, also refers recent discussions about the priesthood of women to the trash can. This subject is indeed high on the wish list of modern circles in the Church, feminist and other. But despite the fact that they struggle against clericalism on many other fronts, in their claiming for the appointment of women priests, they remain stuck in the omnipresent web of that clerical Church and its two-world scheme without being aware of it. This contradiction is due to a lack of insight. They feel rightly that women have to be freed from their ecclesiastical tutelage, but, wrongly, they don't question the existing practice of ordination, because they don't see that this practice and this tutelage stem from the same root: the two-world thinking scheme. For the exclusion of women from leading positions is nothing but a product of the purely heteronomous idea that church leaders have received from on high the certainty that God only accepts men as authorized go-betweens. Similarly heteronomous is the idea that a consecration, descending from on high, is necessary to act as such an agent. The priesthood itself, as well as the consecration that in the Catholic and Orthodox traditions is deemed necessary for this, can therefore only be maintained in an obsolete heteronomous world of thought. This holds for male as well as for female priests. What a believing community needs is not a consecrated priest or priestess, but a believing and inspiring pastor who wants to dedicate him- or herself to arousing and keeping awake belief *in* Jesus Christ. And that holds for married and unmarried persons alike. For nobody will question that a married man or woman can also be an excellent preacher and pastor in faith. For that you only have to look at the pastors in the Churches of the Reformation. From a theonomous perspective it is therefore twice meaningless to stick to the compulsory celibacy of priests.

5. Matrimony

Every culture sees marriage as something that is related to the divine domain: sexual urge and fertility are experienced as divine forces that surpass humankind and to whose grace or disgrace they are delivered. It is not surprising that at the occasion of marriage the medieval pious prayed for a blessing from above, and especially the blessing of children. Nor is it surprising that at such an important occasion the official mediator between below and above should be present. He didn't come to consecrate the marriage, because it had already been solemnized before he arrived, but to bless it.

Because Jesus relates this human bond to God's plan with creation, marriage tends to become an indestructible, divinely sanctioned unity. The unknown author of the Letter to the Ephesians, who writes under the name of the apostle Paul, takes this even further and depicts this unity as the representation of, and the participation in, the unity between Christ and the Church, that is, as a reality of salvation. Indeed, by this bond the couple participates in the basic attitude of the glorified Jesus—an attitude of love and faithfulness—and this means becoming a new creation.

Until the eleventh century, matrimony was essentially a social event, despite the fact that it was often crowned with a priestly blessing. But through a process that has been analyzed by the French historian Duby, this blessing gradually gained more ground in the wedding ceremony, until at the end it became a consecration without which a wedding was deemed invalid. And after that it didn't take long until the scholastics included Matrimony in the list of sacraments and thereby completed the number of the Holy Seven. Thomas Aquinas still calls it a special sort of sacrament, and rightfully so. Because, to start with, it is historically not possible to speak about the founding of matrimony by Christ, as marriage exists as long as living memory. Jesus only gave it a specific character and a much richer interpretation with specific demands following from this richer view; but in doing so, he referred to marriage as a state, not to the rite. Moreover, this sacrament is the only one in which one cannot meaningfully speak about administration on the one hand, and acceptance on the other. For the sacrament resides in the ritual affirmation by a man and a woman of their existential bond, interpreted by the author of the Letter to the Ephesians as a symbol of the even more existential bond between Christ and his Church community. The announcement that bride and groom are going to 'administer to each other the sacrament of Matrimony' which is sometimes seen in print on invitations for Christian weddings, therefore doesn't make much sense.

A theonomous approach to this sacrament involves fewer problems than the other six. For we are dealing here with a social and thus inner-worldly event that wasn't considered a sacrament until the second millennium. Any problems that might arise here will rather be situated in the domain of ecclesiastical practice.

Indissoluble Bonds

To start with, there is the emphasis by the (celibate) hierarchy on the absolute indissolubility of marriage, decisive support for which is derived from the words of Scripture. In that view, the bonds of marriage would continue to exist, as an effect of the once given word, even when love has faded into complete indifference or turned to enmity. Indifference, and all the more so enmity, are not existential bonds at all; only love deserves that label. Without love, not understood as a spontaneous feeling, but as goodwill and fidelity, there are no bonds of marriage. And just this bond is the symbol of the unity between Christ and his Church and therefore in it resides the sacrament. Evidently, the church community, through its leadership, can determine that a person can only marry once, and not within certain degrees of family relationship, or when one has received a certain consecration. They could even decree that it is not permitted to remarry after one's spouse has died. But not being allowed isn't the same as not being possible. Marriage is a social reality and whether a relationship is a marriage or not is determined by social consensus, not by ecclesiastical decrees. In that consensus marriage means that two people promise to live together forever, also sexually, and that this promise is not in stride with social consensus, as would be the case, for example, if such a commitment would take place between brother and sister, or father and daughter. Part of that consensus, at least so far, is also that marriage binds one woman and one man. As has already been said, church authorities can refuse to recognize a socially accepted marriage as a marriage (but does that mean it is no marriage?); they can brand socially recognized marriages as concubinage and damn the *concubinarii* as public sinners (but are they therefore *concubinarii* and sinners?). They can even exclude them from receiving sacraments, but are they right in doing so? This becomes even more doubtful when one sees that crimes against humanity, such as those committed by General Pinochet, are in the eyes of the same church authorities no reason for a similar exclusion. A prohibition that cannot hold up against faithful reasoning, loses every ethical bearing.

Speaking about 'the sacraments' in plural is, for that matter, a huge generalization. The prohibition is in reality restricted to only one sacrament, communion, because those excluded are already baptized, confirmed and even married, and confession has all but served its turn. And even concerning the Eucharist, according to the same authorities, *concubinarii* have the strict obligation to be present at the liturgy.

Among the basis, and even among that part of the hierarchy that is sensible to the evolution that is happening, a different approach is emerging, which explains that nowadays doubts about the justification of that view are voiced publicly. These are signs that betray the (often still unconscious) transition from heteronomy to autonomy. It can be expected that, early in this third millennium, celibate Church authorities will lose their last bit of power over all matters relating to marriage that they had gradually gained in the second millennium.

It is maybe more correct to say that marriage contains a dynamic to become indissoluble and that in ideal circumstances it indeed *becomes* indissoluble, rather than that this is already the case only because the couple has said 'I do'. Real indissoluble bonds reveal themselves when a couple that has been separated by force, does not find any rest until they are reunited. When Jesus quoted the words from Genesis that a man should be united with his wife and that both are no longer two but one body, and that humans cannot separate what God has united, he did not think about the as yet nonexistent Roman Catholic sacrament of Matrimony. His words pertain to all marriages, also to those of the (as yet) only civilly married or that of divorced people who remarried. Nevertheless, despite Jesus' words, such marriages are not considered indissoluble by the Roman Curia. On what do they base themselves, then, to enforce that indissolubility on those married in the Church? Besides, it is questionable whether Jesus' words referred to a juridical minimum requirement, and not rather to an existential ideal. And we can only wonder how Jesus would have formulated and interpreted indissolubility in this twenty-first century.

No Divorce, but rather Nullification

Related to this illogical clinging to the absolute indissolubility of matrimonial bonds, and for modern thinking equally obsolete and thus bound to die in the third millennium, is the Roman practice of the nullification of marriages. Questioned by fellow Jews (which means that neither their question nor his response have to do with sacramental marriage) Jesus not only forbids remarriage, but even divorce (Mark 10:9). Based on these words, Church authorities don't accept divorce under any circumstances either. Juridical divorce, that is. They do accept marital separation, although that too doesn't leave anything intact of the existential bonds, which Jesus explicitly sees as the essence of God's plan for marriage.

What they also do is annul marriages. That is, they determine with certainty that there never has been a marriage, not even after the couple has lived in wedlock for ten years or more, and nobody has ever questioned its validity, and even if same the church tribunal that passes the sentence would not have had the slightest doubts about its validity before the crisis started. They even go so far as to deny the existence of the existential bond, only because certain prescribed formalities in the ritual protocol had not been observed. Moreover, in one country, 9 out of 10 marriages that are brought before them are nullified, and in another only 1 out of 10, which means that there is a great deal of subjectivity involved. Is it possible that the subjective opinion of the canonical judges, no matter how full of good will they are and how well they have studied the file, can change objective reality? The whole practice of ecclesiastical nullification is strange, to say the least. Outsiders, as a rule celibates without the slightest experience of married life and its problems, will decide on the basis of second hand knowledge of what has occurred between husband and wife, whether a married couple has ever been a real couple, and whether a second marriage will be a sanctifying sacrament or a concubinage loaded with mortal sins. To arrogate to oneself so much knowledge is only possible in a heteronomous climate in which one believes oneself to be invested from on high with the necessary insight and power. The impression that is given here by Church authorities is that of a failed trick to solve a problem that they had first created themselves, by distilling out of Jesus' words about the indissoluble bonds of marriage, the heavenly determined minimal requirements for a marital relationship, only to be confronted with the bitter reality of human fault, inadequacy and misery.

But why do the Church authorities interpret these words of Jesus so strictly and in so oversimplified a way, while they could just as well read in them a holy and pursuable ideal? Why don't they interpret in the same strict manner his words about the left and the right cheeks? And not only these words from the Sermon on the Mount, but many other words of Jesus they take with several fat chunks of salt, like, for example, his many warnings against the accumulation of wealth. They are probably led here by the unfortunate trend that has crept into the Church with Augustine and Jerome, to consider everything that has to do with sexuality as an invitation to sin, to weigh it scrupulously, and to find it never too light, while they have always been very tolerant about greediness and the abuse of power; in other words, always fishing the gnat out of the cup but carelessly swallowing the camel.

It is high time we left this past rigidity behind and take a different perspective on the indissolubility of marriage, not juridically, but existentially, really, as the ripe fruit of growing together for years, until the two are no longer two but one. And they should stop with this policy of nullifications and rather recognize that a marriage has, alas, ceased to exist. And they should not allow all baptized couples so lightly to get married in the Church. For in the vast majority of cases these don't want this out of a desire to confirm and live their relationship as people that believe *in* Jesus, but only because the Church has developed such a festive ritual for this.

Civil Marriage No Marriage?

A third vexing point is the refusal of the Church authorities to recognize a civil wedding of baptized people as a wedding. Nevertheless, everything that makes a wedding a wedding is present there: one man and one woman that are capable to do this according to society, promise each other lasting fidelity. The ecclesiastical rite (which only surfaces after a thousand years of Church history) cannot take away anything from this reality, only add to it. The desire of Church authorities to identify marriage and sacrament at any price can have all kinds of good and bad grounds, but it presupposes in any event the idea that a consecration from-on-high qualifies these authorities to make, on their own accord (but of course always, as they say, illuminated by the Spirit of God), binding statements about what is and what is not, what is good and what is bad. But only what is good by itself is good, and only what is bad by itself is bad. And to find out what something is by itself, that is the work of all concerned parties together.

Related to marriage is, of course, the whole complex of sexual morality, which in the course of many centuries the celibate Church leadership has dug out to the smallest corners, and filled with innumerable prohibitions and threats. The gap in this matter between the opinions of the traditional Church leadership and those of the modern faithful could not be more vast. The tension between heteronomy and theonomy also plays a role here, but it would lead us too far afield to occupy ourselves with that topic at this point.

Chapter 15

Taking and Eating, Taking and Drinking

Last Supper and Eucharist

If we leave aside the near extinct practice of confession, then the Eucharist is the only sacrament that each and every Christian in the West encounters throughout his life, unfortunately in a presentation that is soaked with heteronomy and therefore indigestible for modern people. For according to the *Catechism of the Catholic Church* which has been mentioned before, it is indeed a real sacrifice, and woe to the one who cannot subscribe to this. But with this sacrificial presentation we irrevocably end up in heteronomy. Therefore, in preparation of the treatment of what has been named the 'Sacrifice of the Mass', the analysis of this cultic notion and some of its branches such as peace offerings, supplicating offerings, and the Sacrifice of the Cross, is due first.

Sacrifice and All that Relates to It

A historical anecdote as a preamble: Near the end of the Second World War, when Allied forces carried out destructive bombardments on German cities, the entire community of Carmelite nuns of Mainz offered themselves as a peace offering to God, so that he (or the Allied forces?) would spare the city. At the very last bombardment on February 27, 1945, a 2,000 pound bomb exploded next to the shelter of the convent in which the nuns had sought safety—one may wonder why, as they had offered themselves as a peace offering—and prayed together. After the bombardment they were all found together, killed on the spot by the high pressure of the air because of the nearby bomb hit. Mainz was spared from further bombardments. The reaction of the inhabitants was unanimous: "God has accepted their sacrifice and saved us". Maybe this would also be the spontaneous reaction of many of us. But what God are we talking about then? Apparently a God who can be moved through sacrifices, and more specifically human sacrifices, to abandon his destructive plans. But is that the same God as the compassionate God who loved the world so much that he has gratuitously given us Jesus and with him, everything? Can notions of sacrifice and peace offerings withstand the radiation of this compassionate God?

Cultic sacrifices of animals that are slaughtered in honor of God, such as were prescribed in the Old Testament or still exist in Islam have never existed in Christianity and are therefore all but non-existent in Western society. Christians never slit the throats of sheep or goats to testify to God's power over life and death, nor did they pour out libations of wine or milk in honor of subterranean gods, or burn fat or flesh so as to make a pleasant smell rise up to the halls of the heavenly palace. For modern people, cultic sacrifice has, therefore, become a totally void concept. Even lighting candles or putting money in a collection box are barely felt as a sacrificial acts by most faithful, even though these pious actions are something of that kind. Only mass is still called a 'sacrifice', and the Roman documents insist that we continue calling it thus, and that it remains the reserved territory of the consecrated priest, because cultic sacrifice has always been the domain of the priest, and this is the reason and justification for the existence of his office.

What was characteristic of cultic sacrifice, apart from its relation to a super-terrestrial or sub-terrestrial deity? That one parted permanently with something of a certain value and usefulness to give it to the deity, which happened most efficiently by destroying it. For in that way, in any event, they wouldn't be able to use it themselves any more. In all this, it was assumed that the deity enjoyed it when he saw the sheep whose throat was cut bleed to death in convulsions, as a token of honor to his greatness, or that he was pleased when he sniffed up the smell of the burnt offering. Just as one sought to obtain something from a human ruler by giving him gifts, people hoped to gain the goodwill of the deity by these sacrifices and move him to grant the favor they prayed for or to obtain that he would turn a blind eye to a transgression and omit deserved punishment.

As has been said, in Western society sacrifice has long been dead and buried. In our language, the term survives in a few expressions but no longer with a religious meaning. 'Sacrificing our time' doesn't remind us of cutting a throat, pouring out a libation, or burning meat in honor of a deity, yet it does retain two of the essential characteristics of cultic sacrifice. For 'sacrificing something' always means: to give up with a heavy heart something that we would rather have kept or saved; in any case it means depriving oneself, a little or a lot. And this is the first element of the idea of sacrifice: the idea of pain, of detriment, of loss. We do so, not because we like to do so, but as in cultic sacrifice, in order to gain something else that we find more valuable. And this is the second essential element of the idea of sacrifice: the idea of gaining by exchange. We sacrifice our time to serve as a sounding board, because we want to help someone who is depressed, and that weighs up against the burden; we are willing to bring the sacrifice of stopping smoking, on doctor's orders, because we do not like the idea of getting a heart attack or because we want to get rid of that terrible smoker's cough. And to make the final or supreme sacrifice means to die to uphold our holiest convictions or to save your fellow human.

THE UNCONSCIOUS PRESUPPOSITIONS OF CULTIC SACRIFICE

Sacrifice is no doubt a central notion in the cult of all religions and must therefore respond to a deeply rooted need. Etymologically it is derived from the Latin noun *sacrificium*, which goes back to *sacrum-facere*: to make something holy. This making holy is done by offering it to a deity, thus transferring it to his domain. The *Oxford Advanced Learners' Dictionary* defines 'sacrifice' as: "The act of offering something to a god, especially an animal that has been killed in a special way; an animal, etc. that is offered in this way." But in this cultic definition, an essential element seems to be lacking, namely the fact that this offering happens to the detriment of oneself. Spontaneously, religious sacrifice is indeed perceived this way: what you offer, you lose. It is in any case withdrawn from its daily use: poured out, burned, killed, destroyed, or consumed by the representatives of the deity, that is, the priests. If I don't give up something to which I am attached, then sacrifice is out of the question. This would be the case, for example, if I would offer something to the deity only to be rid of it. Or of course, if I would chose someone else's lamb to be the sacrificial lamb. That would no longer be sacrifice but cutting long thongs of other men's leather.

If one starts to think about this widespread practice of cultic sacrifice, some remarkably strange things come up. First, this practice suggests that the relation between the human and the deity are imagined after the model of human competitors, in which one man's breath is another man's death. For the deity seems to lack what we possess, otherwise we wouldn't give it to him. And that which is given away, is gone forever. This mutual exclusivity is related to the spontaneous assertion that things in the heavenly realm happen more or less in the same way as in ours. And in our world it happens to be the case that my possession cannot be at the same time someone else's possession. One who doesn't play according to these rules will be dragged to court. It is also related to the material nature of the sacrifice. For spiritual assets, such as knowledge, experience, or happiness can be possessed together and shared with others without anyone losing anything. In those matters, sharing even means multiplication. In a human relationship of love, it is, moreover, possible to possess material goods together. So why is this not possible in the relationship between the human and his God? Is that not also a loving relationship? All this raises questions as to the correctness of the image of God behind sacrificial practice.

Secondly, the deity is apparently keen on material things. To give something to someone only makes sense when the receiving party appreciates the gift. This should especially be kept in mind when the gift is intended to win someone's favor. One will get nothing out of a teetotaler by giving him a bottle of brandy; or out of a deaf person by giving him a load of CDs. Therefore, if the deity likes, or even demands, that sheep, bulls, gold, silver, wine, oil, frankincense or whatever else be offered to him, this must mean that he loves those things. But maybe what the deity really wants is not that specific material object, but rather the acknowledgement of his absolute supremacy and his full right to dispose of someone's entire possession, including his life. One acknowledges this by destroying something of that possession by killing, burning, or pouring it out. In this way he pays honor to the deity, and praises him, and the deity loves that, so that it is possible to win his favor by doing so. All this does not present a very lofty image of the deity.

Thirdly: the deity even seems to be keen on human lives. This explains human sacrifices. People offered the gods a human life, preferably that of someone else, in order to move him to spare their own life, or that of their loved ones, or of the entire community: clan, tribe or nation. A life for a life. The offer of the Carmelite nuns of Mainz—take our lives but in exchange spare the town—fits perfectly well in this concept of a god-pleasing human sacrifice. But this sacrifice has already been humanized in that the nuns offered their own lives to save that of others, and not the other way around. When we look at it this way, the idea that God wanted Jesus' death on the cross to serve as a 'peace offering for our sins', fits the frame of human sacrifice too. But human sacrifice is characteristic of a still primitive cultural stage with a corresponding primitive image of God. With the progress of humanization, this practice has been gradually left behind and replaced by animal sacrifice. The deity still receives the life that he apparently desires, though not that of the human himself, but that of a creature that is close to him and that can, therefore, take his place: that of domestic animals such as bulls, sheep, pigs, he-goats, pigeons, even horses, but strangely enough not that of pets like cats, dogs or canaries.

Fourth, and closely related to the previous remark: the term 'peace offering' in particular evokes a doubtful anthropomorphic image of God: that of a lord who is easily vexed and whose anger needs to be placated with the presents he desires so much that his joy of receiving them outruns his wrath.

The fifth remark concerns supplicating offering. Just as with earthly rulers, gifts make it possible to get something done from the deity that he would otherwise not do. He can, for example, be moved to reconsider a plan or a decision. But that would mean that his former decision was not based on reason and justice (why else would he reconsider it?); or, if it was based thereon, that we could bribe him away from it. But should it not be expected from a deity that at least he has clean hands?

Modern Belief and Cultic Sacrifice are Irreconcilable

The surprising fact is not that a long time ago people started to bring offerings to the unknown power or powers they felt vaguely above them, and that they have continued to do so for thousands of years. They apparently spontaneously imagined these powers after the model of the earthly rulers who can be bribed and placated with gifts.

The surprising fact is not even that ancient Israel, and from the Babylonian Exile until the destruction of the Temple in 70 CE also the Jewish People, upheld the sacrificial cult as something entirely natural. Despite the depth and the transcendence of their image of God, it remained indebted to the image that prevailed in the entire Middle East, where God was a mighty monarch and ruler. Eloquent witnesses to this are the titles which Israel attached to its God: Lord of Hosts, King, the Most High, the Almighty, and so on.

The surprising fact is, rather, that the concept of sacrifice succeeded to strike such deep and strong roots in the Christian community. For the image of God that was preached by Jesus is at odds with sacrificial practice. No wonder he adopted the Prophets' criticism of the sacrificial cult: 'I desire mercy, not sacrifice'. (Matt. 9:13) Nevertheless, after some time sacrificial thinking not only knew a strong revival in the Church and infused its entire piety, but it even managed to become the official and exclusive explanation of Jesus' death, as well as of the central Christian cult: the Eucharist. This explanation of the death on the cross and the Eucharist as a sacrifice became an essential part of the Tradition, which allows it to make claims to authority.

But like everything that lives, a living tradition has an inner vitality, which may lead to surprising transformations. And loyalty to the past can become disloyalty to the Tradition. A caterpillar is only loyal to its nature when it becomes a butterfly. We should always ask ourselves: what is the genotype behind the changing phenotypes; in other words: what remains constant in the Tradition? One who condemns a new phenotype because it is so different than the previous one, ignores the essence: the genotype. To insist that Jesus' crucifixion and the mass be presented as cultic sacrifice at any price, is taking the phenotype for the genotype. Because the term

'Sacrifice of the Mass' is so closely related to the term 'Sacrifice of the Cross', the latter has to be examined first.

SACRIFICE OF THE CROSS

The explanation of Jesus' crucifixion as a sacrifice, and more precisely as a peace offering, is already found in Paul. This is not strange, considering that the Church in its interpretation of Jesus' life and death let itself float on the stream of the Old Testament. And because cultic sacrifice infused the entire ancient Jewish religion (the Pentateuch is filled with its regulations), the Christian scribes, in their search in the Old Testament for 'prefigurations' of Jesus' role as a savior, often ran into sacrifice. This interpretation was, moreover, supported by contemporary religious culture, in which sacrifice and peace offerings were deemed essential components of every religion. As long as one didn't question the obscure backgrounds of the sacrificial cult—and no one did that before modernity—Jesus' death could without any problems be presented as a sacrifice and specifically as a peace offering. The question is if this is still possible today.

To start with, cultic sacrifice in the form of libations, slaughtering and burning, has disappeared from Christian practice and therefore also from the experience of reality that was connected with it. But if something has no experiential content, it is not suitable to illuminate and fill with existential meaning something so disturbing and ugly as the killing of Jesus of Nazareth, so that his death can touch, inspire and enrich someone's life. We therefore urgently need different and better schemes of interpretation.

It gets even worse moreover, when Jesus' blood is turned into a ransom, a cost of discharge, demanded and collected by God. Certainly, Scripture supplies us with many texts that support this presentation. But this brings us straight into the quicksand of anthropomorphism. And by following this line of interpretation, God shows an even scarier and a for modern people even more reprehensible face. Because he does not mind treating a human life as a piece of merchandise, thus running counter to the modern sense of respect for the sanctity of the human person and his life.

Is there a more existential interpretation of Jesus' death on the cross in which modern people can find a source of poignancy and inspiration? Probably this one. As is proven by his prayer at Gethsemane, Jesus hoped and prayed that he would not have to die. He could have fled. He did not do it. In the full knowledge that they would arrest him, he stayed were he was, not to sacrifice himself, but out of loyalty to his mission: he had spread the good news of God for whom every human being is important, however disappointing he may be. This meant the death sentence for every form of dominance and self-preservation at the cost of others. He had to keep on affirming this, even if that message would make him the object of hatred and persecution and would cost him his life. His life should not be worth more to him than his loyalty to his mission, his loyalty to God. This is liberating in a very different way than the heteronomous interpretations in the past, in which our debts were paid with human blood without us being involved, and the closed gates of Heaven would open again without anyone noticing anything. The liberation consists in the radiation of that attitude of life that moves and changes people, and in the creative power of his message, which thereby appears to be fully reliable. This power generated a world in which love sets the tone, a world of human salvation that in Scripture is called 'the Kingdom of God'. This is how Jesus became our 'Savior'. Therefore we may forget about what we were told in the past: that Jesus has paid the divine creditor with his death, that he has destroyed the bond or erased it with his blood, that he has tempered the divine wrath. This is the language of a world-view that splits up reality into two different domains. This heteronomous world-view puts modern people off instead of attracting them, and that therefore brings about more harm than benefit. We have to let ourselves be touched by the power that emanates from Jesus' life and especially from his death, which summarized and sealed his life. In this way we *become* saved. We *aren't* saved yet.

THE EUCHARIST AS A SACRIFICE

The traditional doctrine, formulated at the Council of Trent, understands the Eucharist as a sacrifice, and more specifically as the 'representation of the Sacrifice of the Cross'. What has just been said about the interpretation of Jesus' death on the cross holds, therefore, also for the Eucharist: to call it a sacrifice is of no use for the modern Christian. Not only does the one-sided repetition of this now empty image hinder our access to a more honest and vital interpretation of this event; it even furthers, unconsciously, the pre-Christian view of God that hides behind the ideas of sacrifice and peace offering. True, Tradition has been emphasizing the sacrificial character of the mass since time immemorial, and ecclesiastical authorities never miss a chance to underscore this. But is it possible to subscribe to modernity and at the same time maintain that premodern, heteronomous view?

In all of this, it is not claimed that this view is incorrect, only that its correctness is relative, depending as it is on the departing axiom, and that it becomes incorrect as soon as the axiom of heteronomy and the anthropomorphism that is connected to it, are left behind. Therefore, a modern Christian can't get anywhere with the traditional reading of the Eucharist as a cultic sacrifice. He has to come up with a different and better one. And for this, he will not find help in the official language of the liturgy of the mass, for that overflows with the idea of sacrifice. And to make matters worse, the Vatican regularly issues warnings that not a jot or a tittle of the official texts is to be changed. The exodus from Sunday mass could well be explained by the ever growing gap between the unconscious intuition of modern people, and the pre-modern language and schemes of interpretation of the liturgy of the mass.

SOME OF THE PROBLEMS RAISED BY THE TRADITIONAL PRESENTATION

But there is more than this gap. Even if one makes an effort to think along the lines of the pre-modern interpretation, one stumbles upon all sorts of problems and contradictions. For, in that view, the mass is called a sacrifice of infinite value, the apogee of all sacrifices that one can bring to God, because it is, according to the Council of Trent, the bloodless representation of the Sacrifice of the Cross. And there the problems begin.

First problem: what hides beneath the word 'representation'? Does it refer to a symbolic enactment, like what is done on stage? But then the mass is not a *real* sacrifice. Is it rather, a form of actualization? But historical events are rooted in their own time (which is what makes them historical) and they cannot be transferred into an earlier or later time. This is only possible with mythic events from primeval times, and then only where mystery cults flourish. Did the bishops at the Council of Trent maybe purposefully choose a vague term, to camouflage the tricky problem of the relationship between Jesus' death on the cross and the Eucharist, seeing that the problem became unsolvable if both were understood as sacrifices? However it may be, the result has been that the ordinary proclamation, out of a need for clear language and terms, started to speak about a bloodless renewal of the Sacrifice of the Cross. This is certainly clearer, but from a theological perspective totally untenable. Jesus' dying can and need not be 'renewed', neither in the sense of 'repeated', nor in the sense of 'restored'.

Second problem: for a cultic sacrifice, a sacrificial animal and someone to execute the sacrifice are necessary. Where are these to be found here? That is not a problem in Tradition: the sacrificial animal is, of course, Jesus. And the one who executes? Perhaps his hangmen? Not at all: the sacrificial priest is, again, Jesus. This is guaranteed by the Letter to the Hebrews. But by speaking thusly, his death on the cross is turned into a cultic suicide, something like a self-burning in honor of God, which is certainly not the intention of the Tradition. That Jesus himself, at his Last Supper, interpreted his death as a (peace) offering, at least insofar as his words have not been colored by their later liturgical use, is no reason to continue doing it: as a man of his time he could not but read his relationship with God and his fellow people in a heteronomous way, and as a Jew he could not but express that relationship with images of the Old Testament.

Third problem: what could be the sense of the repetition (at least a million times a week) of a sacrifice of infinite value? Multiplying an infinite value is as meaningless in theology as it is in mathematics. A cherished presentation of the efficacy of the mass is, moreover, related to Purgatory, as almost all the 'intentions of the mass', that is, what the priest wants to obtain by celebrating, have to do with liberating a soul from Purgatory. If the value of a sacrifice is identical with its efficacy in obtaining what one intends with it, the question rises as to how this value can be infinite, because it consists of a very finite liberation, and because its efficiency must seemingly still be reinforced over and again. These three problems give an idea of the quicksand in which one ends up if one starts speaking about the Eucharist in the theological language of the past.

This sacrificial theology is also the source of tons of inauthentic words and practices. What could it mean, when the priest, after the so-called offertory, exhorts the community to pray that God may 'accept mine and your sacrifice'? What sacrifice does he mean? That of the bread and the wine? But these were not even his; they had been provided by the church wardens. But leaving aside who provided them: parting with a piece of bread and some wine in honor of God is a very meager sacrifice indeed. And if the priest intends to say that he and the faithful will soon sacrifice Jesus again in a bloodless way, then the sacrificial priest suddenly ceases to be Jesus himself. And why need God be asked to accept this sacrifice (of Jesus)? Is his acceptance maybe doubtful? Moreover, how can we possibly give something to God who gives everything himself, and what can it mean that he accepts gifts? Equally inauthentic and insincere is also a practice that is sometimes recommended in pious writings, namely to put oneself on the paten during the offertory; because what is the priest parting with, when the faithful is laying there? And parting should be the essence of the idea of sacrifice. It is indeed a strange kind of sacrifice, to take back home as if nothing has happened that which one has just given to God. The same is the case when one has school children bring their books and their toys as an offering to the altar. All this betrays that we have grown far away from the cultic idea of sacrifice. To try to explain the Eucharist with the help of this now empty concept is trying to explain something unclear by means of something equally unclear. Sacrificial language is no longer authentic language. And a lack of authenticity is the mother of pretense and verbiage. A tree that produces such fruits can in the long term expect to share the fate of the trees in Matthew 7:19.

THE DOCTRINE OF TRANSUBSTANTIATION

Enough has been said now about the problems that will be met by a theology that interprets the mass as a sacrifice. Yet another pillar of the traditional theology of the mass leans so much on heteronomous presuppositions that it cannot remain standing in a theonomously thinking culture: the doctrine of transubstantiation, which was originally brought up in scholasticism. The term transubstantiation has been under fire for a while now, indicating that modern Christianity shows resistance against this category, and even more against the pre-modern world view that supports it. Transubstantiation implies that certain words, when pronounced correctly—not by anyone, but by a man (women are taboo) who possesses special powers—can effect an invisible but essential transformation. The bread would be changed into the body of the (bodily!) resurrected Jesus, and the wine into his blood, which, although shed, is yet present in that body. We do not merely stand here with both feet in heteronomy, but already with one foot in magic. In order not to end up there completely, we need to take recourse to the emergency solution of well-oiled cooperation between Heaven and Earth that has been described in Chapter 13. The picture is completed by the idea that the man who possesses such power of transubstantiation, does not owe this to his own talent, to training, or to any form of inner-worldly activity, but exclusively to consecration, that is, to the intervention of God-on-High. With each step into Eucharistic theology, the modern Catholic bumps into heteronomous images that obstruct his way to the evangelical message.

The Eucharist as Remembrance

It is possible, though, to speak about the Eucharist in a much more meaningful way than Tradition does. For sacrifice is only one of the possible interpretations of the Eucharistic ritual, and not even the oldest one. Just as old, for example, is the equally heteronomous reading of the Eucharist as a mystery, in the sense of the Hellenistic mystery cults. But that reading is only accessible for one who is familiar with those cults—which definitely doesn't include people living in the twenty-first century. Even older than these two is the reading of the Eucharist as the 'meal of the Lord'; this is already found in Paul's First Letter to the Corinthians. Can't we get somewhere with this concept? It has the advantage of being inner-worldly, because Paul uses it for a real meal in which the Last Supper was remembered, and thereby Jesus' death. But the consumption of a thin host, into which the communion has degenerated in the course of time, cannot honestly be called a meal, or 'sitting at the table of the Lord'. Just as calling the Eucharist a 'celebration', is mostly a violation of language. For centuries it has been urged on the faithful as a strict Sunday duty, under penalty of a mortal sin, and for many of them it has become much more a mechanical ritual than a celebration. Words have a meaning, and if one uses them for something else, one is guilty of counterfeiting. Authenticity comes first: call things by their proper name. A cat is a cat and no tiger. Otherwise we create an atmosphere of insincerity, whereas God is absolute sincerity. Speaking about things that relate to Him therefore demands sincerity.

In theonomous language it is probably best to use the term 'remembrance'. Because the Eucharist is the ever repeated execution of what Jesus has instructed us to do: to remember him. And this remembrance takes more precisely the shape of taking and eating, taking and drinking. Even though barely anything is left of the eating and the drinking, yet this is what makes the Eucharist what it is. The intention of this eating and drinking is, after the words of the story of its institution by Jesus, to commemorate him, which means concretely: to create a living memory of him as someone who wanted to be like bread and wine for people. This living memory, this remembrance, will render him present and creatively active in the life of those in whom it is evoked. Nothing in this approach reeks of magic. Neither is there any need for a supernatural intervention: everything occurs in the inner-worldly, existential realm and has illuminating parallels in our daily experience. The thankful remembrance of a great and noble person renders this person psychologically present and arouses in us the desire to become a bit like him and to follow his way. In the Eucharist, eating and drinking is the means, while the remembrance, the living memory of Jesus with its enriching influence on our life, is the goal. And the goal is always more important than the means. For there is only one goal and the means can be many. Also this kind of remembering is not the only one. There are more ways to remember Jesus and to render him present, and in doing so to be moved by the power that emanates from his love of humankind and of God. The liturgy of Good Friday that comports no Eucharist, and the praise of the Easter Candle, are good examples of this. That the Eucharistic form of this remembrance plays such an exclusive role in Catholic piety has many reasons, as a rule of heteronomous origin, and usually without any connection to this remembrance—such as the intention of saving a soul from heteronomous Purgatory. To rely today, in theonomous culture, on heteronomous Tradition in order to maintain the absolute priority position of the Eucharist as the main form of remembrance, is *a priori* hopeless; and the prescription of the daily mass to which canon law binds the clergy and that is based on this priority position, loses its justification.

WHAT COMES INSTEAD OF THE DOCTRINE OF TRANSUBSTANTIATION?

The above question can be divided in two others: how should we understand Jesus' words in the so-called institution of the Eucharist; and what do they teach us about the Eucharist? As regards Jesus' words in this story, it should not be forgotten that they are already marked by their liturgical use in the earliest Church and that they are, moreover, not Jesus' own Aramaic words but (originally Greek) translations. Therefore, they should not be overtaxed. Nevertheless, the doctrine of transubstantiation poses with resolute and uncritical realism that by saying 'This is my body, this is my blood' Jesus transformed the bread into his material body and the wine into his material blood. This doctrine originates from a time when everybody automatically assumed that 'body' in Scripture meant the same as what it means for us: a physical unity of flesh and bones, enclosed by skin. That the theological tradition thought this way, shows, among other things, from its emphasis that this transformation of the bread into Jesus body also contains his blood, not because of the (in fact, magical) power of his words, but *per concomitantiam*, literally: by companionship, because a body is unthinkable without blood. But is it possible to imagine that Jesus was physically reclining at the table and at the same time equally physically, with muscles, skin and hair, lying on the table in the form of bread? And this not once but as many times as the amount of the pieces in which the bread was broken. The same holds for his blood, in which again *per concomitantiam* his entire body was present, and evidently also his soul and together with his humanity also his divinity. If these images are more than problematic for us, how then can we explain Jesus' words in a sense that we find meaningful?

To start with, modern exegesis has furthered our insight into the early Jewish conception of the body, which features the bodily-spiritual person, the self. Thus far there are no problems. When 'body' means 'I', what Jesus says, amount to: 'This bread is my self, this bread is I.'

But how should we understand *that*? Jesus does not give an answer to this question. Catholic Tradition does, however, and claims that we should understand this very literally, because the copula 'is' would attribute to both terms the same degree of reality. But how can Tradition be so certain of this? For there are other possibilities, as will soon become clear. Moreover, we immediately stumble upon the impossibility that has been outlined before: that at the Last Supper two or even more physical bodies of Jesus would have been present.

If we pay close attention to Jesus' words at the cup in the version of Paul (the oldest of the four versions in the New Testament), and, very probably inspired by him, in Luke (the most recent of the four), we see that Jesus does not say there: 'This is my blood', as he does in Mark and in Matthew, who depends on him, but rather: 'This is the cup of the New Covenant in (that is, founded in, sealed by) my blood'. If those two traditions are equally valid, then also the two formulations are equally valid, and the formulation 'This is my blood' need not be taken as realistically as heteronomous Church doctrine wants it. This indicates that also Jesus' words about the bread should not be taken too realistically.

But which other way is there to read this 'is' sentence? Maybe this is a way. Imagine this: someone points at a picture that shows him, maybe in disguise, or as part of a large group, or before a diet, or still as a boy, and he says: 'This is I'. Of course this is not the same as what is meant by the instituting words of the Eucharist. But it shows that 'This is I' need not always be understood realistically, as if the speaker wants to say that he is two times present: once in real life and once, equally physically, in the picture. He merely wants to say: 'This is a picture of me'.

A similar natural explanation is thinkable in the case of Jesus' words: in the bread that he breaks for his disciples, he recognizes himself; this bread is his full-body portrait, the eloquent sign that he is really (albeit not physically) bread for them and for all people; that he nourishes them, sustains them, and that he surrenders himself for their cause. In that moment, the bread in his hands receives a new and endlessly richer sense, and an entirely new meaning, not that of a physical source of energy but that of an intense encounter and relationship between the disciples and their teacher and master, from whom they will soon be separated. Therefore, in the last decades, the terms 'transignification' or 'transfinalisation' have become preferred over 'transubstantiation'.

That the entire Tradition has read the transmitted words of Jesus in a physical sense (those who tried to do otherwise, like Berengarius in the tenth century, or the Protestants in the sixteenth century, had to pay for it with excommunication or execution), is obviously closely related with the heteronomous axiom of another world that, at will and in the most miraculous ways, can intervene in our world, and indeed does it, if necessary without us noticing a thing. But with the shift to the axiom of autonomy, the unanimity of such a Tradition loses its weight.

THE REAL PRESENCE

Thus far about the Last Supper. But we are only halfway there. Because what happens in every mass? Are those merely ritually enhanced remembrances of what Jesus has done during the Last Supper, when he eloquently summarized his life and his person in one meaningful gesture? For with the breaking and the passing of the bread he testified that he wanted to distribute himself as bread, and with the blessing of the cup, that he was ready to give up his life (because blood means life) for the sake of the 'many'.

But if so, is he still 'really present' in those guises of bread and wine, as the Tradition unanimously teaches it? Or is he only symbolically present? For closely linked to the doctrine of transubstantiation is the emphasis in the Tradition of Jesus' real presence in the host and the wine. This emphasis should not blind us from the truth that all presence is real, as the *Catechism of the Catholic Church* reads, for example, in paragraphs 1074 and 1088, a presence in symbols as well. One is either fully present or not at all. To characterize the specific form of Jesus' presence, the *Catechism* therefore quotes the formulation of the Council of Trent that he is present 'in a true, real and substantial manner', in which only the term 'substantial' distinguishes Jesus' presence from a symbolic presence.

The problem related to this 'substantial' has already been mentioned in relation to the Last Supper, when the unthinkable multiplication of Jesus' human person was pointed out. Moreover, even a physical presence (which is after all the real meaning of 'substantial') is only a presence in signs, that is, a symbolic presence. Because the body is the sign of the person, not the person himself.

Therefore, despite the heteronomous Tradition, Jesus' presence in the Eucharist is not substantial, but symbolic. But a symbolic presence presupposes always that the symbol is recognized as symbol, as sign. Otherwise there would be no sign but merely a thing. And where there are only things and no deeper reality, there is no presence at all. Presence is always related to word and counter-word, to being addressed and to answering, that is, to recognition. In this way, a country is recognized as present in its flag, anthem, and its ambassadors. Similarly, we recognize Jesus' presence in the crucifix, otherwise we wouldn't venerate it on Good Friday; and in the Easter Candle, otherwise we would not cense it and praise it; and in Baptism, otherwise it would not be a sacrament; and in the altar, and in the Book of the Gospel, and in the icons that represent him. And also in the bread of the Eucharist. Always present and always in a different way. In the Eucharistic bread, he is present as an appeal to do as he has done. But in that sign, he is only present in so far as it touches us and we, touched by it, answer it, recognize and affirm him in that sign. Otherwise bread and wine remain what they are: food stuff.

It is of course possible to contemplate that sign in prayer and let oneself be touched by it: this is the whole purpose of the Adoration of the Holy Sacrament, with at its climax the display of the Host in the monstrance, and the solemn procession with it through the streets. But only in eating and drinking will its full evocative power develop. For Jesus did not say: 'Look, contemplate, pray, and parade me in a procession through the streets', but he said: 'Take and eat'.

One aspect of this presence should not be left aside: the vine does not exist without its branches. The Jesus who has grown to his fullness (in biblical language: glorified) and as such has been established as 'Lord and Christ', does not exist without the community of those who believe in him and who are grafted onto him, and in whom he lives and operates creatively. Without his effective presence in a community, no representative of that community would ever be able to change common things as wine and bread into creative symbols of Jesus' presence. Only I myself, and nobody else, can turn something into a present that embodies my self and my affection. What has been called 'transubstantiation', therefore, presupposes that Jesus, in his historical shape of local and universal community, operates actively through certain community members who by that same community have been mandated to do so. The question as to when exactly this kind of 'transubstantiation' occurs (in the past this was conceived as a lightning strike at the pronunciation of the words of consecration), is as difficult to answer as the question when exactly the roses that one buys in a shop are transformed from mere merchandise into a gift that symbolizes love.

CHAPTER 16

GUILT AND PUNISHMENT

TWO DIFFERENT PERSPECTIVES ON SIN AND CONFESSION

Our treatment of the sacraments so far has left Confession aside, for it is inextricably related to the concept of sin, and first we need to settle things with that concept. This is all the more necessary because sin takes up such a central position in the Christian doctrine of faith, for attached to it are a whole cluster of very important, but mostly heteronomous concepts, such as salvation, pardon, justification, original sin and all that is related to it, as well as many less important ones such as punishment, atonement and mortification, indulgences, Purgatory and Hell. And also Confession, which in its turn is embedded in a complex of heteronomous ideas: law, punishment, judgment, penalty, and jurisdiction. Most of these are waning since the decline of the so-called sense of sin. In conservative circles this decline, and especially that of Confession, is being regarded as a disaster. But this decline is not at all a loss if it merely implies a replacement of the heteronomous presentation of the embodied reality by a more modern and theonomous presentation. Instead of trying to maintain these familiar concepts and names, we should be concerned with polishing the dusty reality they conceal. This requires that the thoroughly heteronomous, and therefore provisional character of the concept of sin comes to light, and with it the desirability of leaving it behind. Afterwards, this concept needs to be detached from its heteronomous context and rephrased in theonomous language. The following analysis is restricted to the Jewish-Christian world of thought; that of other religions remains out of consideration.

Because of its primeval past, the idea of sin was born in a heteronomous context. It was used to translate the sense of frightening chaos in the most fundamental relation there is: the relation between the human and his origin, God. This translation, just as everything else we say about God, unconsciously uses metaphors. The image that is evoked is that of trespassing against an omniscient ruler who is enthroned above him, by not listening to his commandments and laws. In doing so, he elicits the righteous anger of that ruler, loads guilt upon himself, and hence should expect punishment. This image originates from experience with earthly rulers. Those that eat cherries with great persons shall have their eyes squirted out with the stones. This means that a person in power cannot be offended without consequences. And this holds also for God. As long as God has not forgiven his sins, the human feels a dark cloud hovering above his precarious existence. The concept of sin is therefore surrounded with a frightening and dark aura. It evokes a feeling of threat and danger because of its context of anger and punishment. The human wants to get rid of that threat and makes efforts to settle his disturbed relationship with God. He knows how that works with the earthly rulers he has offended: he has to make himself small, admit his fault and show regret, beg their pardon and offer gifts, in an effort to remove the disturbance that he created and to reclaim at least partially the lost goodwill, so as to escape the punishment that hangs above his head. What works with human beings will also work with the (anthropomorphously conceived) God, he thinks, and the offering of gifts takes the form of peace offerings.

The expected answer is forgiveness. But that forgiveness does not imply that the guilty person himself experiences an existential change. If a change happens, it does so exclusively on the side of the judging ruler. He does not avenge, he grants amnesty for the offense or the injustice done to him, so that the guilty person escapes the punishment deserved on account of his misbehavior. The Greek word *amnèsteia* literally means: not remembering, forgetting. The divine ruler acts as if he had forgotten. He acquits remaining debts. But that decision is conditional: the guilty one has to show regret, even if the motive for his regret is not very lofty. Fear for the punishment that would otherwise come upon him is enough.

For Immanuel Kant, such a fear seriously undermines the ethical and thus existential value of the human deed. This too shows that the guilty one needs not undergo an existential change, read: conversion. From him, all that is required is the promise that he will not undertake similar transgressions in the future. This explains the important place of good intentions in this way of thinking.

This analysis not only lays bare the heteronomous content of the concept of sin, but that of the other concepts in its semantic field as well: guilt, punishment, penitence, regret, forgiveness, acquittal. All this depends on the heteronomous presentation of God as an outer-worldly ruler, dressed up in the garb of inner-worldly rulers. If, from a theonomous perspective, one becomes aware of the untenability of this anthropomorphous idea of sin as transgression of a divine law and offense of the most holy legislator and ruler, then all the above-mentioned terms in the semantic field of sin, will founder also. And with them the practice of Confession, in as far as it is saturated with these ideas. This justifies the suspicion that the swift waning of the practice of Confession in the West is related to the fast advance of autonomous thought, and that all efforts to modernize Confession, such as dressing it up as a therapeutic conversation in a cool confession room, are of no avail.

FROM SIN TO EXISTENTIAL NEED

Is it possible to translate 'sin' and maybe also some of the untenable concepts that are related to it into the language of autonomy? As has already been said, 'sin' is a metaphor for a painful existential experience: that of a rift in the relationship between the human and his highest Good. In heteronomous thought this highest Good appears in the disguise of a legislator, and the rift corresponds to a transgression of the law. But all that is not the essence. The essence of it is, that in the light of the human's total dependence and his fundamental sense of threat, this rift that is translated as sin is a catastrophe, and even the ultimate catastrophe.

To get a sense of the seriousness of this catastrophe, we need another image than that of legislator and transgression, an image that has the advantage of being less extrinsic and more existential. We can use the name God for the Primeval Ground (which is again imagery!) of the entire cosmic evolutionary reality and hence also of our essence. Then the rift in the relationship will really start showing its depth. It is nothing else than our existential alienation form our Primeval Ground, through which alienation our deepest being has become wrecked and disrupted and we have ended up in a dreadful fundamental crisis. Compared to this, transgression of a law remains something more external and superficial, for we can undo it by doing something in return. Punishment too is an extraneous intervention, necessary to make someone physically experience that transgression is not child's play. For the fact that one has transgressed so lightheartedly implies that one has, wrongfully, not taken the transgression very seriously. And forgiveness remains something extraneous as well: it is the dismissal of deserved punishment, albeit on the condition that one has admitted his guilt and promises improvement. Ethically sensible liberals can sometimes be heard criticizing Catholics for the fact that they make light of ethical faults, as if confession to a priest would be enough to free them from the evil they have done. This criticism originates in the appearance of externality that has just been described, which is closely related to the metaphor of sin as the transgression of a law and forgiveness as acquittal. The fact that 'forgiveness' is an existential process, demanding internal change, does not easily permeate a heteronomous frame of thought.

In an approach that is no longer heteronomous, precisely this internal transformation is at center stage. The internal rift is being healed, the fundamental need relieved. One rises up from the emptiness, the darkness and the chaos, and obtains access to light and harmony. This transformation occurs in the kernel of our existence through unification-in-love with the radiating Wonder that is the ground of our being. We had become estranged from this ground by giving in to our inclination to be ourselves without being Him. Only in this unification can we find our completion, the fulfillment of our deepest need; doing without this unification is therefore the worst of all disasters. 'You have made us for yourself, and our hearts are restless until they rest in you.' (St. Augustine in his *Confessions*), or: 'My soul thirsts for you like a parched land' (Psalm 143:6)—these quotes are able to express more correctly than the term 'sin' what is really the matter: that we find ourselves in a state of need, loss, incompleteness, insatisfaction (which we try to satiate with all kinds of fake means), and of a powerless desire to be liberated from it. This experience of need is proportionate to our fundamental inadequacy to love—the latter not understood as a feeling, but as the self-abandonment for which we are created. For thanks to Jesus, who has opened our eyes to this, we dare to confess that the essence of this creating Wonder is a self-abandoning Love that aspires to express itself in everything, to make everything congruous with its Being, God-alike. But instead of letting ourselves be permeated, we stay in our closed shell. And precisely therefore we experience that we are still in need of the essential and we remain deeply unsatisfied, needy, and pitiable. If He would not attract us towards loving, we would not be torn between the gravity of our thirst for self-preservation on the one hand, and attraction towards love on the other; between what we merely are now, and what He wants us to become. We would not experience that kind of need, unknown to the animals, that 'quiet desperation' (so the philosopher Henry David Thoreau) that characterizes most human lives. Here, this analysis meets up with the more traditional idea that the only real sin is selfishness, which is refusing to heed God.

Where an existential state of loss and need replaces sin, the self-assured resolutions also disappear from sight, as well as the weighing of the measure of one's own guilt, which is again a term borrowed from jurisdiction, where it is decisive for the correct determination of the punishment. We do not even know in how far we can speak about guilt, that is, to what degree we are truly free in what we do, and to what degree we are dependent on forces in us that control us. And even the guilty abuse of our freedom is still related to our fundamental condition of need, which exists in the not yet abolished alienation between us and our deepest Ground. Instead of making good resolutions, as in our heteronomous past, now we cry out for mercy, liberation, and fulfillment. This cry is born from our incompetence to fulfill and heal ourselves. And the more intensely this cry rises up from within ourselves, the more we become recipients of the nourishing living stream of Love that meanders in us, and the more we will be united with it.

When sin makes way for loss, need, misery, and malady, the metaphor of forgiveness and acquittal has to make way for that of salvation, healing, and remedy, because those refer to the existential change for the good that comes about in our depth.

HEALING RATHER THAN FORGIVENESS. SO WHAT ABOUT REPENTANCE?

A thorough analysis of the human process that is called 'forgiveness', makes clear that we cannot automatically apply it to our relationship with the creating Love. Forgiveness presupposes that one party feels vexed, mistreated. When a dog barks at me, I do not need to forgive him: his barking may frighten me, but it does not offend me. If a human being barks at me, I *do* feel offended. This touchiness (because that's what it is: I do not become internally different, lesser, threatened in my depth because somebody else is unfriendly) and the need for revenge that goes together with it, demonstrate that I feel disparaged, hurt in my sense of dignity, and threatened. My reaction is a form of self-defense; I deem it necessary to prove that one has to reckon with me, that my little self is important.

Forgiveness is cutting across this inclination, not taking revenge, not making the other suffer for his deeds, to act as if nothing has happened. This is generosity, but it presupposes a previous narrow-mindedness, a previous vexation, the frightening impression that the precarious existence of my little person is at stake. And how could we ascribe such a reaction to God? He is not vexed by what we do, which is, moreover, usually done out of a lack of freedom. He is pure radiation, only caring for our good, not for his own honor. In a truly theonomous way it is, therefore, not possible to speak about His forgiveness. Moreover, God cannot act *as if* nothing has happened. He is the uppermost reality. What has happened has happened. Closing a chapter is human business. God has no place for that.

On the other hand, he is not indifferent to what we do; for him we are not like barking dogs. Simply because he is Love, he cannot accept that we are not yet love, that we harm and diminish ourselves and close ourselves off from him. And he keeps on pushing us against our will, until we change, open ourselves up, transcend our need, heal from our disease. This existential language is occasionally found in the Gospel. Jesus defends his association with 'publicans and sinners' by replying that not the healthy, but the sick need a doctor. Moreover, his healing is much more than the activity of a sympathetic miracle worker: for the evangelists, this healing activity points to the existential salvation that occurs within people through him. Even the Council of Trent used the terms 'sick', 'wound' and 'remedy' for sin and forgiveness, albeit only as metaphors. Forgiving is apparently not the only way to describe the internal human process of recovery.

Does this mean the end of repentance, which is the ecclesiastical synonym for the primeval human notion of regret? Quite the opposite. Etymologically, the word *regret* comes from the Old French *regreter*: to lament; and lamenting is done because one has lost someone. Not something, but someone. We regret, we lament the death of someone we love. True lamenting does not happen at the surface of our existence, where we deal with material profit or loss, or even health, but in the depth. It is grief for the end of a human relationship, the loss of a loved one whom we consider to be indispensable for us. Perceived this way, regret has nothing to do originally with fear for the loss of advantages, for sanctions and punishment, even though that meaning has gradually pushed the other aside. If we leave the heteronomous notion of sin behind for the painful awareness of being separated and alienated from our beloved origin and indispensable fulfillment, regret will receive an existential dimension that it usually doesn't have in the heteronomous view. It becomes an expression of the wish to change. We regret what we have lost and would like to make this loss undone. In this, we don't look so much at our deeds, as we do in heteronomous regret, because these can no longer be undone. But we look at what lies behind those deeds: our unwillingness (inextricably mixed up with impotence) to let ourselves be moved by the Love that attracts us. And the dynamic of this grief already begins to remove the alienation and to bridge the gap. In this sense, it remains true that repentance (or regret) forgives sin, as the heteronomous formula teaches us. A true 'act of repentance' is, in theonomous view, nothing else than an 'act of love'.

CONFESSION

This has brought us to Confession, for that is the sacrament in which the Church symbolizes and grants God's forgiveness to the guilty. As has already been demonstrated, this immediately evokes the heteronomous image of the extra-cosmic legislator and ruler, who feels wronged and now judges, but who, instead of punishing, lets mercy prevail over righteousness and grants amnesty. Evidently, the heteronomous slant of that sacrament colors the entire theological and liturgical language of confession. One needs to show regret, in traditional language to repent and to plead guilty, revealing all the awkward circumstances and details. For the priest sits there as a justice who needs all the information to judge how serious the offence was, and whether the conditions for God's amnesty are fulfilled; he evokes God's acquittal, remission and forgiveness and determines a fine. Besides, confession as we know it today is nothing else than a further development of the tariff system of the early Middle Ages, which was basically the administration of justice of the former Druids in Christianized Scotland and Ireland, dressed up in a Christian garb by the priests who had inherited their role.

Pessimistic cultural critics blame the fast disappearance of Confession on secularization, which would exclude God from life, resulting in the disappearance of the awareness of sin. Certainly, the awareness of sin is disappearing, but not because God no longer plays a role, but because a heteronomously disguised God-judge has become a foreign concept in the modern cultural climate and with him inevitably the traditional notion of sin too.

The name of the sacrament of confession itself betrays its heteronomous slant. The Latin word *confessio* literally means 'admitting', that is, one's own guilt, and therefore belongs to the realm of jurisdiction. Moreover, the word confession is invested with a negative aura; it exudes an atmosphere of fear, aversion, and shame, not a joyful, enlightening atmosphere of healing, wholeness, and fulfillment by the God who completes us, for whom we yearn as dry soil for rain. Therefore, this sacrament deserves to receive another, better name.

ATONEMENT, AND THE CELEBRATION OF ATONEMENT

A better name would be the 'sacrament of atonement', and maybe even better 'celebration of atonement', because of the joyous associations of the word 'celebration'. But then, the word atonement should first retrieve its original meaning. The Middle English *atonen* was derived from 'at one'—being of one mind, in accord, reconciled. Because of a process of development that should be entirely charged to the account of heteronomous thinking, in religious language it has received the connotation of self-punishment, and hence self-affliction. The stages in this process can only be briefly outlined here: There is a spontaneous consensus in all societies that an offence needs to be amended by an equivalent punishment. For example, a murderer still receives capital punishment in some states. With this 'execution', justice is executed. The validity of the principle can be questioned, because if killing someone is reprehensible, the execution doubles the reprehensibility. But this is the case, and that principle of equivalent punishment is the foundation of the entire system of criminal law. In this system, every offence is regarded as damage to the tissue of the social order, and because that tissue is so precious it has to be repaired. Based on the above-mentioned consensus, this repair, removal of the damage, fixing the tissue, making it good again, requires the punishment of the guilty individual. As transgression of God's commandments and therefore disturbance of the divine law and order, sin calls for the repair of this order, which is punishment. In order to avoid punishment in the hereafter, one can take up an equivalent punishment in this world by afflicting oneself occasionally. In this way, the concept of 'atonement', which originally meant: making one again, restoring the unity, repair, has become a synonym for self-punishment, self-affliction.

The stubborn idea that through self-affliction one can obtain a reduction or acquittal of one's sentence from God-in-Heaven has in its turn brought forth the illusion that in the same way one can obtain from Him other things, too. This is no longer called atonement, but mortification. This concept will be examined in Chapter 17.

The next step in the distortion of the concept of 'atonement' was the idea that God apparently likes to see that we afflict ourselves. Why else would he answer our supplicating prayers accompanied with mortifications? And thus the medieval pious tortured themselves with hunger and cold, sleep deprivation, flogging, wearing hair shirts and pointed chains, and so on, only to make Him happy with that gift, and thus to show how much they loved Him. Also the image of the suffering Jesus drove many pious persons to practices of self-torture out of the urge to identify with him. However much this self-torture has been recommended and practiced in pious tradition, it is based on medieval ideas that modernity has left behind. Besides, can we imagine a relationship of love in which one partner tortures himself in order to show the other how great his love is? A partner that is happy with this is mentally insane. This distortion of the notion of atonement makes it therefore undesirable to redefine confession as the 'sacrament of atonement'. A much better name would be: 'sacrament of conversion', as it is called in the *Catechism*, paragraph 1423, or 'sacrament of renewal'.

Whether 'sacrament of reconciliation' would be a suitable name will be discussed further.

But also the entire external form of that sacrament as a court of law, with (self)accusation and acquittal on the condition of a (ridiculously small) punishment, is so thoroughly heteronomous that it has no future. The traditional confession is, however, historically only the second form of that sacrament, far removed from the original form that consisted of the (once-only) re-admittance into the church community after the necessary proofs that, despite the previous proofs of the contrary, one belongs there. That re-admittance served as the creative sign that one stood again in the living stream that goes out from Jesus. If in the third millennium we stubbornly want to maintain that second historical form of the sacrament, we will experience its demise. It can only survive if it takes up a third form.

Something can already be suggested: a celebration in which the semantic field of sin makes way for that of illness and healing, or calamity and rescue, or need and fulfillment, or captivity and liberation. All these concepts are closely related to the origin of the word atonement as stemming from *at-one*: becoming one, whole, again, with oneself, one another, and God. But becoming whole is a long process. This idea is totally lacking in the imagery of pardon and acquittal: the promised forgiveness at confession gives the false impression of something instant and extrinsic. The celebration of atonement, on the other hand, with its emphasis on slow inner healing, aims at an existential improvement. This is obtained by the inspiring atmosphere of the rite, in which prayer, song, meditation, and proclamation play a creative role; and by the co-operation of the attendant congregation. It also doesn't pretend to establish salvation instantly, as it were with a magic formula: it wants to be nothing more than an intense moment in a life-long process of healing.

In the celebrating congregation, the glorified Jesus is active. A ritual sign, such as, for example, the imposition of hands that often accompanied and established Jesus' healing activity, can make its saving effectiveness visible and in this way contribute to existential healing. The process of healing consists in essence in this, that we, out of our mixture of impotence and guilt, in deep longing for healing and salvation, put ourselves in the hands of the God who seeks us, so that he can lift off this alienation between us and his Love that attracts us.

MERCY AND RECONCILIATION

Speaking about forgiveness implies speaking about God's mercy. This connection is so close that the prayer 'Lord, have mercy' in the beginning of the Service of the Word has become the full equivalent of the old *Confiteor*, so that it has usually pushed away and replaced that confession, as well as the following prayer for forgiveness. And 'have mercy on us' has become also the official continuation of the supplication 'Lamb of God, you who take away the sin of the world'. Leaving the semantic field of sin and forgiveness for that of existential need, therefore, doesn't imply that we better cease to speak about mercy also. Quite to the contrary. And that the 'Lord, have mercy' supersedes the *Confiteor* with its self-accusation and its plea for forgiveness and for mediation by the saints, is even a gain rather than a loss. But only, of course, when it is prayed as an honest cry for rescue from the existential need in which we have become entangled by our obstinacy and impotence.

The *Catechism* uses still another term for the sacrament of confession, calling it the 'Sacrament of Reconciliation' (par. 1424). This biblical term has made a remarkable come-back in modern religious language. But reconciliation presupposes a previous quarrel. Two parties have had a fight and want to make up. But a quarreling God is equally as untenable as a punishing or amnesty-granting God. Again, He would be diminished to a vexed and aggressive opponent, who would certainly not turn his left cheek when stricken on the right one, and who, contrary to what the First Letter to the Corinthians testifies about Love, doesn't bear all things. And from our human side towards God, quarreling and fighting should also be out of the question. We may occasionally protest what befalls us, and argue with God as Job did; but that is generally not our sin. Our sin is, rather, the refusal to obey his call deep inside us to forget ourselves and to turn towards our neighbors. Reconciliation becomes stuck in an anthropomorphism that belongs to a heteronomous world of thought, and is not the proper term in modern thought to define the process of recovery in the relation between us and the God who attracts us. Nor is it the proper term to supersede the heteronomous name of Confession.

CHAPTER 17

MENTALLY ILL OR CLOSE TO GOD?

MORTIFICATION AND ASCETICISM

In the above treatment of the Eucharist, the notion of ritual sacrifice has been dealt with. Characteristic for ritual sacrifice, aside from the effect one expects it to have in the other world, is also its painful character: it hurts to separate from something that one likes to keep, even if one hopes to receive something better in return, such as is always the case in ritual sacrifice. Gradually, in the Western world, the ritual meaning of sacrifice has been replaced by its non-ritual meaning in which both elements of loss and gain are retained, for example, sacrificing smoking for health reasons; or making a sacrifice for one's children. Mortification is closely related to this meaning of sacrifice; they are like sister and brother. Only the sister is religious, and the brother is usually secular. In traditional piety, mortification, like its brother, sacrifice, means to deprive oneself in this world, to give up something or to take up something painful, in short: a bit of self-torture, in the hope of attaining something valuable. Only, now the intended effect is no longer in this world, but in the supernatural world, namely soothing God and trying to get something done from Him. This expectation is based on the strange presupposition that God is particularly happy with our self-torture and likes to see us suffer rather than flourish. From a Christian perspective this is a flagrant misconception. Our God is a God of well-being, even of bodily well-being, as the healing activities of Jesus made visible. In the final analysis, the completion of God's work of creation exists in a world without mourning, crying or pain, as is testified in the Book of Revelation

(21:4). If this is the case, we need to be done with mortification, as far as it is based on an untenable image of God; and also with the practice of self-torture that is incorrectly called atonement, a practice that flourished widely in the Middle Ages but that has sequels today, as we occasionally learn from astonishing examples. Some of those practices are still part of the spirituality of Opus Dei, which casts doubts on the value of this spirituality for the Third Millennium.

But can we simply condemn a tradition that has such ancient credentials? Throughout the centuries, mortification has not only been practiced fervently, by saints as well as by the average Christian people, but it has also been emphasized as indispensable by the spiritual masters, whereas pleasure has been in the bad books since Augustine. Those spiritual masters can hardly all have been wrong. And a practice cannot have flowered for so many centuries without the experience that it made sense. Not all the supporters of mortification can have been pathological cases. Can we today discard more than 1500 years of human wisdom without damaging ourselves? This presents us with the task of finding out under which circumstances mortification, so praised in the past, can still be meaningful today. And these are two in particular.

Two Conditions that Keep Mortification Meaningful

The first is this. Mortification is still defendable in a modern world, if it can be shown that the deprivation that it always entails, serves an inner-worldly cause. Take, for example, refraining from smoking during Lent, an example of traditional mortification. This becomes meaningful if one does it to serve one's own health, or that of one's housemates; or if it helps to regain that part of one's freedom now lost to nicotine addiction; or if one reserves the saved money for charity. Health, freedom, and solidarity with the poor are now experienced as a greater good than the pleasure of smoking. But if no demonstrable and therefore inner-worldly gain corresponds to abstinence from pleasure, then that mortification is no more than senseless self-torture. Modern people, Christian or not, won't hear of this. They will find it meaningful to follow a diet that prohibits all sorts of goodies on doctor's prescription. Or to fast as a form of solidarity, in order to experience personally how it feels to be hungry. Or to sacrifice part of their much-needed sleep to sit up with an ill person in order to guarantee his safety. But they wouldn't think of calling this mortification. They find it a natural thing: for to do so corresponds to the ethical principles of civilized people. But to give up smoking, not for the earthly gain it will resort, but to please God by this self-torture to make him more generous (while our fellow beings have to live with our greater irritability) is for modern believers equally as incomprehensible as it is for unbelievers.

This criticism of the efforts to please God by self-torture should not obliterate that the relationship with God remains an essential part of the concept of mortification: an ascetic practice without relation to the Transcendent cannot be called mortification. Therefore a second condition needs to be met as well, lest mortification becomes identical to secular sacrifice, its twin brother. At least in the background, the consciousness needs to be present that this humanly founded abstention has to do with God, intends to be a step towards him. But how do this inner-worldly profit and that 'love for God' match?

NOT SELF-TORTURE, BUT WISDOM

The answer to this question is offered by the almost untranslatable saying of the third-century church father Irenaeus: *Gloria Dei vivens homo*, freely translated: our humanization honors God. And we may add: and it is also God's will. Whoever directs himself towards God and makes His great desire of bringing the world to its perfection his own, cannot but want to grow in humanity, which means also: in solidarity. Every sacrifice that helps him to become more human and to progress in solidarity, therefore, implicitly receives a dimension of God-encounter.

Indeed, our humanization requires from us an ever-repeated choice for the more valuable, at the expense of the less valuable, however strong the latter may attract us. When we realize, for example, that an inner life is a deeply human need, and that prayer is therefore as important as breathing, we not only have to make time for it at the cost of other interesting activities, but we should also be able to say 'no' to the seduction of nourishing the eyes and the imagination with worthless television shows. This means renunciation and thus sacrifice. The at least latent presence of that desired God-encounter in that effort to become more human, allows us to keep using the term mortification. Allows it, but doesn't make it necessary. And because of the centuries-old connection between the term mortification and a self-torture that no longer makes any sense, the former will still be under taboo for a long time. In this sense, Buddhism appears to hold a wiser philosophy than the traditional Church. It teaches that pleasure should not be sought after, but neither should suffering. The only thing one needs to seek is what leads to the goal one wants to reach. The only thing one needs to reject is what obstructs that goal. If love for our fellow humans demands effort, burden and suffering, then it is good to take these upon oneself. This is what Maximilian Kolbe did when he took the place of a father of seven in a starvation bunker. He did not do it out of self-torture, he did not choose *for* suffering and death; he chose *despite* the suffering and death this would bring him, for something that in his eyes (and ours) was worth suffering and death: the rescue of a despairing fellow human. One who fasts out of solidarity with the countless hungry people in the world will not say that he practices mortification. He would find himself sounding ridiculous, so much has that term become obsolete. As has been said above, the first condition that the old mortification needs to fulfill in order to meet our modern sensibilities is: inner-worldly meaningfulness. The example that has already been given was sacrificing sleep in order to take care of a sick person. Can a modern Christian find such wakefulness equally meaningful when it means sacrificing sleep to pray at night? Certainly, but only if sleep deprivation enhances his praying experience and not if it turns it into a difficult struggle to keep his eyes open. Otherwise we end up on the inclined plane that traditional mortification really is. Because, if it pleases God that we deprive ourselves, then it will please him even more if we deprive ourselves even more. And the end of that is usually the hospital or the madhouse. How do religious orders even today justify the practice of nightly choral prayer, the daily torment of waking up at ungodly hours and chanting psalms, half-asleep (and in periods of fast also hungry) in a sometimes icy convent church? One can only hope that the motive is no longer the unconscious idea that a monk, by suffering these unpleasant experiences, does a God-pleasing work, something 'meritorious' for which he will be royally rewarded in this and the coming world.

In short: the word mortification in the sense of a God-pleasing choice for the unpleasant would better disappear from the Christian lexicon. It is too closely related to a pre-modern and even pre-Christian image of God which the defenders of mortification usually reject themselves. The former idea and practice of mortification should be replaced by an attentive attitude of reason, consequence, wisdom, which will often require more mortification than the mortifications and penances of the past. For these do not necessarily train the inner freedom that characterizes a real human being. It is even possible that, instead, they create a subconscious protest and attraction towards the opposite. This might explain the strange phenomenon that members of religious orders, who have been raised with such practices of self-affliction, in their later lives often show an unreasonable and unexpected lack of freedom when being confronted with the many seductions of the consumer society.

ASCETICISM

The collapse of the concept mortification does not necessarily need to imply the downfall of asceticism too. Those two should be detached from each other. Admittedly, there is often an undertone of rigorous harshness in the term asceticism. An ascetic would be someone who doesn't allow himself anything, who, when able to choose between the pleasant and the unpleasant, in principle chooses the unpleasant. This is due to the historical association between asceticism and mortification. But this changes when we return to its origin, the Greek term *askèsis*. For *askèsis* simply means 'exercise'. In spirituality it deals with the practice of inner freedom. This practice opens the way to what the Buddhist calls 'enlightenment', and the Christian, not without danger, 'sanctity'. For we are still far removed from this harmonious condition, in which our impulses and passions are willingly and in the end almost effortlessly embedded in the process of reshaping our being. Indeed, as Nietzsche said, 'The dogs bark wildly in the basement', referring to the violence of the impulses deep inside of us. If this embedding of the impulses doesn't go effortlessly as yet, then it will have to go with effort. And that's where asceticism comes in. It is the effort that is necessary to control the impulses that pull us in all directions, so that they do not divert the heart away from its way towards God. Again, some by now well-know terms appear on stage: sacrifice (in the non-cultic sense), in which the more valuable is chosen at the expense of what the impulses want; and mortification, as the indication that in all this a deeper reality is seen and sought after than the athlete who abstains from cigarettes and alcohol and while training goes as far as the limit of pain in order to built up and maintain an optimal physical condition. Also that may be called asceticism, but Christian asceticism is something else.

In his first letter to the Corinthians, Paul explains in an aside the Christian attitude towards enjoyment: Nobody has the right to criticize me, he says, if I eat something for which I thank God (I Cor. 10:30). In this way he indirectly says that everything is good, as long as it is enjoyed in gratitude. Gratitude presupposes that one doesn't snatch something avariciously, hold on to it stubbornly, and demand still more and more of it. Gratitude is an attitude of receptivity, joined with a two-fold awareness: the awareness that we cannot make claims to what we receive, so that we don't get vexed when it is not available; and the awareness that what we receive has been given with love, and that this love is even more important than the gift itself.

WERE THE MEDIEVAL PENITENTS SO OFF THE MARK?

Our rejection of medieval self-affliction that justified itself with the pious names of penance and mortification, confronts us with a dilemma. For we cannot accept that the rich ascetic and mystical tradition of the medieval Church was a complete mistake, its mysticism of suffering a collective mental illness that obstructed all spiritual maturity. Because if so, how can we explain the superior humanity of so many of those penitents? To mention only one example (but there are hundreds like that): the marvelous and so human character of the Poverello of Assisi. Was he a pitiable pathological case, he who chastised his 'brother donkey', as he used to call his body, starved it, exposed it to freezing temperatures, deprived it from sleep, and mistreated it in many other ways, whereas he would have become very angry if someone would have done this to a real donkey? Should they have closed him up in a madhouse? How can a modern believer escape from that dilemma?

The answer appears to be that his greatness and that of his peers is not due to their self-castigation, but rather to the consistency of the love with which they sought God and approached their fellow men. In their heteronomous way of thinking, in which God is pleased by sacrifices, part of that consistency was their readiness to atone (distorted into self-affliction) for their own sins as well as those of others, yes, of all humankind. The inner peace and fulfillment that issued from their love of God were strong enough to make them capable of the impossible and to stand the whole gamut of afflictions which they imposed upon themselves without collapsing psychically. But they often collapsed physically. Francis of Assisi wasn't even 40 years old when he died, entirely exhausted. The fire of his willingness to do what he thought was utterly pleasing to God, had consumed him completely. But it had at the same time enriched his life immensely.

That their way of thinking and doing differed a lot from ours was not exclusively the result of their heteronomous idea that God would prefer to see suffering rather than pleasure. What also played a considerable role was the fact that the world in which they lived was very different from ours. Life was hard, suffering a daily companion and therefore nothing to be upset about, while nowadays pain counts as the biggest of evils. Their earth was really a valley of tears. They had to cope with rudimentary medical care, surgery was very poor and happened without anesthesia, tooth aches had to be endured stoically, painkillers were unknown, as were the domestic comforts of electricity, central heating, refrigerators and freezers, air-conditioning, washing machines, vacuum cleaners and so on. Corporeal punishment was deemed a normal practice, and torture the standard course in justice. Nobody had ever heard about human rights or would have understood what Amnesty International was about. Executions under hellish tortures, the burning of a witch or heretic at the stake, the quartering or the breaking on the wheel of a convict were spectacles that attracted crowds. Sadism ran rampant, only the word wasn't known yet, nor its detestability. The same holds for the amount of hidden masochism in pious self-torture. In such a climate, things are perceived differently than in ours. Differently, not at all more correctly. And whoever has become stuck in a certain frame of thinking, usually finds in that framework a seemingly logical place for something that runs counter to the rest of his thinking. Despite the influence of the Gospel on the Western world, protests against slavery and torture, for example, were not heard here for a thousand years. Not even from the pious, the church leaders or the theologians. Shaping reality after one's own theories is a common fault of humankind. Moreover, in the *a priori*-science of pre-modern times, pioneered by scholastic theology, visible reality played almost no role in contrast to the dominating role of the tradition. Galilei had to learn that to his own cost.

CHAPTER 18

WHERE DO WE GO IN TIMES OF TROUBLE?

WHAT REMAINS OF SUPPLICATING PRAYER AND GOD'S HEARING OF PRAYER?

Leaving the axiom of two worlds behind implies that God is no longer perceived as enthroned above our earthly reality. This threatens to be the end of supplicating prayer, and therefore also of God answering our prayers. For these two seem inseparably connected with the idea of a second world in which God-on-High, or an angel or saint, would mingle with earthly business and grant the supplicant what he needs. In order to move these powers to intervene, the needy person sends prayers and complaints upwards, often and with great pressure if necessary. Sometimes he accompanies these prayers with presents, either immediately given or otherwise held out in prospect, that is, he brings offerings or promises something on the condition of being answered. If what he hoped and asked for effectively happens, then he concludes that this other world has heard his supplications.

A HERITAGE FROM OUR CHILDHOOD?

This model of thinking is clearly an extrapolation of something we know all too well from daily life. Someone has problems that he cannot solve himself, but he has a good relationship with someone who can help him. Of course he will draw the attention of that other person to his situation. Already in the crib we learn that this is the way to solve problems. Helpless, needy and totally dependent on the care of others, the baby signals his need by crying loudly and his mom or dad will soon come and give him what he needs. Even long after our infancy our parents keep on playing this role of the *deus ex machina* who solves our problems and is always ready to throw himself into the breach for us. Considering this, supplicating prayer seems a reflex from our childhood. But the role of the caring and seemingly almighty dad and mom is now played by invisible powers in an equally caring but this time really almighty world. The metaphors of 'God, our Father' and 'Mother Mary', under whose cloak we can take refuge, are instructive of this. In front of them, we relapse into the role of the helpless child who asks for what he needs because he is not capable, or deems himself not capable of obtaining it himself.

This heteronomous scheme of invoking the help of supernatural powers is so familiar to us that we are heedless of the problems it presents to the critical mind. If God really loves us, and knows better than we what we really need (so Jesus in Matt. 6:32), why would we pray for it and, therefore, what sense does supplicating prayer make? Is it not, rather, a proof of our lack of confidence? And do we know better than God what we really need and that we are not dealing with illusionary needs or even dangerous or harmful wishes? Or do we maybe want him to change his mind? In criticizing sacrifice, Chapter 15 already pointed out the nonsensical implications of the latter. Indeed, if God rightfully does not want to grant us what we ask for, for example because it would do us more harm than good, then we cannot possibly expect that our pressing and presents would against all reason get it done from him. Such an anthropomorphic image of God is only the projection of the leniency of incompetent parents or the corruptibility of authorities. Which is therefore totally unacceptable. With the help of so much anthropomorphism it is not possible to say anything meaningful about God. And that is leaving aside the statistical rarity of the so-called hearing of prayers. How many thousands of sick persons make pilgrimages each year to Lourdes, Fatima, Medjugorje or Padre Pio, to pray for healing, and how few return healed? That rarity seems to confirm the right of those who think that coincidence is the right word for what the faithful call answered prayer.

Of course the classical presentation of supplicating prayer totally collapses once the heteronomous axiom has been left behind.

If there is no other world, then it doesn't make any sense to send prayers to a deity who is located there and to ask him to please intervene in this sublunary world. One can just as well send an e-mail to the man in the moon. Together with this illusory second world, the possibility of finding help there has also vanished, and the so-called hearing of prayers has become nothing but an illusion. Moreover the autonomy of the cosmos implies that one cannot meddle with the inner-cosmic chains of cause and effect. As soon as the bomb bay door of a plane opens, it is already inevitably laid down where each of the bombs will land. That point is defined by the speed and the height of the plane, the weight and the shape of the bomb, the strength and the direction of the wind, the pressure of the air, and so on. If so, asking and begging will be of no avail. No angel will come and change the trajectory of the deadly engine. At the same time, saying farewell to the classical idea of supplicating prayer makes a clean sweep of the problems and vexations with which it inevitably burdens the critical mind.

YES OR NO TO SUPPLICATING PRAYER

But does the twenty-first century suddenly know everything better than 100,000 years of human history? For indeed supplicating prayer is a primeval fact of all religions. And it must have been perceived as meaningful all this time, despite the rarity of prayers being answered. And what should we, Christians, do with the admonitions of Jesus himself to take supplicating prayer seriously and to practice it intensely? These two questions are only rightfully asked when we leave aside the fact that in the past everyone, including Jesus, spontaneously thought in heteronomous schemes. At the switch-over to the axiom of modernity, those two remarks lose their strength. For they don't relate to the meaningfulness of the practice, but only to the meaningfulness of the interpretation. Another interpretation could maybe rehabilitate the practice. In the theonomous presentation we should try to conserve the rich human experience that lies behind supplicating prayer, as well as the phenomenon of the so-called hearing of prayers. At the same time, that new presentation should cut off the infantile excrescences of the traditional practice. For these are legion, such as praying to Saint Anthony to find lost keys, or the magical idea that there are prayers with guaranteed success, or that certain numbers of repetitions, such a the number 9 in the novenas or 30 in the Gregorian masses would have a particularly high efficiency.

An interpretation based on the theonomous axiom is grounded in the fact that a fundamental need in us makes us look forward incessantly and reach for fulfillment. In good Christian formulation this means that we are created towards God, drawn towards unification with that primeval Wonder, and that only this unification can fulfill our essential need. As long as we are still estranged from our Primeval Ground (in traditional language this alienation is called 'sin', in theonomous language 'essential need'), this feeling of being unfulfilled keeps the desire to be fulfilled awake in us. But the encounter with this magnetic pole that attracts us is not in our hands. It is a gift, in the form of a merciful approach. Therefore we react spontaneously with begging and crying for help. There is nothing against crying for help. We cannot do without it and we cannot avoid it. We only have to stay aware that what happens then is something entirely different from the idea we have formed about it since childhood. There is no Other whom we have to move. Rather, this Other is always trying to make us move towards Him, attracting us. His attraction and our longing are one and the same thing, perceived from opposite poles. The expression of our longing (in the form of supplication) not only actualizes this latent desire but coincides with God's approach towards us. The more we open ourselves up longingly, the more richly he will be able to fulfill us. In a sense, the *horror vacui* of physics holds here also. Just as air automatically fills up all vacuums, we become filled with God the more we become empty of ourselves. And becoming empty of ourselves is just what happens to us when we reach towards encounter with Him. Put in more traditional language: we will always be heard if we pray, because praying, even if we are not actually conscious of it, is always seeking for an encounter with God, and it is already the initial realization of that encounter. This corresponds to Jesus' word in Luke 11:23 that God will doubtlessly give the good spirit to those who pray for it. Besides, this encounter with God is the only thing that deserves to be the true object of our desire and therefore also of our supplication, because that encounter is our destination and ultimately our fulfillment. That we have only reached it in a very insufficient way so far is the reason for our fundamental destitution. And to experience it actively opens us up for that fulfillment.

CAN SUPPLICATING PRAYER CHANGE THE COURSE OF EVENTS?

But do these lofty speculations also hold when we ask for something else: for example, healing, a job, good weather or whatever else? Will we not end up, that way, in the quicksand of the problems of supplicating prayer that have been set out above? Not necessarily. Because what are these good things we ask for? Very limited concretizations of that absolute good, that they embody more fully, the more they relate to our real humanization. For this is at the same time our divinization. Praying for good weather because of a planned excursion cannot be compared with praying for rain in a period of drought that threatens to ruin the harvest, with starvation as a result. Indeed, the failure of a planned trip is a much lesser menace to a dignified human existence than starvation. The first embodies absolute good far less than the second. Maybe one can imagine in this way what happens in the event of such a supplicating prayer. The dissatisfaction with our incompleteness in the deepest layer of our being creates, by resonance, dissatisfaction with every form of incompleteness in us, in the less deep layers as well, in the layers of our psyche and our body. We want to be happy and cannot but want to be so. In this way, our urge to fulfill our fundamental need takes the shape of concrete desires to relieve suffering and needs in all their forms. Without being aware of this, these concrete desires are born from our fundamental longing for total liberation, for a salvation that can only be found in our unification with the Absolute. But the less we are aware of this deepest need and its absolute surplus value, the more we will get the impression that salvation exists in the fulfillment of our psychical and physical needs. Nevertheless, even in those supplications, a far echo of our longing for that deepest fulfillment can be heard. And every desire of that kind will be fulfilled depending on the measure of its sincerity.

If we can speak about such concrete desires being heard in prayer, then also this hearing consists in the first place in the growth of our encounter with God. Because that is what we did seek, unconsciously, in and through our begging for that more superficial fulfillment. In our psyche, this being heard can take the shape of surrender, resignation, even peace. But it can take also other forms. Precisely our unity of body and mind makes it possible that this psychically beneficent experience penetrates into the closely related physical level, and appears there as healing. Modern science has no problem with that: such influence of the physical state by the psyche is the object of psycho-somatic medicine. The miraculous healings in Lourdes and elsewhere can probably be explained in this way. Moreover (this is an important insight of Aldous Huxley in *The Perennial Philosophy*), the very intense spiritual activity of millions of people directed towards God can load an environment with something like spiritual energy, which can arouse in the pilgrim a psychical and through this also a physical wellness.

THE JUSTIFICATION OF PRAYING FOR OTHERS

We can go a step further still: no creature is an island, isolated from the rest of the cosmos; everything is connected to everything, the cosmic reality is a worldwide web of an endlessly richer and more complex design than the Internet. Whatever occurs in one of us, spills over to others and can even influence the material world, the latter always being more than material: it is the initial and still primitive manifestation of the one spiritual reality that carries and connects everything, being creative in each and every one of its parts. For just this is what we say when we speak about creation by God. This shows the meaningfulness of supplicating prayer for others, which includes intercessory prayers in mass. In most Sunday masses they may have been petrified into a dead ritual: often the answer is recited by a congregation that isn't the least aware of the need that is brought before God. Moreover, in most cases any desire that God may effectively alleviate the need is lacking entirely. But this practical erosion of intercessory prayer does not undermine the meaningfulness of the practice in itself. Because what happens when we pray sincerely for others? Our longing for the salvation of humankind and the world, aroused in us by God, opens us up (depending on the sincerity of the desire) to the stream of energy that He is. To the extent of our existential connection with our fellow human beings, we become good conductors of that stream of energy towards them. It is therefore not remarkable when that creative energy effects a change outside of us also.

But why does that change occur so rarely that it seems to be the result of coincidence and therefore no hearing of the prayer at all? In the heteronomous frame of thought one can seek refuge in the pure mystery of God's unfathomable but wise decision. God just wants one sick person to be healed and the one next to him not to be, and His will is always the best. Such recourse to the impenetrable darkness of divine decisions is characteristic for a way of thought that doesn't have any problems with extrapolating the arbitrariness of human rulers to God. But it is more honest to say that we don't know. In autonomous thought, the problem is not much smaller, but maybe a meaningful answer can be found in this direction. The carry-over effect of salvation into corporeality will encounter less obstruction in one constitution than in another. This can be ascribed to random factors. The healing itself is no random event, though, but the result of creative forces that flow from the creating God into the universe.

In this way, Jesus' admonition in favor of supplicating prayer (for example, Matt. 7:7 or Luke 11:9) and his certainty that it will be heard, can be given its due in theonomous thought as well. To be sure, Jesus' thought is also permeated with heteronomy—for he happened to live in a culture that thought heteronomously—but his words translate his own experience of wellness with supplicating prayer, the same experience theonomously thinking Christians still have today, but which they formulate in a different frame of thought.

INTERCESSION, OR SUPPLICATING PRAYER IN THE SECOND DEGREE

Our Catholic tradition is not only full of supplicating prayer; it is equally full of intercession and mediation. The 'pray for us' returns as an obstinate refrain in the prayer concert of the church. It is directed at all kinds of intercessors, male and female, of whom a mediating role is expected in the securing of the ardently desired but inaccessible good. Because of its immemorial use, this practice has become self-evident; but at a closer view it raises some questions. Intercession is a common practice, or misuse, in politics, justice, and social life. This is not only so today. It was even more common in the past, when everything depended on the whims of an autocratic ruler enthroned so high that the ordinary human didn't have much hope of getting to him and getting something done from him. If one was so lucky as to be on friendly terms with someone who enjoyed the ruler's favor, and he succeeded in engaging that relation as an intercessor on his behalf, one had already gone a long way. This experience was then uncritically projected from the earthly onto the heavenly domain. God became the highly-enthroned ruler for whom the human was just a tiny runt. And that runt could moreover fear that he had made himself a *persona non grata* in the eyes of the fearful God by doing something wrong. Things changed when a go-between could take the case of the supplicant to heart. But such a person needed to be found first. Fortunately, plenty of them could be found. In the first place, there was the 'mother of God', who as motherly intercessor should have a natural influence on the fatherly strict God. It didn't seem to matter that in Scripture not she, but Jesus is mentioned as the only intercessor. A mother is always more motherly than a savior and therefore a better go-between. Eventually it was even forgotten that she was merely a go-between, and not the one who herself had to grant what was being asked. The 'pray for us' imperceptibly received the meaning of 'give to us'. She herself became the giver, who was afterwards thanked for the gift, not for the intercession. And this did not happen only with Mary. It happened with all the popular saints, such as Saint Joseph, Antony, Rita, Padre Pio and many others. In fact, it was a mere continuation of what was customary before the arrival of Christianity: calling upon one of the many gods for help, trying to get something done from them. Those gods didn't need to pass on this request to the upper-god Zeus, Jupiter or Wodan: they could act on their own initiative. It was therefore important to remain on good terms with them. To get access to them, and the same held for the saints, one didn't need another intercessor. This explains in large part the enormous success of devotion to saints and their relics throughout the Middle Ages.

Lex Orandi, Lex Credendi?

For this medieval form of piety, one could not refer to the ancient Church, either to its practice or to its confession of faith. There it failed completely. But for the faithful that did not matter. And Rome let flourish what flourished and didn't react, didn't praise or blame the practice. Not until close to the year 1000 do the first documents appear in which Church authorities agree with the practice of seeking the intercession of saints, and in this way officially validate what had already been in use for a long time. It apparently didn't disturb Church leaders that this custom teems with ideas that are strange to the Gospel. 'Through the intercession of' has since become a refrain in liturgical prayers. But for the theonomously praying Christian this *lex orandi*, this practice of prayer, is certainly no *lex credendi*, a rule of belief. In fact, it denies what the Gospel says about our relationship with God. For Jesus does not know Him as a highly-enthroned ruler, who can only be approached through intermediaries. For him, God rather resembles a father who cares for his children. And in which good-functioning family does a child need an intercessor or go-between to get something really necessary from his understanding parent? But the use of intercessors has other flaws, too. Not only does the notion of intercession have a bad reputation in a democratic society (it all is too often a synonym of favoritism and nepotism); applied to our relationship with God it is a clear product of heteronomous thinking. Indeed, the above criticism of the traditional view of supplicating prayer returns here, even in the second degree. Not only does it locate God (in a very anthropomorphous shape at that) in a world above, but also the saints are projected there and get a job with the God who is enthroned there. All too often they themselves are, moreover, treated as the half-divine granters of the desired good. But if God is the love that permeates the cosmos and that aspires to grow in each human being, why do we still need such intercessors?

IF THE SAINTS ARE NOT INTERCESSORS, WHAT ARE THEY?

The success of the saints in the popular church has always been due to their aura of intercession and protection. That they were only the delegates of the power above, was often forgotten and they were addressed as if they themselves distributed the favors. This blew up their importance, and that of their material remains, their relics, to an extraordinary degree. Sometimes there were literal fights over these remains. They were treated as if loaded with creative, even magical, power. Through these, one received contact with the heavenly energy of the venerated saints. And that contact would pay off, so one thought and hoped, in the form of concrete advantages. And so the veneration of relics enjoyed an uncontested success during all those centuries. In a society deprived of technology, medical care worthy of that name, insurance or safety, people in need could not but set all their hope on the mercy of the other world, which had the power to save where every human endeavor failed. In every old sacristy, therefore, plenty of relics can be found, some with a certificate of authenticity, even if it is a feather of the Holy Spirit, drops of mothers' milk from Mary, or the umpteenth head of John the Baptist. The heyday of relic devotion is over. But not much is left of the cult of the saints, either. Where have all their holidays gone, their fraternities, the pilgrimages to their shrines, the prayers to beg for help in the problems and diseases of man and beast? Nothing but some meager remnants. Only some Marian pilgrimage sites still draw crowds. The holiday of All Saints is being supplanted by its bastard offspring Halloween. And the services of All Souls draw far more crowds than those of All Saints. The dead bodies in the graveyard are clearly much more important than all the living saints in Heaven together.

A New Role

The cult of the holy intercessors and protectors may be declining with uniformly accelerating speed; nevertheless, the last popes have been stubbornly adding ever more saints to the heavenly host. The Roman slogan seems to be: 'Less demand? Increase the supply!' However the Roman intent is not to boost the slacking demand. Also there, it has been accepted that saints have traded their prior role of intercessors for a new one: that of examples. They were already considered so in the past, but now it has become their almost exclusive function. Saints are now role models. With the full weight of ecclesiastical approbation, a certain type of attitude or behavior is now brandished as highly admirable and worthy of imitation. In this sense a canonization has acquired the function of a rallying slogan: 'Faithful of all nations, think and act as they did!'

But do we really have to think and act like Pius IX with his stubborn resistance against the declaration of human rights? Or like Pius X, who gave his blessing to the persecution and condemnation of the so-called modernists, based on anonymous accusations, imputations, and evil distortions of the truth? Or like Marquis Escriva de Balaguer and his very dated Spanish spirituality, embodied in Opus Dei? Fortunately, besides those, some really admirable people have been canonized and hence rightly held up as models, such as Don Bosco, Maximilian Kolbe, and Mother Teresa.

Help from Another World

To guarantee the reliability of this ecclesiastical approval, the second world has to lend a helping hand. For there has to come a sign from Heaven, even though at the sound of this word, texts such as Matthew 12:38–39 and 1 Corinthians 1:22 will start flickering as warning lights. This sign, required as the official stamp of the heavenly chancellery, is the so-called miracle. There cannot be a canonization without one or two miracles, one for a martyr, two for a confessor, which serve as the unmistakable proof that the other world approves solemnly of the papal declaration that that person has effectively arrived in that realm (albeit without a body for the time being) to settle there forever. In the case of a confessor one sign from Heaven apparently will not suffice. Heaven has to confirm someone's sanctity two times. This is how the Vatican administration wants it. The heteronomy of the canonization practice does not require further explanation.

Such a miracle never consists of a sign in the moon, sun or stars, such as mentioned in Matthew 24:29: it has to be a medically observable miraculous healing. In this, it is forgotten that inner-worldly processes always have inner-worldly causes, even if we are not yet capable of tracing these. In this context it should be remarked that already in Scripture miraculous healings are related to belief. No miracles without belief. Think about Matthew 13:58: Jesus cannot work any healings in Nazareth because most of the inhabitants do not believe in him. Or think about the word: 'Your belief has saved (or healed) you', which recurs as a refrain in the biblical healing stories. Whether we read this belief as an existential faith in Jesus-Messiah, including the readiness to follow him, or as the belief that he can and probably will heal, it always remains a psychological process. And this is where psychosomatics comes in, the science of the healing or sickening influence of psychological states. Even though we do not know exactly how this influence works, it lends us at least the beginning of the long and still hidden thread of explanation that ends with the healing. That beginning is apparently something deeply emotional. Healings in Lourdes or Medjugorje always happen in a very intense emotional climate, all the more intense because it is of a collective nature. But also in the case of other healings by invocation of (not yet canonized) saints an intense connection with these is always presupposed.

Back to canonizations. Does Rome not grossly overestimate their importance? They undoubtedly serve their purpose as mediagenic events and tourist attractions. But do people like Mother Teresa, Oscar Romero or Martin Luther King, or so many others need a solemn declaration by Rome in order to be admired? Doesn't a modern Christian do that automatically? The so-called 'honor of the altars' (an expression that nobody still understands) does not change anything in our feelings towards them. And if canonization should encourage imitation, it belabors an obvious point. For if we truly admire someone, then this does not remain a noncommittal attitude: admiration automatically and often unnoticeably entails at least a bit of imitation.

Conversely, where there is no admiration, there cannot be imitation. But how can we admire people we don't know at all? And how can we celebrate them? This exposes the meaninglessness of the detailed ecclesiastical calendar, issued yearly by the Congregation of the Sacraments, that prescribes the people of God almost every day the liturgical celebration of one or another almost unknown saint, thereby adding with precise detail what, according to the Roman office concerned, we have to do or omit. This liturgical office, as well as the office for canonizations and the many other well-known, lesser known, and totally unknown offices behind the walls of the Vatican, has at least one useful side: it provides plenty of employment.

CHAPTER 19

CLEARING AWAY THE TRANSFORMER

THE OLD CREED IN A NEW GARB

Sunday after Sunday the ever declining herd of churchgoers recites its confession of faith, docilely, usually murmuring it mechanically as a forced exercise rather than consciously proclaiming the good news that is expressed in it. But even when the modern believer really wants to express that good news, he feels that these words are no help to him. Indeed, in that brief summary of our Christian view of God and humankind, he finds concentrated as in a focal point all the difficulties which biblical heteronomy has in store for him. The uneasiness that issues from this has led in progressive churches and chapels to a proliferation of locally-made confessions, one more modern than the other. What follows here is not the umpteenth endeavor of that kind, but only a theonomous reformulation of what we confess in the ancient symbolum, because we will not be done with that creed in the near future. The traditional faithful, and those are the majority of the Sunday church crowd, are not exactly dying for a new creed. They only feel safe with the familiar. And the hierarchical keepers of the faith are not (yet) ready to pour the old wine into new wineskins, even though the old skins are burst and leaking. The modern faithful therefore have no other choice but to switch on a spiritual transformer when reciting the so-called 'twelve articles', the shorter Western form of the old creed that is used in Sunday mass.

In the eyes of the Vatican keepers of the liturgy, however, this symbolum is only a stepchild that wrongfully takes the place of the longer Eastern creed of Nicea-Constantinople. The latter 'credo', after its initial Latin word, is occasionally still heard in the rich polyphonic masses of Western musical history; one enjoys it, but doesn't confess it. In that sense it doesn't burden us with problems. Problems only arise when the twelve articles are intoned on Sundays from the altar or the lectern, as an invitation to confess them once again. This last chapter is meant to tackle the problems that arise when this happens. To that purpose, it will follow faithfully the order of those twelve articles in an effort to free us from the necessity to switch on the above mentioned spiritual transformer, which is more a necessary evil than a desirable good.

But an important remark is due first. A creed is no confession of adhesion to a system of thought; it is our 'Amen' to God's self-revelation, and this from the first sentence on. It deals with God. And God is never a third person, about whom we can speak. He can at the most become so grammatically, as in the previous sentence; and in our language this happens, alas, far too often. In reality, God is always the second person, whom we address with You (or Thou), and whom we ought to approach with great respect. While confessing our faith in Him, we stand before his face and should be aware of this.

I Believe *in* God, the Almighty Father

For the modern faithful no less than in the past, the phrase 'I believe *in* God' formulates in a nutshell the essence of his existential attitude of faith; and therefore it should remain as it is. But immediately thereafter we already stumble over the epithet 'almighty', which might evoke the image of a mighty sorcerer, who can uproot the cosmic order as he pleases. However, the Greek term *pantokratoor* that is translated here, can equally well be rendered as 'dominating everything'. And the primeval Wonder indeed dominates everything, because it generates and permeates the entire cosmic order, not because it could uproot those at will.

This generation of the cosmic order evokes the concept of Creator, whom we should not dress up in the philosophical tailcoat of 'Maker out of nothingness'. Not only is this idea foreign to Scripture, but moreover the essence of the inner-worldly term 'creation', namely self-expression in matter, is lacking there. Furthermore, modern believers would do better not to think here of human (artistic) creations such as paintings and sculptures that can lead an independent existence away from their maker. When we address God as 'Creator', we should think of the primeval Wonder that expresses Itself in all the wonders of the evolving universe (in the creed: 'Heaven and Earth') and therefore also in us, and gradually makes Its invisible essence more visible.

This all-creating and all-dominating Wonder is called 'Father' in the creed. For the sound mind, considering all the horror and evil that resides within the cosmos, this is incredible and almost unthinkable. Calling God 'Father' is only justifiable if we refer to the deep mystical experience of Jesus of Nazareth and his Jewish tradition. If so, we must learn from him what that name should evoke for us. And it will become clear that it not only expresses the certainty of being loved gratuitously, but also involves the demand of obedient surrender to His impulses.

I BELIEVE *IN* JESUS CHRIST, HIS ONLY SON, OUR LORD

Also the above 'article' is totally acceptable in theonomy. Indeed, the Nicean reading of that 'only son' as 'true God from true God' and the Trinitarian doctrine that goes with that, are not essential here, despite the fact that this might seem so. We only have to read 'son of God' as in the Old Testament, where it is a honorific title of the king of Israel, and of the whole people of God, and of the angels, and—in Jesus' pedigree in Luke—of Adam. To be the 'son' means in all those cases, to be His image and likeness, and also the object of his special love and care.

Jesus is further called 'Christ'. This is not a standard epithet and even less a surname. It is a title. *Christos* is the Greek translation of the Biblical honorary title *mashiah*, which means 'anointed'. This title originally only referred to Israel's king, as a result of his anointing when he was installed. After the exile it referred to a savior of royal blood, the so-called 'messiah', a descendant of King David, whom God would send to his people and whose coming everybody in Israel yearned for. Therefore the name Christ is heavy with the promises of messianic well-being and happiness.

Finally, we call him 'our Lord', with which we declare the transcendent greatness of this laborer from Nazareth. For us, he is incomparably more than a wisdom teacher such as Socrates or Buddha, or than the founder of a religion such as Mohammed, or than a prophet such as Moses or Elijah. He is God's mighty self-revelation in the middle of our unwilling humanity and insofar as this he shares God's lordship.

What is further declared about Jesus in this article needs some re-thinking. Not that he was conceived and that he was born from Mary. These are historical data, and a historian doesn't confess, he records things. Confession is only at stake in the additions 'by the power of the Holy Spirit' and 'virgin'. To clear away these heteronomous stumbling blocks we must stop thinking physiologically, and no longer conceive God's Spirit as a replacement of Joseph. What we confess here is the creative work of God in the person and the activities of Jesus, the son of Joseph and Mary, but projected back with the aid of mythical images to the first moment of his existence. If this article of faith is understood thusly, the word 'virgin' will also lose its physical resonance. This has been explained more extensively in Chapter 10.

What follows seems again to belong to the category of historical data, far removed from any dimension of faith. The date 'under Pontius Pilate' reinforces that impression even more. Upon a closer view, however, there is much more at stake than historicity. For in this article we confess our paradoxical faith in a messiah who has suffered the extreme defeat, in a savior who could not save himself, which is a daring attitude of faith, to say the least! His disturbing death is even further underscored by the mythological addition (which is remarkably missing from the long Nicean Credo) that he 'descended to Hell'. Nobody knows what to do with that. So everyone makes the best of it. The best for the Byzantines was to follow the bizarre track of 1 Peter 3:19, which states that after his death Jesus took up preaching to the spirits in the underworld. The Byzantine icons portray this literally: the Risen has just torn the hinges off the very material gates of Hell (which is not a fiery Hell but rather a Limbo) and slammed them down, so that the poor guard-devils at the gates lay flat as pancakes underneath, and he is seen leading the patriarchs out of Sheol. These pictures illustrate the rich idea that Jesus' fullness of life opens up a new future for humankind. But the imagery is too heteronomous for us to take in. Another possible reading is that of the official *Catechism of the Catholic Church*, paragraph 636. There it is understood that the 'descent to Hell' would be the repetition and reinforcement of 'died and was buried'. Which is quite plausible, because 'Hell' is only the misleading translation of *inferi*, the ancient underworld, the abode of the shadows. And that ancient underworld was in its turn the visualization of being dead and buried.

ON THE THIRD DAY HE ROSE FROM THE DEAD

The above mentioned historical statements about the death of Jesus of Nazareth are closely connected to the incredible statement that follows. Therefore, the historical part would better be preceded with 'despite' and what follows with a contrasting 'nevertheless'. One who cannot affirm the contrasting second panel, can also not believe *in* the executed. He can at most acknowledge his existence, maybe admire him, and try to discover what else can with fair reliability be said about his life. But is it possible to believe *in* someone who died and was buried almost 2000 years ago? Certainly, because despite his death, he has ever since consistently manifested himself as living. To be sure, this 'living' can no longer be understood in a biological way, but in the way we ascribe life to God, which is certainly not biological. Evidently, this does away with the corporeality evoked in the heteronomous language of the creed by the verb 'risen', and therefore also with the bodily reality of the glorified Jesus, despite the series of apparitions related in the Gospels that picture him as solid and tangible, able to march many miles and to eat fried fish.

The confession that Jesus 'on the third day rose from the dead', requires, therefore, that the theonomous believer forget about the empty tomb and all its surrounding stories. And that he thinks resolutely symbolically, by understanding the 'third day' as symbolic language for God's saving presence in human dead-end situations. And that he understands 'rose from the dead' as the symbolic rendering of 'fully creative', through a total unification with God, who is measureless life and measureless creativity. The symbolical reading should also be applied to 'ascended into Heaven', by thoroughly forgetting everything that reminds us of astronauts. This is easier because in Scripture 'Heaven' often stands as a respectful synonym for Yahweh, whose name should not be pronounced lightly. 'Ascending to Heaven', then, becomes another expression for being totally absorbed by God, for total unification with the primeval Wonder. The mythological 'seated at the right hand of the Father' is a third synonym—this time borrowed from the royal psalms—for the unification with God, accomplished by Jesus through his freely accepted death that manifested his love 'to the end'.

FROM THERE HE WILL COME TO JUDGE

If the preceding was already loaded with mythology, what follows is one big tangle of mythological images. The origins of the formulation have already been laid bare in Chapter 12. Can we still do anything with this today? For we no longer live in the apocalyptic climate of the first century. First, we should detach from its mythological background the 'coming' that each year fills with its sound the four weeks before Christmas. In fact, this detaching already begins in the New Testament. The prior expectation of a sudden appearance of the messiah 'on the clouds of Heaven' makes way already there for the idea of a slow inner-worldly process of growth of the kingdom of God, and thus of Love. Also the 'judging' must be detached from the physical images that surround the Last Judgment. And that is possible, because judging is in fact (trying to) repair violated justice. In the still primitive human legal order that unconsciously serves as a model here, this unfortunately has to happen by means of a painful punishment. In the divine order of Love, to the contrary, this means healing of the disease, repelling evil from human hearts by the power of love and thus leading humanity towards its fulfillment. From the addition 'the living and the dead', finally, it can be derived that this completion concerns all of humankind, past, present and future.

I BELIEVE *IN* THE HOLY SPIRIT ...

The last articles clearly belong to the 'good news'. But they too require being freed from the heteronomous smell they exude. First, there is the belief *in* the Holy (or holy?) Spirit. The nascent church confessed its belief *in* the holy (lowercase) Spirit long before the Council of Constantinople in the year 351 formulated and fixed the classical Trinitarian doctrine. Until then, speaking about the Spirit was speaking about God himself, as creating, saving, and sanctifying. And there is no need for us to confess more than the church of the first three hundred years.

The 'I believe *in*' applies grammatically also to 'the holy Catholic Church'. This is testified by the oldest Greek confessions. That lends the Church a divine aura, because in this way the movement of surrender to God, to Jesus Messiah, and to God's Spirit flows over to the Church also. The addition of the word 'holy' underscores this even more, because 'holy' refers to God's secret essence. But when it comes to 'Catholic Church', the average believer, alas, thinks wrongly that these words deal with the human, all too human, institution directed from Rome, which even among Catholics provokes ever more criticism and ever less support. But 'Catholic' does not at all refer to the Roman Catholic Church. The Greek word *katholikos* means 'universal', in contradistinction to 'local, particular'. The adjective 'Roman' rather evokes the opposite, not the whole of all true believers in Jesus Christ and his God, not the universal, but the local and the particular. Belief *in* that universal church, which consists of humans, (and where there are humans, things might get a little too 'human'), presupposes that we recognize in its imperfect shape the presence of the living Jesus Christ. The image of the vine can help us to look at the church in this perspective.

The addition 'communion of saints' can be interpreted in two ways. This expression can be read as a grammatical apposition to 'church' and thus as its synonym. In doing so we would follow the New Testament in which Christians are called 'the saints' more than 40 times. For Christians are (or should be) people who through their union with Jesus have admitted God into their lives the sanctifying God. It receives another meaning if the Latin term *sanctorum* is read as a neutral form. Then the translation would be 'of the holy things', referring to the ritual signs and especially to the bread and wine in the Eucharist. If so, 'communion' receives another meaning, too. Instead of meaning a closely-knit group, it means then the common participation in these holy things.

The 'forgiveness of sins' we confess, most certainly doesn't refer to the sacrament of confession. This sacrament had not yet been born at the time when that formula entered the creed. The young Church, rather, saw that forgiveness realized in baptism. We can do this also. But then forgiveness should not be understood as amnesty, that is, as an escape from condemnation and punishment. Whatever does not touch and renew our deeper essence does not save us. Forgiveness is therefore to be understood as an existential process, involving the inner healing and re-creation of our core, as the result of a love that gradually reduces our selfishness. If we apply this to baptism, then we first have to free it from the layer of half-magical images that through the centuries has been deposited onto it. Only then is the forgiveness of sins rightly understood as being the good news that the divine Wonder wants us to grow, despite our resistance, from being the *missing link*, which unfortunately we still are, into those liberated and godlike humans, which we really want to become.

As to the 'resurrection of the body' at the end of time, the modern faithful can no longer subscribe to that at all. That a body that has decomposed into its billions of molecules would suddenly be totally restored after interminable time, has become simply unthinkable for him. Fortunately, as an enriching synonym for this unthinkable resurrection of the body, the creed adds the notion of 'life everlasting'. 'Everlasting' as well as 'life' are metaphors borrowed from our daily experience. We know what 'life' means. In itself it is something biochemical and bound to come to an end, but we have the experience that it can transcend that biological level so completely that we can apply it to God, thus transcending time, so that we can then call it everlasting. And thus in that last article of the creed we confess the good news that these metaphors refer to: that the human (in biblical language: the body) by the power of God's breath, which is love, is called to transcend death. At the same time, however, we are profoundly aware that we do not really know what in the order of the last reality corresponds to it. We only know that 'life everlasting' points to something that is absolutely good, akin to being at our fullest, unthreatened, unharmed, complete. That it is akin to be love and to be God.

From what precedes, it appears that only at the cost of a continuous process of internal translation a modern believer can still recite the creed as it stands and this way is too laborious. We therefore need a reformulation that can make that internal transformer superfluous. What follows is an attempt at such a reformulation. It has the advantage of staying in the living stream of the Christian Tradition, yet escaping from the heteronomy that permeates almost every sentence of the ancient creed.

I believe *in* God, endless Love,
Primeval Wonder that expresses Itself in an amazing way
in the evolution of the cosmos and the human.
And I believe *in* Jesus Christ, our Messiah,
God's unique human image,
born from human parents,
yet entirely the fruit of God's initiative of salvation.
Who has accepted suffering and death,
was crucified by order of Pontius Pilate, died and was buried,
but nevertheless fully lives, because he merged into God,
and thus became an all-healing force,
that will lead the entire humanity to completion.
I believe *in* the inspiring activity of God's holy breath of life,
And *in* the worldwide community in which Jesus Christ lives on,
and *in* God's offer to heal us
and to transform us into real human beings.
And *in* the divine future of humankind, a future of life.
Amen.

EPILOGUE

After reading this book many will probably be angry or upset and exclaim that it uproots all but the entire content of our faith without the least respect for the wisdom and sense of faith displayed by two thousand years of Church History. The question is whether it is at all possible to speak differently, having left the previous axiom behind and embraced a new one. Yet there is no reason to panic. What is uprooted is merely the presentation and formulation of the message of faith as it was in vogue in the Middle Ages. The rock of modernity inevitably shatters the grand statue of this medieval presentation and formulation of our faith. This does not mean, however, that the wisdom or even the correctness of this past presentation is being denied. Usually (not always!) the early Christian and medieval theologians did interpret the original message of faith correctly, and even with amazing depth and richness, but they necessarily did so in the light and with the tools of the axiom of heteronomy. They didn't know any other. And they were not even aware that their point of view was only an axiom.

Therefore there is nothing against an effort to formulate the message of the past in today's language, on the basis of the new axiom that has taken over the old one. The justification of such an effort becomes even more obvious when we realize that many elements of the traditional content of our faith are not as original as they are usually thought to be. Several of those needed a long time to become the officially accepted doctrine. For example: it took more than half a century before the divinity of Jesus won acceptance; the acceptance of the personal nature of Yahweh's Spirit took more than three centuries; that of the doctrine of original sin almost four centuries; that marriage is a sacrament took more than a thousand years; and the Marian dogmas even longer. Was it impossible, then, to be a true Christian in the time prior to their fixation?

Some may also think that the present author is ridiculously arrogant in trying to put his private opinions above the wisdom and the unanimity of the entire Catholic Tradition. But then they overlook the fact that this book does not formulate the ideas of one lonely individual. What he writes lives subconsciously, not yet explicitly, in many seeking Christians. The loud and persistent echo that was provoked by this book in the Dutch- and German-speaking regions proves that many recognize themselves in these new ways of presenting the Christian faith. This proves that the present author is only a wave in an already wide and deep river. And that river swells incessantly. Hopefully also the reaction of the English speaking readers will affirm that it is perfectly possible to be a true believing Christian without sticking to the formulations of faith of the late Roman Empire.

HONESTY

Moreover, it is not in the least the intention of this book to be destructive or iconoclastic. It truly wants to serve the cause of the faith. If we endorse human rights, democracy and the theory of evolution, and don't bother about the prescriptions of *Humanae Vitae*, we only say 'yes' to the basic ideas of modernity and thus to the axiom there is only one world, and an autonomous one at that, and not two. If so, we should also say 'yes' to what logically flows from this axiom. If we say 'yes' to this new axiom, we can no longer say 'no' when becoming aware of its consequences.

No doubt the ideas that are presented here will arouse resistance. For they shatter certainties that are very deeply rooted in the Tradition, that have always been accepted as self-evident, that are so central that we must fear to distance ourselves from our faith and the Church if we give them up, that seem so sacred that they cannot allow criticism. These are as many inner resistances that make us inclined to stay with the old. But if we say A we have to say B. Otherwise we run the danger of contradicting ourselves.

A fine example of such self-contradiction, albeit in the reverse order, is the sensational ordination of seven women in 2001 on a boat on the Donau. Accepting ordinations-from-on-high and digging up for their validity a bishop who in his turn has been invested with the episcopacy from on high, those women not only unconsciously accepted a two-class church with ordained priests and unordained lay people, but also the two-world system that is at the basis of these concepts, including the absolute power of a pope seated in Rome. If so, they could not at the same time deny that power by putting aside the strict prohibition from Rome. And that is what these seven 'priestesses' have done. What they did was maybe brave, and inasmuch justifiable, but it was inconsistent, and inasmuch wrong.

A RELATIVITY THAT DOESN'T AFFECT THE ABSOLUTE

The great majority of churchgoers and virtually all church leaders accept from childhood, and therefore without question, the existence of a second world, and that it operates through channels that descend from Rome. This existence is as a rule an essential part of their faith. Woe to the one who dares to put into perspective the formulations and statements that are based on this two-world scheme, and who ventures to open a door towards other, for modern people more accessible, but also more relative, formulations.

Indeed, meanwhile a revolution has taken place, announcing a new era. Humanity has discovered the autonomy of the cosmos and with that its own autonomy. As a result, everything that had been built on the axiom of heteronomy lost its validity, the traditional formulations of faith as well. But not the message of faith itself. Because that has sprung from the historical and therefore inner-worldly experiences of the people of Israel with the Depth of reality, culminating in the God-experience of its greatest son, Jesus of Nazareth, and after his execution also from the experiences of his followers. The testimony of these experiences need not necessarily be transmitted in the language of heteronomy. For modern people, this should happen in the language of modernity. This backs up the desirability and the legitimacy of the effort to formulate the same message as of old in today's language.

Doesn't this shift of perspective affect the absoluteness of our faith? Not in the least. Christian faith is and will always remain an attitude of complete and therefore absolute turning towards the saving God, whose approach to us lights up in the life of Jesus of Nazareth. This absolute faith was initiated in the young Church and found its orientation there. We should not lose that orientation. For as Christians we are always heirs to that beginning. But when people undertake to formulate this original turning towards God through Jesus, they can only do this in the language of their particular culture. And the culture of modernity speaks a different language than the two-world culture of the past. Nothing forces us to accept modernity and its culture and to speak its language. The Amish, for example, refuse to do this and therefore they decline the achievements of modernity such as electricity and cars. They continue to live in the time of horses and carriages and preserves. They consistently keep on cultivating the language (in the broad sense of that word) of the past. And therefore they are fully justified to reject the ideas of this book.

But if we accept modernity in all its forms day after day, we can no longer afford to do so, at least if we want to be consistent. One who doesn't think and act consistently can still be truthful, at least for a while. But only until the contradiction in which he lives dawns upon him.

ACCOUNTING FOR THE HOPE THAT IS IN US (1 PETER 3:15)

Christians have to be ready to give a meaningful answer to the neo-pagans of modernity, 'who demand an accounting for the hope that is in them'. In other words, they should be able to explain to these non-Christians the meaningfulness and the richness of what they confess. But does such an undertaking stand any chance of success if they have to do it in the two-world language of two natures in one person, of three persons in one substance, of unity of essence as distinct from identity of essence, of being generated but not created, of a mother who remains a virgin despite conception and birth, of bodies that have turned to dust but miraculously will come back to life, of rituals with invisible workings but guaranteed everlasting effects? Yet all these articles count as central pillars of the Christian faith. And they are only a few specimens of the multitude of Christian statements that are so infused with heteronomous thinking that the modern unbeliever can only be flabbergasted that one can take them seriously. This is the most decisive argument in favor of the desirability of this book. We have not received our faith in order to keep it safely hidden in the burial ground of the past, but to make it yield. Today this means to make it penetrate the culture of modernity so that this culture can become a provisional form of the Kingdom of God. To that effect, the Good News has to be translated in the language of modernity. For otherwise we have to fear that it will not much longer remain Good News, not even for us.